THE SELF-CARE WORKBOOK FOR HELPING Professionals

The Self-Care Workbook for Helping Professionals is a how-to workbook of tools to help the helpers. Emphasizing that the problem of stress is not a reflection of the depth or quality of a helper's resilience, the book provides readers with assessment tools to identify problematic reactions and develop personalized self-care practices that enhance resilience. Readers will come away from the book with a variety of activities and techniques for identifying focal points and developing personalized self-care practices. *The Self-Care Workbook for Helping Professionals* is an essential resource for any helping professional, including first responders, medical personnel, mental health professionals, child welfare workers, social workers, judges, law-enforcement officers, educators, and clergy.

William Steele, PsyD, MSW, is an author and consultant who has trained thousands of helpers and developed evidence-based, trauma-informed interventions that are used in 55 countries.

"This book offers a rich menu of options that can truly make a difference! Its grounded, thoughtful, evidence-based approach skillfully emphasizes the individual responsibilities and self-care opportunities helpers have while acknowledging the role the workplace environment plays in risk and resiliency factors that influence or mitigate helpers' stress. I strongly recommend this workbook and trust that if helpers implement its wisdom, they can experience relief from helper stress while increasing both compassion satisfaction and fulfillment too."

Lynda Monk, MSW, RSW, CPCC speaker, facilitator, and director of the International Association for Journal Writing

"Dr. Steele provides a very useful and accessible toolkit to support helping professionals exposed to trauma through their work. This book allows professionals to engage in and determine the self-care strategies that work best for them and their well-being."

Paul Gavin, PhD, programme leader for criminology at the University of the West of England Bristol

"It's refreshing and empowering to see the way this book presents self-care as a strengths-based approach and celebrates what draws people to being helpers. Evidence-based research, real-world experience, a plethora of targeted assessments, and resources make this a multifaceted framework for customizing self-care practices that recognize the unique responses experienced by helpers in the field."

Misty Ramos-Saviano, ATR-BC, LPCC-S, ACTP, executive director of PALS for Healing

"Dr. Steele provides a clear, practical guide that recognizes the complexities of helper stress. His work provides useful tools and insights that truly support resilience. This is an invaluable resource for anyone who wants to care for themselves while caring for others."

Amy Priest, MSW, LISW-S, LICDC, past director of the Mental Health and Recovery Services Board of Lucas County, Ohio

"This is a great resource for helpers! The author has a knack for taking what's complicated and making it understandable through personal experiences. Insights from his training about self-care, research on self-care and best practices and his experiences with survivors of catastrophic and traumatic events reveal his understanding that helper self-care should never be a 'one size fits all' model."

Anthony Salvatore, EdD, retired public school administrator (Newtown, Connecticut) and current board member of The Coalition to Support Grieving Students

"With real stories, practical advice and actionable techniques, Dr. Steele's latest book demonstrates that self-care is not just possible but essential, empowering practitioners to maintain resilience in their challenging roles."

Barbara Rubel, MA, BCETS, DAAETS, author of But I Didn't Say Goodbye and coauthor of Living Blue

THE SELF-CARE WORKBOOK FOR HELPING Professionals

Different Stressors, Different Solutions

William Steele

Routledge
Taylor & Francis Group
NEW YORK AND LONDON

Designed cover image: Getty Images

First published 2027
by Routledge
605 Third Avenue, New York, NY 10158

and by Routledge
4 Park Square, Milton Park, Abingdon, Oxon, OX14 4RN

Routledge is an imprint of the Taylor & Francis Group, an informa business

Library of Congress Cataloging-in-Publication Data
A catalog record for this title has been requested

ISBN: 978-1-041-14276-8 (hbk)
ISBN: 978-1-041-14222-5 (pbk)
ISBN: 978-1-003-67369-9 (ebk)

DOI: 10.4324/9781003673699

Typeset in Warnock Pro
by Apex CoVantage, LLC

Access the Support Material: https://resourcecentre.routledge.com/books/9781041142225

To all the courageous survivors and helpers who allowed me to spend time with them, to learn what was most helpful to them in the midst of their stress, trauma, their terror, fears and worries immediately following what they were exposed to when life, as they once knew it, had completely changed. They are the creators, the voices of this work. They taught me early on that self-care was personal, that what worked for one did not work for everyone, that too many times too many assumptions were made as to what would be most helpful for them personally. They taught me that whatever I had to offer them had to be immediately useful and helpful in some way; that what I offered aligned with what they indicated mattered most to them. They taught me that their greatest strength was the effort they engaged to keep trying, exploring, searching till they found what worked best for them. They were the best teachers I ever had.

Contents

Acknowledgements

I want to acknowledge my family's support and encouragement over the last thirty years to pursue my passion. They were always there despite my many hours and weeks away from home helping trauma survivors and training those wanting to be more effective with the help they were providing. And they were there to slow me down and remind me to take better care of myself when needed, something their nursing, law enforcement and physical therapy professions also required they do for themselves. We've been quite the team.

I certainly want to thank Anna Moore at Routledge for her encouragement to write this latest work and all her excellent suggestions along the way. And of course, thanks to Sophie Dracott and all the other team members at Taylor and Francis for their expertise and advice for sustaining the quality and integrity of this work.

Foreword

Dr. Steele has created something rare and valuable here; a workbook that is both scientifically rigorous and immediately practical, recognizing the complexity of helper stress and honoring what helpers actually experience rather than prescribing what they "should" do.

What makes this work so valuable is the core insight that different stressors demand different solutions. This premise shifts everything about how we approach self-care. Dr. Steele dismantles the myth that a single intervention, whether meditation, exercise, or cognitive reframing, works for everyone. Instead, he guides helpers through a systematic process of identifying their specific vulnerabilities across the spectrum of helper wellness challenges: burnout, compassion fatigue, secondary trauma, and empathy distress. Only then does he help them match evidence-based strategies to their unique needs.

The comprehensive nature of this book is remarkable. Dr. Steele reminds us that helper stress is as much physiological as cognitive, that toxic organizational structures and practices can undermine even the most resilient practitioner, and that our reactions to stress are often not a conscious choice. No matter how skilled or seasoned we may be, our nervous systems respond before our awareness catches up. His emphasis on nervous system regulation as the foundation of all other self-care represents a paradigm shift from traditional approaches that prioritize thinking over sensing.

Drawing from decades working with helpers responding to catastrophic events, from 9/11 to school shootings to natural disasters, Dr. Steele writes with both hard-earned experience and expertise. One critical aspect often missing in wellness and self-care literature is an acknowledgment that helpers are, more and more, providing services outside of controlled outpatient settings. Self-care suggestions like "Get away from your desk to have lunch" completely miss the challenges of providing direct services in the field and in the moment, to people impacted by crises and trauma. Dr. Steele is one of those professionals who has been present with people as they are experiencing the worst day of their life. He understands what helps clients in those moments and the challenges helpers face. Through this workbook, we benefit from that experience in the form of strategies that actually work. His integration of trauma-informed supervision, organizational assessment, and individual self-care planning creates a systemic view that acknowledges a truth many avoid. Sometimes the problem is not the depth or quality of the helper's resilience, but the constellation of challenges that tax that resilience.

This workbook offers a much-needed resource that prepares helpers across professions, inclusive of students preparing to be helpers, not just to survive, but to sustain compassion satisfaction across careers increasingly marked by exposure to collective trauma. The assessments provided allow for insight that moves beyond generic wellness checklists and self-care activities to genuine support.

This book introduces self-care in its truest sense—care that gets to the source rather than managing symptoms, that honors the subjective experience of stress, and that positions self-care not as indulgence but as ethical responsibility. Steele has given us a map for the journey every helper must make from awareness to action, from fatigue to fulfillment, and from merely coping to genuinely thriving. I am genuinely grateful that Dr. Steele took the time to address a gap that was not well understood, and I'm excited to share this book with my students and colleagues.

Gerard Lawson, Ph.D., LPC, LSATP, NCC, ACS
Professor of Counselor Education
Virginia Tech School of Education
Past President, American Counseling Association

Author Biography

William Steele, PsyD, MSW, MA, began his work in trauma in the early 1980s when he published the booklet *Preventing Teen Suicide*. In the mid-80s he began working with parents of murdered children and other witnesses to murder. He has assisted survivors and professionals following such tragic and traumatic incidents as the Gulf War, the bombing of the Federal Building in Oklahoma, 9/11 in New York and Washington, D.C., Hurricanes Katrina and Rita, survivors of the worst fire in Texas history, the murders of school personnel and students and the daily trauma children and adults experience that never receive national media attention.

Always a practitioner and passionate about bringing helpers intervention strategies to help them help others in distress while taking care of themselves, led to his founding of the National Institute for Trauma and Loss in Children (TLC) in 1990. As its director for 23 years, he created registered, evidence-based intervention programs and resources used in 55 countries by many of the 8,000 professionals he trained while at TLC. His work has been featured in the *Handbook of Play Therapy, Children in the Urban Environment, Understanding Mass Violence, Creative Interventions with Traumatized Children, Clinical Handbook of Art Therapy* and in varied journals. His publications *Trauma in Schools and Communities: Recovery Lessons from Survivors and Responders* and *Trauma Informed Practices with Children and Adolescents* demonstrate his ability to translate theory into practical, timely strategies.

Introduction

Not Smart Enough: A Reset

I was doing some research about learning when I happened upon a story that took me back to the 8th grade. The story was about Dr. Robert Sternberg, a former president of the American Psychological Association. It turns out that I accomplished what Dr. Robert Sternberg also accomplished. We both "flunked" the IQ tests we were given. He was in the sixth grade. I was in the eighth grade. My IQ test was the entrance exam used by the local high school. But wait, both of us were given the chance to retake it. We both did poorly the second time as well. I can still hear the voice of the admissions counselor when I was with my parents in his office. He was nice enough until he told my parents, "Your son is not college material. He lacks the skills for us to place him in our college prep track." My parents were devastated. All I remember thinking to myself was, "Okay I guess I'm not smart. What are they going to do with me now?"

In the Fall of that year, I ended up at another high school. What happened next changed my life. On the very first day, in the very first class, one of the priests, who taught at the school, introduced himself and then said, "Every one of you are here because you have the potential to do very well. Learning is something you do every day. However, when it comes to school learning, how you go about learning is different than when you're on the ball field or with friends. It's my job to teach you how to learn differently, how to study smart. Do what I tell you and you'll finish the year knowing you are good at learning." I believed him and went on to earn three graduate degrees. I didn't realize, for some time, how that first day reset my mind about "not being smart enough". I share this for two reasons. The first being how a simple resetting of my thoughts about learning made it possible to do what I was told would be impossible. For this reason, I am a firm believer in the power of mindsets. It turned my life around as have many of the mindsets regarding stress and self-care presented in this work. Of course, it demanded some effort on my part but that hopeful mindset provided all I needed. Applying the effort is something I'll have more to say about when talking about self-care. Before presenting the second reason for sharing this experience, there's a bit more I want to say about mindsets.

Think Differently

In her book, *The Upside of Stress: Why Stress Is Good for You and How to Get Good at It* McGonigal (2015, p. xii), a health psychologist, describes how she changed her view, her mindset about stress, from being an enemy to fight and eliminate to being something to embrace. She uncovered a good deal of research as to the importance of how we think about stress. The research showed that people who had high stress and believed stress was harmful to their life had a 43% greater risk of dying. Others who had similar high stress but did not see stress as harmful, had a lower risk of dying than anyone in the study including those experiencing very little stress.

These, and other results she reports, are certainly a strong motivator to check our thinking and approach to helper stress and self-care. I'll leave you to read her work, since she does such an excellent job covering the science of mindsets and how they influence our biology by releasing hormones specific to strengthening our brain under stress, our immune systems and overall wellness. These findings certainly encourage us to evaluate and, as needed, adjust our mindsets about helper stress and self-care. This work provides multiple opportunities to do just that.

I specifically use the term *helper stress* because it is different from, and in addition to, the stress of daily living. This difference demands additional mindsets related to the different forms of helper stress and how they can impact our lives as helpers. This difference also dictates identifying self-care approaches that are specific to what helpers can experience. I'll come back to this in a few minutes. Allow me to share another story about the power of a mindset to help one survivor thrive despite the trauma he experienced.

Land Mines and Resilience

A very good friend and colleague was working with survivors of land mine explosions in Beirut, Lebanon. The purpose was to train these survivors to promote resilience in peer-to-peer projects back in their home communities. When I asked if he would write a forward for my book about trauma-informed practices with children and adolescents, he provided a wonderful example demonstrating how resilience is determined by how we approach adversity in life. He told how, at the beginning of the program, one land mine survivor introduced himself to the group by asserting, "I am not a victim of a land mine. The land mine is a victim of me. I survived—the land mine didn't" (Steele & Malchiodi, 2012, p. ix).

There is no doubt that positive thinking in the midst of distress promotes resilience (Fredrickson, 2003). When we approach stress as a friend letting us know that it's time to do something different, it then becomes an opportunity to get better at what we do, feel better about what we do, improve our wellness and well-being and sustain our efforts and effectiveness as helpers. It's an opportunity to strengthen resilience, compassion and empathy, rather than increase the risk for compassion fatigue, secondary traumatic stress, burnout, empathetic distress and all the physical, mental, emotional and behavioral downsides associated with this stress. Throughout this work a number of mindsets are presented as to how you can resiliently approach the many different reactions associated with helper stress. Many of these mindsets come from my experiences helping those in distress and what they told me mattered the most in their efforts to remain resilient.

The Second Reason

Earlier I said there were two reasons for sharing my IQ story. Two people responded differently to my IQ scores. I was fortunate that one had a far more positive viewpoint. That memory was very much a part of how I have tried to approach life. I can honestly say that I never settled for what did not feel right for me and looked for other solutions when needed. Sometimes that search was immediately successful and sometimes it created more challenges until I realized I needed to move in yet another direction. When I earned a Master's Degree in Guidance and Counseling, it didn't take long to realize the training I received in the counseling area offered limited practical help for the issues those in distress were presenting. I went back and earned my MSW in social work and fortunately walked away with additional approaches to helping others. Having put in that much effort, it just made sense to me to see what yet another different way of thinking might offer so I completed my Doctorate of Psychology. All three provided different approaches to helping. I hadn't formulated a conscious mindset at that time, but I do know my approach was driven by that early experience about hearing something much different about my ability to learn. It was definitely worth the effort to pursue.

During this time, I worked in several environments that included a 24-hour crisis walk-in center, an outpatient community mental health program, a child guidance center, family services, an alcohol treatment center, a suicide prevention program, and as an on call mental health consultant assisting police responding to often volatile mental health crises. All these combined experiences were driven by the following mindset.

Different Stressors—Different Solutions

Mindset: *There is not one strategy that works for everyone. We can both be exposed to the same stressor yet have very different reactions and need different responses.*

Said differently, what works for me may not work for you. For example, meditation does not always help. Reappraisal and reframing may benefit some but not everyone. *Knowing that what works for one does not work for all supports that self-care must be personal.* There is no one best practice, there are many. However, for a care strategy to be effective it must specifically address how stress is being experienced by the individual, especially at the subjective level. By this I mean not assuming we know what is best for anyone because of the outward reactions or behaviors they are experiencing. Sometimes what is more important is what is driving those behaviors. Let me give you another personal experience that happened early in my life to explain this.

Mute

It always amazes me how some of our not so good childhood experiences become discovered treasures later in life. In the early grade school years, there was a period when what I had to say didn't matter, was responded to harshly or in demeaning ways, so I quit talking at home and at school. It was safer not to talk and I actually felt better. It was one way to detach myself from what was quite stressful. They call it selective mutism now; selective because when I was playing ball, especially football, I had a mouth on me. So, when I started working with survivors of trauma and they didn't want to talk about what happened to them, I understood. It was safer, a place where they felt better. Like myself when playing ball, they felt more comfortable in environments where they could exercise, get a massage or otherwise use their bodies to regulate their overly stressed nervous system. Attending to their bodies made it easier to do what they needed to do to move from one day to the next, until they were able to cognitively process what happened. This was the case with survivors I spent time with in Kuwait following the Gulf War, survivors of the horrific bombing of the Federal Building in Oklahoma that impacted so many families, the survivors of 9/11, Hurricanes Katrina and Rita and far too many traumatic incidents in school settings. For many, talking about what happened was not their initial need. These survivors needed relief from the stress holding their bodies hostage. I completely understood why not talking about what happened was so helpful because of what I was experiencing when I wasn't talking.

Getting At the Source

When I chose not to talk, everyone wanted to know what was wrong with me. They even sent me to a speech therapist assuming that's what I needed. All I remember about that adventure was the therapist having me practice trying to touch the tip of my tongue to the tip of my nose. I kid you not. Many years later out of curiosity I discovered this was called *orofacial myofunctional therapy*, known as the "Nose Touch" exercise to improve tongue strength and the flexibility needed for clear articulation and speech production. I never had a problem with articulation or speech production. Just ask those I played ball against. The source of the problem was what happened when I did talk, not what was wrong with me.

No one ever asked what was happening to me that I wasn't talking. If they had, I think I would have told those I felt safe with. It is the source driving our reactions that is sometimes more important than our behavioral responses. Strategies in this work are presented to identify those sources as needed. Getting to the source is also essential to determining which care strategies may be the most beneficial. When self-care efforts do not address what is being experienced subjectively, they are likely to be less than effective. This again means that self-care practices must be personal.

Helper Stress Is Different and Personal

When talking about the stress of everyday life, self-care such as regular exercise, eating healthy and maintaining social connections are all helpful. However, self-care for helper stress has to be in addition to those basic care practices because exposure to those in distress presents different challenges and reactions than those associated with everyday stress. Exposure to those in distress can lead to compassion fatigue, secondary trauma, posttraumatic stress, empathy distress, burnout and a long list of reactions associated with these forms of stress. These reactions need our attention while remembering there is no one solution that works for everyone. Reactions to the same stressors will vary, as will the subjective issues fueling these reactions. It is personal as is the self-care strategy that may be needed.

Self-Care Is Personal

I was in group psychotherapy partly to enhance my helper skills and partly to resolve a few difficulties. There came a time when everything came to a standstill. Talking simply was not helping. My therapist happened to be experienced in Bio-Energetics—using the body as a resource to heal. She experimented with several different body movements and exercises until we found the ones most effective in releasing the tension and stress my body was holding onto. Once that stress was released, I was on my way. For me it made a world of difference, for others not so much. However, had my therapist not been open to using multiple approaches, I'm fairly certain I would not be writing this book today.

Going back to 9/11, when I was meeting with survivors of the Pentagon Attack, they found comfort and healing by approaching their experience differently than those in New York who found talking too activating. Instead, Pentagon survivors found comfort meeting in groups to talk about how they were doing, what was helping or hurting. Again, this supports that self-care is personal. Sometimes it's about using the body as a resource, sometimes talking and sometimes a simple reframing of thoughts do us well, as it did for me regarding learning. There are a wide variety of options we'll explore to help you better determine what may work best for you.

The "What" of Self-Care

Another example about getting to the source is the difficulty many helpers have with not providing themselves with the same care they provide others. When this is the case, we need to ask what might be happening that this is so difficult to practice. We can go back to mindsets as one possibility. For years society has said that self-care is selfish, self-centered, indulgent, uncaring and unproductive. Self-sacrifice, on the other hand, has been promoted as far more honorable and virtuous than taking time for ourselves. If this is our mindset, then saying *yes* to ourselves and *no* to those in distress will likely trigger a good deal of guilt and shame at which point self-care will likely cease. It can be far more comfortable to say *yes* to others in distress than *yes* to our own self-care. It's this mindset, for some, that is driving their resistance to appropriately caring for themselves and their well-being. It could also be that their previous efforts were too time-consuming or unrealistic, such as the old approach of trying to create a work life balance versus approaching self-*care as an effort, not focused on managing our time, but harnessing our energy for supporting what matters most in our lives.* We're going to detail, in the first stage of this work, additional self-care mindsets, referred to as *approach points* for effective self-care that are associated with what is referred to today as *radical self-care.* Its approach is far more personal and appropriate for managing the unavoidable stress of helping and the world we live in today, and one being supported by health organizations worldwide.

When Stress Is Traumatic

The last twenty-three years of my career were spent meeting with thousands of helpers, many who were also survivors. I was also privileged to spend time with many survivors following catastrophic and traumatic environmental incidents, deadly shootings in schools and communities and those who experienced a variety of traumatic incidents not covered by national media. I met with those who suffered from physical and sexual abuse, were witnesses to the murder of friends and family members, and those exposed to non-violent yet traumatic incidents such as car fatalities, drowning, the loss of parents, the loss of a child. They were all my teachers. The ones who taught me that non-violent incidents can also be traumatic. They taught me that *it's not the situation that determines whether it is traumatic or stress inducing; it's how we experience that situation that determines the degree to which it is stressful or traumatic and the self-care that may be the most helpful.*

Not Always a Choice

Survivors also taught me that *how we react to what may be overwhelming or traumatic is not always a choice,* despite our resilience, intelligence or otherwise beneficial coping skills. In other words, all helpers are vulnerable to unexpected reactions that can be frightening and overwhelmingly stressful. For this reason, you'll be asked to view YouTube segments of a number of well-respected, very intelligent specialists in the neuroscience of stress. They'll describe what happened to them that activated totally unexpected responses and what they needed to calm that stress. They introduce the need for us to be effective at nervous system regulation as both a preventative and a restorative self-care practice. This is important because it can be difficult to access the necessary cognitive process to alleviate the ongoing nervous system driven stress associated with all forms of helper stress. Different levels of regulation practices will be detailed. Some of these are recommended daily and others for specific stress forms such as empathetic distress—having too much empathy.

It's Not Always You

The other factor to consider is that the self-care practices you engage in may well be appropriate for generalized stress, yet the culture and practices of the environment, in which you are working, engages in practices that fuel different stressors that are toxic and lead to burnout, compassion fatigue or even secondary trauma. If you are not aware of the toxic practices at your workplace or are aware, but applying ineffective care strategies, *maladaptive resilience* can quickly take over. This only compounds the strength of your distress. This happens more frequently than you might think because *resilience alone will not prevent burnout. Maladaptive resilience* is reflected in the statement, "There's nothing I can do but suck it up." This is why we also need to assess for those organizational factors, those toxic practices detrimental to daily functioning and well-being. This work also helps you to determine those specific practices associated with environments that allow helpers to flourish. This process will allow you to better evaluate the strengths and weaknesses of your environment in order to better determine the focus of your self-care related to the conditions you face daily.

No One Assessment

What will be more informative and helpful for determining where to apply self-care efforts regarding burnout, your responses to sixty questions related to burnout factors or to four? Four responses may indicate the possibility of burnout yet would need further evaluation to determine its actual presence, as well as the many factors fueling that burnout in order to apply the most appropriate self-care practices. This is why we ask you to complete a variety of assessments and surveys for each form of helper related stress presented in this work.

You'll be evaluating six different burnout areas involving helper stress. These include workload, control, reward, community, fairness and values. You'll be able to compare existing workplace toxic practices to those practices that help helpers flourish. These combined outcomes provide the opportunity to see which practices are most dominant in your environment and how they either support your well-being or leave you vulnerable to helper stress. Because personal well-being impacts how we respond to stress in the workplace, you'll also be asked to evaluate five personal well-being areas—physical, mental, emotional, spiritual and relational. Helper stress also involves a number of behaviors and reactions related to self-compassion, compassion satisfaction, compassion fatigue, secondary trauma, post-traumatic stress and empathy distress. These too need your evaluation. All these outcomes make it far easier to identify the areas of self-care that most need your attention.

Patterns & What Matters

When all these outcomes are combined, specific patterns will emerge related to areas of strength and those areas needing your self-care attention. These outcomes are recorded in a way that allows you to see the interrelatedness of different factors. For example, if your self-compassion practices are limited, you're likely to be experiencing lower compassion satisfaction, which will also be reflected in your well-being outcomes. Another example might be if your work engagement level is low, compassion satisfaction is likely not at its best and burnout more likely. A number of possible interpretations of combined outcomes are provided. What will emerge are those areas that would benefit from the focused self-care efforts presented in the final stage.

In essence, it is best to use a broad range of assessments in order to capture the many personal and workplace factors that can contribute to your stress. This will make it easier to identify the patterns of your stressful reactions and behaviors as well as those that support your well-being and sustain effectiveness. This in turn makes it easier to then select care strategies that best fit your unique conditions and reactions to the stressors you experience. However, you're asked to complete these assessments also *knowing that assessments do have some limitations.* Assessments may not always identify the subjective ways you are experiencing that stress, which are also driving your reactions. I talked about getting at the source, the *what* of our responses earlier, yet repeat it here because it is so important to effective self-care. For example, avoiding a particular situation because it stresses you is your response; what is driving that avoidance is triggered by your internal, often immediate, reaction. The challenge is to identify the *what* of that situation that is driving your avoidant behavior. This outcome then becomes the focus of self-care efforts. When this is the case, it will be beneficial to use specific questions to get at these sources. These questions, along with examples are also presented

About The Book

Helpers Defined

For ease of reading, the term "helper" is inclusive of those who serve, protect, heal, teach or care for others in distress. Primarily it refers to first responders, healthcare workers, mental health professionals, social workers, psychologists, child welfare workers, educators, caregivers, judges, court workers, law enforcement, attorneys and other helpers at risk, such as veterinarians and ministers, who face their own unique situations. The terms, *reaction* and *responses* are also used versus *symptoms* to emphasize that helper stress is not an illness but an unavoidable part of being a helper. *Reaction* refers to those quick, spontaneous physiological reactions and *responses* refer to our behavioral and cognitive responses to what stresses us. Our reactions are not a choice, our responses are.

Some Things Change—Some Do Not

Many things change over time, some do not. Six years ago, I wrote about helper stress. Some of that content, while updated, is presented in this work because it is as relevant and as valid as it was years ago. For many, the new reality that emerged from COVID is that self-care is no longer an indulgence, it is a necessity. As a result, helpers are realizing that different stressors demand different solutions, different approaches to self-care. This is in the midst of growing research showing that resilience alone will not prevent burnout or compassion fatigue. It's showing that meditation and other strategies may be beneficial for some, yet not beneficial for all. Given these emerging issues and others, I decided, when asked, to write this work to focus on helping helpers approach self-care in ways experience and science show are associated with low stress and anxiety, stronger well-being, fulfillment and sustainability.

Experience Matters

This work is partially based on personal experiences during challenging times that shaped several positive mindsets about people and possibilities. Today these are science supported, beneficial approaches to stress and self-care. It is also based on my professional experiences as a helper, trainer and trauma consultant for other helpers and trauma survivors across the country who were exposed to countless stressful and traumatic experiences. I wrote about a number of these national and local incidents in *Trauma in Schools and*

Communities: Recovery Lessons from Survivors and Responders (Steele, 2015). What they shared with me, their lessons and challenges, are still very relevant today. In many ways they established critical mindsets about recovering and adapting to the intense stress they experienced.

What Matters Most

What matters most, a favorite phrase of mine, is that I became the student while the helpers and survivors I spent time with became my teachers. In many ways I am simply the conveyor of their wisdom. One of the other things they taught me is that what mattered to them, while in crises, was not theory but practical, doable and immediately useful tools and suggestions. Had I not been able to do that, I would not have been repeatedly called by organizations, various programs and school districts across the country to help them with the stress they were experiencing following exposure to both violent and non-violent incidents. It's their combined endorsements, recovery wisdom, collaboration and positive feedback over the years that have become the voices of this workbook.

Engagement

I am also a firm believer that the best way to motivate others to accept that what is being taught can make a difference is to engage them in activities that support what is being said. The experiences you will be asked to complete have been used many times with participants in trainings I've provided over the years. These have consistently generated the desired outcomes and reinforced the supportive importance of the self-care strategies and mindsets presented.

These activities are free for you to use if you are also a presenter. When introducing activities, I suggest how to present them. Instructions begin with the phrase *If presenting*. As a reader simply read the instructions and begin the activity. Following the activity, I provide suggestions for processing the results. The wording that follows the phrase *My experience* responds to what participants in trainings I've conducted had to say about the activity you just completed, so you can compare your responses to theirs; as readers, you can do the same if you have completed the activity.

Five Stages

There are five stages. Each stage has one to several chapters dedicated to it. The use of stages signifies that arriving at those self-care efforts that best align with your personal needs is a process. If you came to me saying you are experiencing compassion fatigue, it would be foolish of me to give you a recommendation without first identifying the sources causing you to fatigue as well as determine whether it's fatigue or something else. For example, many assume burnout is the result of limited resilience. Science tells us resilience is not always the issue. There was a time when meditation was the universal recommendation to alleviate stress. Not only did it not work for me, the time spent on it and my frustration with the results just added to my stress and the response, "I'll just suck it up." Fortunately, I found mindfulness and reflection to be of tremendous benefit.

Practices related to cognitive and emotional regulation are also presented as these are critical to avoiding compassion fatigue and empathetic distress. The same practices are also critical to co-existing with the stress of helping as that stress does not disappear. In addition, you'll identify ways of approaching life that are associated with low stress, well-being and self-fulfillment. The final stage culminates in your determining which of the self-care strategies presented will best fit your personal care needs. Throughout these stages multiple assessments are completed in order to allow you to identify your specific, non-helpful reactions and responses and to review all outcomes in one place to arrive at possible interpretations of your outcomes. This is followed by an extensive review of care practices for you to select according to the levels of intensity and the responses that matter most in your efforts to minimize the stress of helping.

How Will This Help Me?

I cannot say how this work may be helpful to you personally, nor can everything be personally meaningful for you. However, I can say, with all confidence, that just as one particular stressor can have more impact on you than other multiple ones, one story, one statement, one piece of research, one example, activity or assessment outcome can also bring about a significant change. Examples will appear throughout this work as a way of saying, "If it worked for me, it can work for you." On the other hand, I also stated earlier, "What works for me may not work for you." Therefore, examples and recommendations come from a variety of different sources to help ensure that you find what may be helpful to you in some way.

The Effort

I will say that little happens without some effort. I had to put effort into learning how to learn that Freshman year in high school. This is a workbook that will be asking you to put some effort into determining what areas needing care matter most to you and what care strategies may be most helpful. I can assure you that if you came to me for some help with compassion fatigue, for example, I would spend time asking you numerous questions as to what you have been experiencing. Questions could cover frequency of reactions, their severity, what they make you feel like doing and what the worst part of these experiences have been like for you. I would ask what you have tried doing to help yourself and how that worked out. The list of possible questions would continue before providing any suggestions. I would certainly offer that compassion fatigue does not happen suddenly and is the result of several factors and conditions, some beyond your control and others as a result of your personal responses. I would then let you know that it would take some time and effort on both our parts to identify the sources of your fatigue, as well as the care strategies that might be immediately helpful and some that may take more effort. This workbook is designed to guide you through that effort by providing the tools needed, feedback and suggestions, that I am confident will matter to you.

You'll Discover

You may not find what you intended to find, but I think you will discover what you need to help you lower the effects of the stress of being a helper at a time when the demand for what you do is so much greater than in the past. You certainly deserve to do what you need to do to take care of yourself, your well-being, and what matters most to you. This is not only beneficial for you, it's beneficial for those you are helping.

References

Fredrickson, B., L., (2003). *The Value of Positive Emotions.* Retrieved October 27, 2025 from https://www.americanscientist.org/sites/americanscientist.org/files/20058214332_306.pdf

McGonigal, K. (2015). *Why Stress Is Good for You & How To Get It and Get Good At It.* NY, Avery.

Steele, W. (2015). *Trauma in Schools and Communities: Lessons Learned from Survivors and Responders.* NY, Routledge.

Steele W., & Malchiodi C. (2012). *Trauma-Informed Practices with Children and Adolescents.* NY, Routledge.

STAGE ONE

Approaching Self-Care and Stress

CHAPTER 1

Approaching Self-Care

What Hasn't Worked, What Does, Ten Approach Points

Theme

Old mindsets regarding self-care have created major roadblocks to helper wellness, well-being, effectiveness and sustainability. They have also left helpers far more vulnerable to burnout, compassion fatigue, secondary trauma and empathy distress. This chapter identifies the healthier and more effective approaches to self-care that support the necessary proactive, preventative and restorative practices in the face of the unavoidable stress of helping others in today's world. These will be summarized near the conclusion of this chapter under *approach points.* Each chapter will conclude with its own set of *approach points,* identifying how they align with this overall approach to helper stress.

Self-Care Defined

Let's review how self-care is being redefined. Tygielski (2022, para. 9), defines self-care as "taking an active role in protecting one's well-being, pursuing joy, and having the ability, tools and resources to respond to periods of stress so they do not result in an imbalance and lead to a health crisis." Scott (2025) is a bit more specific as she suggests that self-care is a conscious act people take to promote

DOI: 10.4324/9781003673699-2

their physical, mental, spiritual and emotional health. Spiritual health, or what is referred to as spiritual intelligence (King, 2008; Fidelis et al., 2024), reflects an approach to life associated with low stress, anxiety and depression, and involves the practices and mindsets supportive of well-being and personal fulfillment.

Not An Indulgence

Skovholt & Trotter-Mathison (2016) promote self-soothing, relaxation, and resilience strategies as ways to achieve physical and mental well-being. I think we would all agree these practices are beneficial for everyday stress reduction, however, additional strategies are needed to address compassion fatigue, secondary trauma, problems with empathy, self-compassion and other stressors. As Forman (2021, para. 3) reminds us, "self-care is not an indulgence, it's a discipline that enables you to keep functioning at your best." Obviously, as helpers, this is always the objective.

An Ethical Responsibility

Not only is self-care not an indulgence, it is an ethical duty every helper implicitly agrees to when assuming their responsibilities. In fact, every major helping profession has a stated self-care code of ethics. For example, The American Nurses Association (2022) Code of Ethics indicates "The nurse has moral duties to self as a person of inherent dignity and worth including an expectation of a safe place to work that fosters flourishing, authenticity of self at work, and self-respect through integrity and professional competence" and "Nurses must be alert to the signs and symptoms that their own health and well-being have been negatively affected." The first responder's code states, "These principles declare that it is unethical not to attend to your self-care as a practitioner, because sufficient self-care prevents harming those we serve" (Green Cross Academy of Traumatology, 2010, para. 2). However, knowing self-care is an ethical responsibility is not enough. I like Forman's definition because the term "discipline" reflects that self-care takes some effort, more specifically, *effective effort*, which we will come back to shortly.

Managing Our Energy

An excellent way to approach self-care was proposed by Schwartz & McCarthy (2007), from Harvard Business School, when they summarize that self-care is not about managing our time but managing our energy. It's not about the older concept of work-life balance but managing our energy to sustain what matters most to us. Managing our energy is not about doing more but about doing things differently. In other words, a self-care strategy that does not support or restore our energy to do what we do is not a helpful strategy. Put simply, when we feel good, we do good. When we feel bad, we don't do so good.

It's Personal

The World Health Organization (WHO, 2024, para. 1) agrees that self-care is personal when it recommends self-care intervention through "a holistic approach to the health and well-being of each person, taking account of their circumstances, needs and desires." Self-care must be personalized to each person's specific problematic stressors, reactions and conditions, needs and desires. This is achieved via outcomes from assessments and surveys, subjective questioning and each person's determination of what matters most for their self-care.

Radical Self-Care

Degges-White (2020) talks about radical self-care as "a move away from a focus on self-indulgence to creating a source of self-protection" to "taking care of things at the source rather than just sugarcoating or managing the symptoms" (para. 1–para. 2). Getting at the source triggering our stress is presented in the second chapter when talking about approaching stress; this refers to the way we respond behaviorally, emotionally and cognitively during stressful times that either benefits us or hurts us. Audre Lorde was a Black civil rights activist, writer, lesbian and feminist who initiated the radical self-care concept. Porteous-Sebouhian (2021) credits her with stating, "Caring for myself is not self-indulgence, it is self-preservation" (para. 1). Following this he adds that it "sustained her ability to enact change" (para. 3). In other words, radical self-care allowed her to manage her energy. Nicole Steward wrote in her book, *Radical Self-Care* (2025, p. xxviii–xxix), "Radical self-care invites, allows and demands that we unapologetically advocate for ourselves and be unshakeable in our belief that we are worthy of this care." This is certainly true when dealing with toxic workplace practices and environments that provide little support for their helpers' well-being despite the daily exposure to the distress of others.

As A Helper

Radical self-care, for you as a helper, is about asking what matters the most: a question you will return to repeatedly as you reflect on what you are learning.

Radical self-care is also about asking ourselves how satisfied we really are with what we are doing, how we are doing it and where we are doing it. Satisfaction levels are a good indicator of burnout and compassion fatigue, as well as compassion satisfaction and self-fulfillment. Radical care is also about embracing self- compassion, an absolute essential for sustaining compassion satisfaction. It is about setting boundaries as the only way to make space for ourselves; and working in an environment that aligns with our values (Parker et al., 2023).

Different for Everyone

The National Institute of Mental Health (NIMH, 2025, para. 14) self-care statement starts out by saying that "Self-care looks different for everyone." In essence, it supports the following mindset.

Mindset: *There is no one intervention or self-care strategy that fits every individual or every situation.*

This has been proven to myself and many others, many times over. Listening to the survivors of such traumatic incidents as the 1995 bombing of the Federal Building in Oklahoma City where 168 people were killed including infants and children, revealed the many different ways people coped. Both their reactions and how they coped varied greatly. What I learned when I met with some 200 volunteers helping the 25,000 evacuees in the Houston Astrodome following Hurricanes Katrina and Rita also varied greatly. The stressors they experienced varied from one to another and the solutions they found to be helpful worked for some, but definitely not all.

As indicated in the Introduction, spending time with the survivors of 9/11 in both New York and Washington D.C. was no different. Many in New York directly exposed to that horrific attack on America said talking about what happened only made it worse, while others said that having access to the local workout facilities helped them better than talking. On the other hand, meeting with survivors of the Pentagon attack told me that being together with others in their survivor group meetings mattered the most to their well-being. When spending time with survivors of the 2012 massacre at Sandy Hook Elementary, it was no different. Individuals experienced what happened differently and they had many different ways of coping. For one administrator, it was paying attention to his breathing, for a counselor and mother it was yoga, for another it was being reminded that "recovery was not a race but a marathon" and for others it was reaching out to other helpers in the community (Steele, 2015, p. 91).

Believe me there were times when the lessons I was learning through my experiences with survivors challenged my thinking and changed my mindsets about helper stress, recovery, resilience and self-care. Because this is important, allow me to give you two additional examples.

Cognitive Reappraisal

Cognitive reappraisal and reframing is a recommended self-care strategy related to changing thoughts associated with compassion fatigue, burnout or secondary trauma. Wang & Yang (2023) indicate in their research the limitations of reframing, as no two situations are alike. We know that two people can be exposed to the same traumatic situation yet have very different responses that will demand different self-care strategies. Meditation is also often recommended as a self-care practice for managing stress. However, Farias (2024) points out that adverse effects are not rare and include increased anxiety and depression. He also found that these outcomes happen to those who have had no previous mental health problems. So, once again we reiterate, what works for one does not work for all.

Trial and Error

The National Institute of Mental Health (NIMH, 2025, para. 14) statement goes on to say, "It may take trial and error to discover what works best for you." Arriving at self-care strategies specific to your needs will take some effort on your part. However, you will have the outcomes necessary to determine the focus of your care efforts by completing the assessments and surveys provided in this resource. The strategies you select may be a perfect fit; then again, they may need to be replaced with a different strategy. Let's take a minute to detail the practices and mindsets of *effective effort* as this disciplined effort reflects the characteristics and actions of resilience and radical self-care. Effective effort, by the way, is also a form of *good stress* or what is referred to as *eustress,* a form of stress that enhances our performance, sustainability, resilience and well-being (Cohen, 2024).

Effective Effort

The Director of Professional Learning for Mindset Works provides the following definition of effective effort which is also a mindset.

"Effective Effort is purposeful and targeted. When I am really trying effectively, I am doing a LOT! I pause and quietly think. I problem-solve. I research. I tinker. I figure out what isn't working and change my strategy. I furrow my brow, and I don't stop until I figure it out" (Diehl, 2017, p. 122).

The following categories describe how I recommend approaching self-care effectively.

Curiosity

The first characteristic of resilience described by Diehl is curiosity—*I quietly think, I research, I tinker, I figure out what isn't working.* This is exactly what I am asking you to do related to thinking differently about stress and self-care, approaching these differently at times, trying a variety of cognitive processes, adopting new mindsets, completing a variety of assessments in order to determine the strategies you will try.

Persistence

The second characteristic also found in resilient individuals is persistence—*I furrow my brow, and I don't stop until I figure it out.* When never giving up involves not changing what is not working, it is stubbornness. Stubbornness is rigid, an unwillingness to change one's attitude or position. *Persistence is keeping focused on what we desire even when we need to change how we're trying to make it happen.*

Risk Taking

The third characteristic of resilience is risk taking—*I figure out what isn't working and change my strategy.* Getting out of our comfort zone is never easy and does induce some stress. However, getting out of our comfort zone introduces us to new outcomes, different ways to think and adapt. Risk taking is a form of both good stress and resilience building.

Courage

The fourth characteristic is the courage to continue while vulnerable—*I don't stop until I figure it out.* In many ways, vulnerability defines what we feel when we care for or respond to those in distress. We can't predict the outcome. We may influence it a bit, but we can't control it. We find ourselves in situations where we have no answers, where we ourselves feel overwhelmed at times and yet we continue to respond and care the best we can. Effective effort helps us to be at our best despite the challenges we face. This is demonstrated in the following study by Carol Dweck reported by Regan & Meehan (2018).

The Study

Four hundred fifth graders were all given an easy IQ test. Following the test, half the group was praised for their intelligence (You are really smart), the rest of their group for their effort (You really worked hard at this). Both groups were then given the opportunity to take a harder test or take a test similar to the first one where they would do well. Amazingly, 60% of those praised for their intelligence took the easier test while 92% of those praised for their effort took the more difficult test. What this demonstrated is that those praised for their intelligence heard, *"Oh you value me because I am really smart so I will not do anything to change that."* The kids praised for their effort on the other hand heard, *"You won't criticize me for making a mistake but let me learn from it and continue to work hard."*

In the next step, all students were given an impossible test. What they discovered is that those praised for their effort actually worked harder and longer on this test than those praised for their intelligence who were easily frustrated and gave up early. In the final part of this study, all students were given a test similar to the first one. Once again, an amazing result. Those praised for their intelligence did 20% worse, while those praised for effort raised their average score by 30%.

Mindset: *Effective effort is a wonderful example of good stress or eustress; it motivates, inspires, teaches, enhances performance, self-fulfillment and well-being.*

Self-care is definitely worthy of our *effective effort* and pursuit.

Spiritual Intelligence

Another well researched approach to self-care associated with low stress and anxiety is engaging in the practices associated with Spiritual Intelligence (SI). SI is not about religion but how we approach and live life. It is essential self-care. Pinto et al. (2024) found a significant relationship between SI and low levels of burnout, stress, depression and anxiety. In addition, their research showed SI enhanced resilience, emotional intelligence and mental health. O'Sullivan & Lindsay (2022) also found SI increased resilience, reduced depression anxiety and stress. In essence, the everyday practices of SI are essential preventative self-care practices for supporting our overall well-being and, as such, need to be part of any self-care strategy over and above those specific to burnout, compassion fatigue, empathetic distress. You'll have the opportunity to learn more about SI and evaluate your SI levels when we spend more time on self-care strategies in *Chapter Nine*.

My Final Questions

Go to Appendix B-1 & B-1.2, My Final Questions. Record your answers for the following two questions.

1. Of all that you read or experienced in this chapter what one thought stands out the most for you?
2. Of the mindsets established in this chapter which one stands out the most for you?

If presenting, repeat the process established in this chapter following each chapter.

My experience has been that participants best appreciate the reframing of self-care, thinking of it as a way to harness energy rather than approaching it as a work-life balance issue. Many also indicate that the example related to praise and *effective effort* was quite effective and not what many of them experience in their workplaces.

Approach Points

Given what others have experienced, written about and researched, our approach to self-care is based on the following *approach points* (parallel stress approaches presented in the next chapter are in parentheses).

- ❑ It's not an indulgence (Stress is a friend letting us know it's time to do different).
- ❑ It's an act of self-preservation, self-protection, advocating for ourselves because we're worth it (It's about wellness and well-being, and being deserving of flourishing workplace practices).
- ❑ It's a way of approaching life for maintaining our well-being (It's staying within our window of tolerance).
- ❑ It's about advocating for our well-being because we are worthy of it (Worthy of environments that promote well-being and flourishing).
- ❑ It's different for everyone. It's personal (What works for me may not work for you).
- ❑ It's saying "yes" to what matters most to you (It's saying *yes* to *eustress*).

- ❏ It's about sustainability (Being able to fulfill my purpose and find meaning via my workplace).
- ❏ It's about managing energy, not time (Not doing more—doing different, regulating our physiology).
- ❏ It's about engaging effective effort to determine the self-care that meets our personal needs (It's about assessing, reflecting, doing differently).
- ❏ It's utilizing self-care to get at the source of our stress (It's the *what* triggering our reaction that matters the most).

Summary

Before determining the self-care strategies that will matter most to you, there needs to be an awareness of those sources of stress that need your self-care the most. The easiest sources to identify are workplace practices. The more difficult are your thoughts, emotions, behaviors and your approach to all aspects of your life—professional, physical, personal, relational, mental, emotional, social and spiritual. You'll have the opportunity to evaluate each of these areas in order to better determine what self-care practices may personally be most beneficial for you. However, before we begin that process, we need to think about the way we approach stress and what matters most in that approach. The following two chapters establish the approach this workbook will be guiding you through.

References

American Nurses Association. (2022). *Code of Ethics for Nurses with Interpretive Statements*. Retrieved May 14, 2026 from https://codeofethics.ana.org/provision-5

Cohen, H. (2024, August 13). *Eustress: The Good Stress*. Retrieved July 25, 2025 from https://www.psychologytoday.com/gb/blog/be-the-sun-not-the-salt/202408/eustress-the-good-stress

Degges-White, S. (2020, October 30). *Radical Self-Care to Protect Your Overall Well-Being*. Retrieved July 17, 2025 from https://www.psychologytoday.com/gb/blog/lifetime-connections/202010/radical-self-care-to-protect-your-overall-well-being

Diehl, E. (2017). Growth Mindsets for Learning: Effective Effort. In W. Steele (Ed.). *Optimizing Learning Outcomes: Proven Brain-Centric, Trauma Sensitive Practices*. (p. 122–143). NY, Routledge.

Farias, M. (2024, July 19). *Meditation can be harmful—and can even make mental health problems worse.* Retrieved July 25, 2025 from https://theconversation.com/meditation-can-be-harmful-and-can-even-make-mental-health-problems-worse-230435

Fidelis, A., Moreria, A.C., & Vitoria, A. (2024). Multiple perspectives of spiritual intelligence: A systematic literature review. *Social Sciences & Humanities Open.* Retrieved July 25, 2025 from https://www.sciencedirect.com/science/article/pii/S2590291124000767

Forman, T. (2021, December 13). *Self-Care Is Not An Indulgence, It's A Discipline.* Retrieved July 21, 2025 from https://www.forbes.com/sites/tamiforman/2017/12/13/self-care-is-not-an-indulgence-its-a-discipline/

Green Cross Academy of Traumatology. (2010). *Ethics of Self-Care.* Retrieved August 16, 2018 from https://www.ncbi.nlm.nih.gov/books/NBK207194/box/part2_ch2.box30/?report

King, D. B. (2008). Rethinking claims of spiritual intelligence: A definition, model, and measure (M. Sc.). *Trent University,* Canada.

NIMH (2025). *Caring for Your Mental Health.* Retrieved July 25, 2025 from https://www.nimh.nih.gov/health/topics/caring-for-your-mental-health

O'Sullivan, L., & Lindsay, N. (2022, June 13). The relationship between spiritual intelligence, resilience, and well-being in an Aotearoa New Zealand sample. *Journal of Spirituality in Mental Health,* 25(4): 277–297. https://doi.org/10.1080/19349637.2022.2086840

Parker, B. A., Mohtasham, D., Donnella, L. (2023, April 19). *Real Self-Care Takes Real Systemic Change.* Retrieved July 29, 2025 from https://www.npr.org/sections/codeswitch/2023/04/19/1170063872/self-care-laid-bare

Pinto, C. T., Guedes, L., Pinto, S., & Nunes, R. (2024, February 1). Spiritual Intelligence: a scoping review on the gateway to mental health. *Global Health Action,* 17(1): 2362310. https://doi.org/10.1080/16549716.2024.2362310

Porteous-Sebouhian, B. (2021, October 27). *Why Acknowledging and Celebrating the Black Feminist Origins of Self-Care is Essential.* Retrieved July 30, 2025 from https://www.linkedin.com/pulse/why-acknowledging-celebrating-black-feminist-origins-/

Regan T., & Meehan T. (2018). *Growth Mindset Feedback and Praise.* Retrieved October 6, 2018 from https://trainugly.com/portfolio/peerfeedback/

Schwartz, T., & McCarthy, C. (2007, October). *Manage Your Energy Not Your Time.* Retrieved July 25, 2025 from https://hbr.org/2007/10/manage-your-energy-not-your-time

Scott, E. (2025, November 5). *5 Types of Self-Care for Every Area of Your Life.* Retrieved July 21, 2025 from https://www.verywellmind.com/self-care-strategies-overall-stress-reduction-3144729

Skovholt, T., & Trotter-Mathison, M. (2016). *The Resilient Practitioner: Burnout and Compassion Fatigue Prevention and Self-Care Strategies for The Helping Profession.* NY, Routledge.

Steele, W. (2015). *Trauma In Schools And Communities.* NY, Routledge

Tygielski, S. (2022, February 21). *The Power of Self-Care: A Bridge to Communal Care.* Retrieved July, 21, 2025 from https://nonprofitquarterly.org/the-power-of-self-care-a-bridge-to-communal-care/

Wang, Y. X., & Yang, B. (2023, April 17). A new understanding of the cognitive reappraisal technique: an extension based on the schema theory. *Front Behav Neurosci.* https://doi.org/10.3389/fnbeh.2023.1174585

WHO (2024, April 26). *Self-Care for Health and Well-Being.* Retrieved July 21, 2025 from https://www.who.int/health-topics/self-care#tab=tab_2

CHAPTER 2

Approaching Helper Stress

Navigating Its Multidimensional Factors

Theme

Our approach does matter. Most of us have traveled by plane at one time or another, so allow me to make this analogy regarding this approach to stress and self-care. You've been flying for a few hours when the seat belt sign flashes and the cabin attendant has everyone put their tray tables up and close any overhead bins that may be open. Everything seems to be going fine until the pilot makes a sharp uphill ascent and then banks the plane to the left, that causes everyone to worry. After circling, for what seems like forever, navigating the second approach begins. Your thumbs are buried in clenched fists. You see the runway lights outside your window as the pilot slowly turns the plane to start its descent. When the wheels hit the tarmac, you're still not ready to applaud until it travels a bit further without incident. Your body doesn't begin to relax until the plane reaches the terminal, the seat belt sign is turned off and the cabin door opens. You probably don't feel total relief until you're in your car leaving the airport; maybe not even till you park the car and open the door to wherever you are staying or living.

Before navigating the second approach, the pilot had time to reflect on what went wrong and make the adjustments needed for a successful landing. Consider sustained well-being, effectiveness, compassion satisfaction, self-fulfillment your destination. Whether you reach that destination is totally dependent on

DOI: 10.4324/9781003673699-3

your approach. This chapter presents a detailed strategy for responding to helper stress that takes into account changes from past approaches. However, before we get there, it's important to first appreciate the multidimensional factors of helper stress that can either increase the downsides of our stress, or be used to support an approach to helper stress that becomes a rich resource for growth. The *approach points* for preventing or mitigating the downsides of stress that align with the self-care points presented in *Chapter One* are listed at the conclusion of the chapter.

It's Multidimensional

- ❑ In this era of *The Great Exhaustion* (Ballesteros, 2024), burnout is at an all-time high. Anyone who works is vulnerable to burnout and all its associated stress reactions.
- ❑ Burnout is largely the result of toxic workplace practices and how employees react to these practices.
- ❑ However, not everyone who works is vulnerable to helper stress and its additional stress reactions.
- ❑ Helper stress is different than burnout although it often involves burnout factors.
- ❑ Helper stress is different because of the daily exposure to the distress of those being helped—their stories, the details of what has or is happening to them, how they are experiencing that distress emotionally, cognitively, physiologically and behaviorally.
- ❑ Varied stress reactions cut across five different categories—*burnout, compassion fatigue, empathy distress, secondary trauma, post-traumatic stress.*
- ❑ Just as there is no one solution that fits everyone in distress, there is no one self-care strategy that fits every helper's reaction to the distress of others. What may work for one, may not work for another, even though both are exposed to the same distress.
- ❑ It's not the distress of others or situations helpers face that determine whether it is or is not stressful; it's the helper's personal reaction to that exposure that determines the stressful impact it may cause.
- ❑ Helpers can work in an environment that is fairly supportive and not conducive to burnout, yet still experience any one of the above helper stress categories because of how they are personally reacting and responding to that exposure. If they are also working in a more toxic burnout producing environment, they are even more at risk for helper related stress.
- ❑ Finally, helpers who are responding to those whose experiences have been, or are, traumatic will be more vulnerable to secondary trauma or

> post-traumatic stress if their workplace is not engaging trauma-specific practices supporting their helpers' well-being as well as readiness for the unique stress traumatized individuals and/or situations present.

All these multi-dimensional variables and the many stress reactions they can induce, establishes the following mindsets for approaching these variables.

Mindset: *Different stressors will demand different solutions.*

Mindset: *It only takes one particular stressor and/or one particular way of responding to that stressor to decrease our effectiveness, erode our sense of well-being and challenge our thoughts about self, what we do and who we help.*

A good example of the power of just one not-helpful reaction is that of being too empathetic

Being too empathetic causes empathy distress, the shutting down of appropriate helper responses and puts those being helped at risk along with the helper. This is why our primary focus will be isolating specific stress reactions you may be experiencing in order to select your self-care strategies. This approach more easily allows us to use stress as a resource for growth. For now, I hope you can approach stress as suggested below; it will make a difference as to what you eventually determine needs your personalized self-care.

Enemy or Friend?

For years we've been told that stress is our enemy, one we need to defeat or, at best, somehow avoid. This approach has not worked well. The fact is stress never goes away. It is and always will be a part of life. Helper stress cannot be avoided and most helpers will have some reactions and responses needing attention. During COVID, and following the end of the pandemic, it was reported that 30% of healthcare workers experienced post-traumatic stress (Qui et al., 2021). There was even a rise in post-traumatic stress among the general population during this time (Zang et al., 2021). Studies also found similar increases in secondary traumatic stress (Whitt-Woosley et al., 2022). When interviewed 42% of social workers were found to be suffering from secondary traumatic stress (Ratcliff, 2024). Helper stress cuts across all helping professions. I think it's safe to say that this country's current climate and the issues its helpers face, across all professions, will sustain continued higher levels of stress for some time.

Note: Healthcare does a far better job of researching the stress of healthcare providers than any other helper related profession. However, helper stress across professions has been documented for years. Prevalence data can be found in *Appendix C-3*.

Mindset: *The fact is, helper stress is unavoidable; what we do with it or how we approach it is what matters most. If what you have been doing is not giving you the results you desire, it's time for a different approach.*

As A Friend

The good news is science has definitively shown us that stress can be a friend, a motivator, a positive influencer for change, mastery, self-fulfillment, wellness, sustained well-being and effectiveness, if we approach it as a resource, not something to be feared (McGonigal, 2015; Scott, 2023). Others report that approaching stress as a resource and opportunity for growth significantly lowers the downsides of stress (Crum et al., 2017). The way we think about stress and how we approach it determines whether it becomes an enemy or a very helpful friend we can take with us into any stressful situation with minimal distress. This is not to say that there will never be a time when we don't become overwhelmed by what we are exposed to, sometimes we don't have a choice as to how our mind and body respond. However, "bouncing back" will be much easier when we allow that stress to be a friend that is leading us to new discoveries about us, personally and professionally.

Before we review each specific form of helper stress, we need to clarify some of the issues that have developed around helper stress terminology, such as addressing reactions and responses versus categories and the fact that similar reactions are common across all the categories of helper stress. These and other issues can leave us confused and asking, "So how am supposed to respond?" Let's first look at additional issues that helpers struggle with, and then present an uncomplicated approach to effectively minimize and spend less energy struggling with stress and more energy focusing on what matters most for you personally.

Free-Flowing Statements

Allow me for a few minutes to engage in some free-flowing statements regarding stress, its varied reactions and the issues that our approach to helper stress must consider. I may end up repeating the same things, but in different ways, because when we read or hear things differently, we respond differently. After finishing, I'll indicate how others have responded when this process has been used in presentations.

- ❏ What stresses me may not stress you. What helps me with the same stressors you are experiencing may not help you. This is why there is no one solution or self-care strategy that works for everyone. For example, talking about what has happened can intensify stress and not lessen it for some.
- ❏ Two of us can be exposed to the same stressor yet have very different reactions. My reactions might trigger any number of negative thoughts

about what I'm doing, about my competence, about those I'm helping or about myself as a person. On the other hand, your reactions may be more emotional than mine. Fear, anxiety, worry, anger, disbelief, frustration, feeling powerless, or emotionally overwhelmed are all possibilities.

- ❑ Maybe we have different physical reactions such as fatigue, headaches, changes in heart rates, or difficulty sleeping. Then again, I may not even be aware of some of the reactions I'm having that are not helping me or those I'm trying to help. This is why multiple assessment approaches provide a more comprehensive view of all the possible reactions of being exposed to those in distress.
- ❑ Then there is workplace stress. Are there toxic workplace cultures that lead us to burnout? Absolutely. Stress is not always because of what we are or are not doing in the way of self-care but because of the specific practices in that culture. Those stressful practices may not stress you; they might stress others, just not in the same way they're triggering you. The fact is, resilience alone will prevent neither burnout nor other forms of helper stress. Some thrive in stressful environments because of their perceptions about stress. This makes us wonder, are my reactions to stress defined by characteristics of resilience or are there other factors involved?
- ❑ Then again, we may do what we do in a workplace whose culture is not toxic, whose practices support our wellness and well-being, yet are still stressed by the end of the day. Might the work load be too much for us? Maybe it's time management issues or struggles with completing necessary paperwork? Maybe it's just one person, like a supervisor, who is less than supportive or knowledgeable enough to be helpful, or maybe, for whatever reason, we just don't trust that supervisor.
- ❑ We all go to our workplace carrying unresolved stress in our personal lives, leaving us even more vulnerable to issues that otherwise would not be as stressful. My stress could be the result of relationships or lack of, certain life events, illness, financial or social issues. When this is the case, my self-care strategies need to address those specific areas as well as workplace induced stressors.
- ❑ On the other hand, stress is not always a choice. We could be moving along quite well until one day the person(s) and/or condition(s) we are exposed to catches every part of us off guard, triggering a cascade of reactions never experienced before. Those reactions may have nothing to do with compassion fatigue, empathetic distress or burnout. They could be associated with secondary trauma or what some refer to as vicarious trauma.
- ❑ Then again, that one day of exposure could be triggering reactions associated with some personal experience that we never quite resolved

and could be a countertransference issue, which demands a strategy different from what we are already doing.

- ❑ How do we know what type of stress we are experiencing, especially when some reactions are listed under several different categories? How do we determine what will best help us with that stress?
- ❑ After years of becoming familiar with compassion fatigue, as the term most associated with the cost of caring, we read that compassion does not fatigue and that the term compassion fatigue should be replaced with the term "empathy distress." However, the empathy distress reactions cited in numerous blogs and papers are also associated with secondary trauma, even burnout depending on who you read; it can get confusing. It makes me wonder how I can tell the difference. Then again, does terminology even matter and, if not, what does matter most in efforts to be an effective helper in the midst of unavoidable stress?

I could go on . . . but let's take a deep breath and sit quietly for a few seconds while you reflect on your immediate reactions to these statements (pause). Now let me ask you for your immediate reactions.

My experience when I begin a presentation like this, is that participants have a number of the following responses.

- ❑ It sounds complicated.
- ❑ All those possibilities stressed me out.
- ❑ What did you mean stress is not choice?
- ❑ If folks can't agree on what to call stress, how are we supposed to know what to do or whether it even matters?
- ❑ You said talking about it doesn't always help; what does?
- ❑ How are we going to determine our own specific stressors?
- ❑ The workshops I've gone to usually recommend meditation. I've tried that and it doesn't work for me. I get what works for one doesn't work for everyone. Are you going to be showing us different strategies?
- ❑ How do I know if my workplace is toxic? What do I do if it is?

These responses reflect the areas we'll cover, such as toxic versus flourishing cultures when stress is not a choice, and the ways that stress becomes problematic, not because of poor self-care but because of other factors. And of course, we'll answer whether terminology matters and what does in our approach to stress as a friend. A number of positive, outcome driven mindsets (shifts in thinking) about approaching and responding to these questions and concerns are addressed throughout our time together. These mindsets will support stress as a resource for change and well-being. Let's begin with possible helper stress reactions and stress inducing workplace practices.

Activity One: Possible Reactions

If presenting, the following set of examples can be shown on several slides. Pause on each one for just a few seconds. The purpose is not for participants to read through each one but to be a bit overwhelmed by the sheer number of possibilities, which happens in reality when exposed to multiple stressors. Following this activity, you can ask for their reactions and then compare those with the ones identified under "my experience" Use the instructions below to prepare participants. *As a reader just continue reading.*

I'm going to present you with a lengthy list of reactions and conditions that represent a sampling of some of the many possible stressors and reactions associated with helper stress. I don't want you to read this to identify stressors you face or reactions you may have; simply give the entire list a quick glance. I'll ask for your response afterwards. (Take no more than 15–30 seconds.)

> Difficulty concentrating, focusing on details, gaps in memory, missing essential details, trouble sleeping or staying asleep, outbursts of anger or irritability, becoming more impatient with clients, becoming more critical and judgmental, feeling more detached, emotionally numb, flat, anxious about making life changing decisions for clients, feeling responsible for client's lives, experiencing thoughts of, "I've heard all this before. Let's get this over with." I stop listening after a few minutes, distrusting my ability to any longer be helpful, finding it difficult to shut off work mode when home, withdrawing from activities and friends once enjoyed to the point of negatively impacting personal relationships, thinking about client experiences even when I don't want to, too many deadlines, exhausted, expected to respond to emails after regular work hours, limited opinions don't count for much. The only time I hear from management is when things go wrong, lack of control over work methods, heavy work load. I'm not as calm as I used to be. It's taking me longer to calm down when I do get upset. I'm paying more attention to my reactions than to who or what I'm dealing with. I've heard way too many bad stories from clients. I'm constantly in a "survival" mode, worried about physical threats, worried about law suits. I'm avoiding

thoughts, feelings, people, conversations, activities or situations that carry reminders of what some of my clients tell me. I'm easily startled, more irritable, on edge all the time. I never used to get headaches. My energy level is non-existent. I wake up dreading going into work. My mood is no longer up. I'm drinking to relax. Clients are aggravating me. I'm doubting myself. I'm thinking about leaving the profession more than I ever have. I'm not satisfied with what I'm doing any more. I feel stuck. My resilience is not resilient. I'm happiest when I can get home and just sit in front of the TV. Pleasure is hard to come by. Joy is just a word. My personal life is not what it used to be. Emotionally, I'm all over the place. I can't shut it off. I no longer know what will set me off or take me down. I'm overwhelmed by seeing only high-risk clients, the increased demand to do more in the same time, the limited flexibility, too much paperwork/computer work, increased isolation from other staff, insufficient training for dealing with client content, situations and reactions. Managers and supervisors are difficult to access. They seem too busy to make time for me. Supervision is inadequate. My voice doesn't matter much. I am not reimbursed for outside training pertinent to what I do. I'm not provided time for regular skill building training. I'm rewarded by getting the difficult clients. Once assigned a supervisor, I can't change to another, if issues arise. I have little control over my work or those I'm assigned to help.

Now, what is your immediate reaction?

My experience with the most common immediate responses from participants in training, are likely similar to your responses.

- ❑ *"This stressed me out." "It's overwhelming." "We don't have a chance."* My reply is, "Absolutely. It's a bit overwhelming." Think about this being what happens with repeated exposure to distressed individuals or trauma inducing situations. However, we're going to get you through this distressing maze to those self-care strategies beneficial for you, that lower your stress while improving your well-being.
- ❑ Another frequent response is, *"I guess with a list that long, I'm bound to have a reaction or two."* I say, "Yes" to that. It is unavoidable, yet normal, to experience several of these reactions as helpers.
- ❑ And someone always asks, *"So how many of these indicate I'm in trouble or have stress overload?"* My response is, it's not the number of reactions that always matters, it's the particular reaction that is most

> problematic for you that matters. If, for example, you begin having more concern for how you are feeling rather than how those you are helping are feeling, it's going to certainly have a negative impact on your effectiveness and even your decision making. If this is the case, those you are trying to help are not getting your best; that's problematic for both of you. Now this response, of having more concern for your reactions, could be a sign of empathy distress and the need to develop some compassion related skills or skills related to emotional and/or cognitive regulation. On the other hand, it could be a sign of secondary trauma resulting from exposure to trauma content in need of different care responses. Just maybe, that situation is triggering reactions from some unresolved past experience demanding yet another response, or perhaps you are in need of more training related to the issues or situations you are presented with. In either case, the assessment and surveys you'll complete will focus in on what needs your attention.

I always end this activity by saying that we may not be able to control what is happening in the work place, but we can control how we respond, and the self-care practices we engage until we are able to find an acceptable and helpful outcome. You may not have heard the term, *maladaptive resilience* which refers to the response, "I'll just suck it up, work harder." As the term suggests, this is a maladaptive care solution; there are other more helpful responses. However, to be as effective as possible these care solutions must address what it is that is triggering a response that only increases the negative effects of that stress. (For readers, this workbook will guide you through the process of determining which self-care practices may matter most to you personally.) Following is one example.

Not Sure

Sometimes, we can't be sure what is driving a reaction until asked specific questions about the subjective ways we are experiencing what is happening to us. Assessments alone do not always reveal these subjective ways. Consider "subjective" to mean the source driving our reactions. In the introduction we used the resistance to self-care as an example of how older mindsets regarding self-care can create that resistance. The response itself is not the source; the source is the reaction it triggers, which often matters the most when trying to change the response. If self-care is addressing the resistance and not its source, then that self-care strategy is likely to have little effect. So, the question remains how do we go about determining the source driving our reactions?

How To?

Let's say you were asked to complete an assessment and you checked the response *"There are days I don't return a client's call."* The question then becomes, how do we know what this response reflects? Is it fatigue, a normal response to a tough day, or something else? The above response is certainly understandable given all helpers are exposed to and required to do day after day. However, it could signal more is going on than a momentary regrouping. If I ask you what is happening that is keeping you from returning a call and you tell me, "*. . . because all they want to do is talk and I don't have the time,"* your response could reflect a burnout reaction. This same statement could be empathetic distress if the rest of the statement read something like, "*. . . because what happened to these clients just triggers too many unwanted personal reactions that I have trouble controlling."* And, the same statement could be considered compassion fatigue if the rest included, "*. . . because I don't think any amount of caring will change anything."* This leads us to the following mindset.

Mindset: *Assessments can be very helpful in identifying potential stress indicators. However, sometimes what matters most is asking, "What is happening to you, what are you thinking, what are you feeling, what do you feel like doing when you have this reaction?"*

For now, we're going to provide a brief description of each helper stress category and in subsequent chapters go into greater detail. These descriptions provide a brief history of their origin and how each is different from the other, yet part of what constitutes helper related stress. In subsequent chapters you'll be provided the opportunity to complete assessments for each category in order to identify the specific stress sources needing your self-care the most.

Helper Related Stress Categories

Burnout

The term burnout, established in the early 1970s by Herbert Freudenberger (1974), existed long before the term compassion fatigue was established by Joinson (1992). Burnout consists of three components: emotional exhaustion; depersonalization (cynicism); and feelings of ineffectiveness, diminished professional efficacy or lack of personal accomplishment. Burnout is listed as a disease in the World Health Organization Statistical Classification of Diseases and Related Health Problems 10th ed. (WHO, 2025). Burnout is the result of toxic workplace practices that induce fatigue while reducing the satisfaction derived from working in that environment. As stated earlier, resilience alone does not protect from burnout. When possible, changing one's response to that environment's practices, or replacing those toxic workplace practices with flourishing-based practices will improve satisfaction while decreasing burnout. On the other hand, changing environments may be needed.

Compassion Fatigue

The reactions initially associated with compassion fatigue in 1992, were expanded by Charles Figley (1995) three years later. He expanded the concept to cover a wide range of professionals in various settings and roles, such as those who care for animals. This type of fatigue is specifically focused on the reactions of those responding to, or otherwise helping, those in distress. The primary reactions here are physical, emotional and mental exhaustion, in addition to a diminished satisfaction or the desire or capacity to be helpful to those in distress. Now, what is interesting is that compassion fatigue is determined by evaluating one's satisfaction with helping others; the fatigue component is determined by the level of burnout. Compassion fatigue is not only the desire to be helpful to others but also being actively involved in helping. Therefore, we could be working in a toxic environment, be fatigued yet remain compassionate about lending a hand. At some point, toxic practices will have a negative impact on one's satisfaction and effectiveness. The issue is that the reactions associated with the concept differ from burnout yet include burnout.

Secondary Traumatic Stress

Secondary traumatic stress was added to compassion fatigue reactions in 1995 by Figley. However, secondary trauma can stand alone and is not the direct result of fatigue but caused by indirect exposure to traumatized individuals, via the details of their experience and/or as the result of being associated with those who have been traumatically victimized. This can happen suddenly, via a single exposure, leaving the helper overwhelmed physiologically, emotionally and mentally. As bad as that may sound, it is important to remember the following mindset.

Mindset: *Secondary trauma is not a pathologic condition but a response considered not to be at all unusual among those caring for trauma populations, and/or responding to potentially trauma inducing incidents, and/or repeated exposure to those in distress.*

Post-Traumatic Stress

Closely associated with secondary trauma is post-traumatic stress. It was formally recognized as a diagnostic category in the Diagnostic and Statistical

Manual of Mental Disorders (DSM) in 1984 (American Psychiatric Association, 2022). Post-traumatic stress is a response that some people develop after directly experiencing a life-threatening event, like combat or various forms of violence. It can also result from witnessing violence and/or non-violent yet traumatic events, such as natural disasters, car accidents or being exposed to the details of what has, or is happening, while helping victims of these incidents. Post-traumatic stress is most prevalent among first responders—such as law enforcement, rescue workers, child welfare workers responding to situations of abuse. Intrusive memories and images, hypervigilance, avoidance of anything or anyone who is a reminder of what happened and negative changes in mood and cognition are a few of its reactions.

Empathy Distress

Effective helpers are those who have learned how to maintain a balance between compassion and empathy. Too much compassion with too little empathy, or too much empathy with too little compassion, results in a variety of stress reactions that are detrimental to those being helped.

Empathy distress is a term originating around 2011. The authors, Singer & Klimecki (2011), psychological neuroscientists, conducted fMRI scans to see which parts of the brain respond to compassion and then empathy. They found that too much empathy (dysregulated empathy) led to overwhelming emotional states, increasing vulnerability to psychological distress or empathetic distress, inclusive of internalizing disorders such as secondary trauma and post-traumatic stress, as later reported by Huang et al. (2024). The primary reaction of empathy distress is that the helper becomes more concerned about their own reactions to helping than about the distress of the person they are helping. In other words, the helper becomes too distressed to be helpful.

Terminology Issues

Compassion Fatigue or Empathy Distress?

Authors Singer & Klimecki (2011) suggested that compassion does not fatigue and as the term is a misnomer it should be replaced by the term empathetic distress. Whether empathy distress should replace compassion fatigue is a debate that will go on for some time. In *Chapter Seven*, I'll present significant research indicating that when either self-compassion or compassion for others decreases, empathetic or personal distress increases, and when compassion is strengthened, empathy distress decreases. Abundant research supports that empathetic distress is a reaction to changes in compassion and that when compassion fatigues, empathy distress emerges.

Vicarious or Secondary?

The term, vicarious trauma was coined by Pearlman & Saakvitne (1995) around the same time secondary trauma was established. The primary reaction associated with vicarious trauma is the loss of a sense of self and a negative change in one's view of self and others (Herman, 1992). Today, vicarious trauma and secondary trauma are terms which are often used interchangeably. There is an ongoing debate as to whether there is a significance difference between them. For our purposes secondary trauma will be inclusive of vicarious trauma, independent of compassion fatigue but often associated with the presence of compassion fatigue.

The Question

All the reactions previously listed are associated with these categories. As we stated earlier, many of these reactions can be applied across categories. Reactions of secondary trauma can be associated with compassion fatigue. The reactions of secondary trauma are also the reactions of post-traumatic stress. Reactions of compassion fatigue can involve burnout and secondary trauma, yet both reactions can also stand alone. So, is it empathy distress we should be now using instead of compassion fatigue? *The more important question is, does terminology matter when it comes to relieving and/or utilizing our stress to grow, or does what we are experiencing matter more when trying to determine what self-care practices are most appropriate for our reactions?*

My immediate reaction is that terminology does not matter as much as identifying the specific reactions and sources causing us the greatest unwanted stress. This is what matters most in order to apply the most appropriate self-care practices.

An Uncomplicated Approach

By identifying the specific stress reactions and responses being experienced, it becomes much easier to apply the appropriate care strategy. Over the following chapters you'll have the opportunity to complete assessments and inventories to determine which of your reactions and/or responses need your care, in addition to those that need to be watched because of their potential to become problematic. During the process you'll also identify your areas of strength. Patterns will emerge for you, as will the inter-relationship between different stress forms such as self-compassion and compassion satisfaction, or compassion and empathy.

One Ancient Universal Reaction

Mindset: *Stress is as much a physiological response as it is a cognitive, emotional or behavioral one.*

Our nervous system responds to stress before we become aware of that stress. Our primal survival response is actually quite amazing and quite good at what it does. *I consider it imperative to our self-care* that we understand and appreciate the value and use of the neurophysiology of stress to regulate our nervous system's response to daily stress, as well as effectively defusing those moments of dysregulation—difficulty managing what we are experiencing.

Mindset: *Nervous system regulation must be the foundation supporting all other self-care strategies.*

Stress regulation controls our energy and sustainability, emotions and behaviors. It is a protector, a "food" that feeds our cognitive processes, allows us to adapt and heal. When our nervous system goes unregulated, we are likely to experience an array of reactions: headaches, anxiety, depression, difficulty managing our emotions, brain fog, difficulty focusing and remembering, changes in sleep patterns, and blood pressure. Our physiological response is the one universal response to stress that must be attended to regularly by helpers, regardless of other existing reactions. For this reason alone, the next chapter is a continuation of our approach to stress, where very convincing personal documentation from leaders in the field will show us that our reactions are not always a choice, no matter how educated or skillful we are as helpers.

Approach Points Aligned with Those of Self-Care (Self-care approaches are in parentheses)

- ❑ Two of us can be exposed to the same situation yet have very different reactions. Therefore, what helps one does not necessarily help another exposed to the same distress (It's personal).
- ❑ Different reactions and responses dictate different solutions (It's personal; it's about managing our energy for what matters most).
- ❑ Sometimes it's not our response that needs attention and care but the subjective reactions driving those responses (It's about getting at the source).

- ❑ Whether it's the stress of daily living or the stress of being exposed to helping those in distress, the one universal response to stress is a physiological one and as such requires ongoing regulation, in order to retain a healthy body-mind response to what is stressful and challenging (It's about managing our energy to be at our best pursuing what matters most to us. It's about self-preservation,).
- ❑ Learning how to stay within our window of tolerance or, how to climb back inside when pushed out, is essential to maintaining lower stress (It's a way of approaching life to maintain our well-being).
- ❑ Approaching stress as an opportunity and resource for growth, significantly lowers the downsides of stress (It's saying *yes* to ourselves, and a way of approaching life to maintain our well-being and effectiveness).
- ❑ Assessments, surveys, research and new findings are used to help determine what specific reactions, responses and sources of stress are most problematic for us (It's about engaging in effective effort).
- ❑ Stress is a reality; it will always be in our lives. What it does to us is determined by how we react and respond to and approach changing what is not helpful (It's about effective effort, a necessity, not an indulgence. It's about self-preservation).
- ❑ Approaching stress as an enemy to be controlled or defeated is equivalent to approaching self-care as an indulgence, a dishonorable act of selfishness. Neither encourages growth, effectiveness, wellness, well-being or sustainability; using stress to grow does (It's a necessity. It's saying *yes* to ourselves, managing our energy to be at our best for what matters most to us personally).
- ❑ How we react to stress is not always a choice; how we respond is a choice (It's about unapologetically advocating for ourselves because we are worthy of it).

My Final Questions

Go to Appendix B-1, My Final Questions. Record your answers for the following two questions. Responses are to be recorded and will be used in the final evaluation process for determining one's self-care strategies.

1. Of all that you read or experienced in this chapter what one thought stands out the most for you?
2. Of the mindsets established in this chapter which one stands out the most for you?

If presenting, ask participants to share their responses to these final questions. Indicate that you will just listen. Sharing responses within the group is a wonderful way for all to acknowledge and reinforce a cross-section of what has been learned and, as a number of them answer each question, they'll realize as a group that they share similarities with one another. They will also hear responses that they perhaps had not thought about. This is a very effective learning approach. It also provides you, as a presenter, with a sense of the group's overall level of experience, interests and issues that can be addressed by you throughout training.

My experience has been, given the different ways to approach and think about stress presented in this segment, that participant responses will address the majority of those approaches and thoughts. Most will indicate that the process used to address the many variables related to approaching stress was very effective in stimulating different ways to think about stress. Most importantly, they are likely to express having a much clearer understanding of what will matter most in their efforts to minimize the negative impact helper stress can induce. They likely will also express an eagerness to know more about the one universal reaction to stress.

Time for a Stress Reliever

- ❏ Put your book down and Google "Funny Stress Management Techniques TEDx speaker Karyn Buxman." It's 2.37 minutes long. Please, don't skip watching this. You'll have a good laugh. *If presenting,* this is a wonderfully funny segment to show participants. It will have everyone laughing and feeling energized and ready for more. Make sure you tell participants to follow the presenter's instructions as if they were attending her presentation. *Readers do watch. It's my favorite stress reliever. Her final statement, "Now is not the time" also reinforces that taking time for ourselves is a necessity not an indulgence.*

References

American Psychiatric Association. (2022). *Diagnostic and Statistical Manual of Mental Disorders* (5th ed., text rev.; DSM-5-TR).

Ballesteros, E. (2024, February 13). *We're More Exhausted Than Ever.* Retrieved July 5, 2025 from https://time.com/6694092/exhaustion-increasing-causes-essay/

Crum, A., Akinola, M., Martin, A., & Fath, S. (2017). The role of stress shaping cognitive, emotional and physiological response to challenging and threatening stress. *Anxiety, Stress and Coping* 2017, 30(4): 379–395 https://doi.org/10.1080/10615806.2016.1275585

Freudenberger, H. J. (1974). Staff burnout. *Journal of Social Issues*, 30: 159–165.

Figley, C. (1995). *Compassion Fatigue: Coping with Secondary Traumatic Stress Disorder in Those Who Treat the Traumatized*. NY, Brunner/Mazel.

Herman, J. (1992). *Trauma and Recovery*. NY, Basic Books.

Huang, C., Wu, Z., Sha, S., Liu, C., Yang, L., Jiang, P., Zhang, H., & Yang, C. (2024). The dark side of empathy: The role of excessive affective empathy in mental health disorders. *Biological Psychiatry*, 2025; 98(5), 404–415. https://doi.org/10.1016/j.biopsych.2024.12.020

Joinson C. C. (1992). Coping with compassion fatigue. *Nursing*, 22(4): 116–120.

McGonigal, K. (2015). *Why Stress Is Good For You & How To Get It and Get Good At It*. NY, Avery.

Pearlman, L. A., & Saakvitne, K. W. (1995). Treating therapists with vicarious traumatization and secondary traumatic stress disorders. In C. R. Figley (Ed.), *Compassion fatigue: coping with secondary traumatic stress disorder in those who treat the traumatized* (pp. 150–177). NY, Brunner/Mazel.

Qui, D., Li Y., Li L., He J., Ouyang, F., & Xiao, S. (2021). Infectious disease outbreak and post-traumatic stress symptoms: A systematic review and meta-analysis. *Front. Psychol.* https://doi.org/10.3389/fpsyg.2021.668784

Ratcliff, M. (2024). Social workers, burnout, and self-care: A public health crisis. Dela J Public Health 10(1): 26–29.

Scott, E. (2023, September 27). *The Benefits of Good Stress: Sometimes, Stress Can Actually Be a Good Thing*. Retrieved June 1, 2025 from https://www.verywellmind.com/what-kind-of-stress-is-good-for-you-3145055

Singer, T., Klimecki, O. (2011). Empathetic Distress Fatigue Rather Than Compassion Fatigue? Integrating Findings from Empathy Research in Psychology and Social Neuroscience. In Oakley, B., Knafo, A., Madhavan, G., & Wilson, D, S. *Pathological Altruism* (pp. 368–383). Oxford, Oxford University Press.

Whitt-Woosley, A., Sprang, G., & Eslinger, J. (2022). The impact of COVID-19 and experiences of secondary traumatic stress and burnout. *Psychological Trauma*, 14(2), 507–511 Retrieved, May 6, 2025 from https://doi.org/10.1037/tra0001183

WHO, World Health Organization. (2025). *International Statistical Classification of Diseases and Related Health Problems. 10th ed. (ICD-10)*. Geneva, Switzerland.

Zang, L., Pan, R., Cai, Y., & Pan, J. (2021). The prevalence of post-traumatic stress disorder in the general population during COVID-19 pandemic: A systematic review and single-arm meta-analysis. *Psychiatry Investig.*, 18(5): 426–433. Retrieved May 5, 2025 from https://pmc.ncbi.nlm.nih.gov/articles/PMC8169329/

CHAPTER 3

One Universal Reaction

Our Reactions Are Not a Choice; Our Responses Are

Theme

This exploration sets the foundation for why our approach to self-care must not only be a cognitive process, but also a physiological one. Extensive research has revealed a great deal about the neuro-physiological reactions to stress and those self-care practices that can help regulate it. We now know that some of these strategies are also beneficial for *managing helper stress on a daily basis.*

Note: Make sure you have access to the internet as you will be directed to several YouTube segments. These video segments introduce you to well-known and experienced stress specialists. The personal experiences they share taught them so much about responding to situations where they had no choice as to the stress responses they experienced. We begin with the fact that our stress reactions can surprise us.

Unthinkable

Twenty-six years ago, as of this writing, a six-year-old boy brought a gun into his classroom and shot and killed a classmate. I had trained a number of the social workers in the county who went to the school to assist. Obviously, all were in

DOI: 10.4324/9781003673699-4

shock and disbelief. Media rushed to the scene and were there for days intensifying the situation by the information they were reporting. Blaming and posting questions about school personnel came quickly as did the removal of this youngster from his impoverished and neglectful home environment. Although these social workers were far more prepared than many of the school counselors as to what would be helpful, they too became emotionally overwhelmed.

The social workers recommended to the superintendent and principal that it would be helpful for staff if they had the opportunity to meet with me, to help process all they were exposed to and were experiencing. There were approximately fifteen staff, including those social workers, identified as in most need of some intervention. When asked, I recommended to the principal that helpers be placed into three different groups from the most exposed to the least exposed. This afforded more time and attention to each, as issues facing the most exposed would be different from those facing the other groups. He resisted this request indicating he wanted everyone meeting at one time. Knowing that some intervention was better than no intervention in a traumatic crisis, I agreed. I will have more to say about this in a few minutes. Given the size of the intervention group dealing with this horrific murder, there were only two objectives—a) normalize as many reactions as possible including those they might not mention, and b) allow them to discover they were not alone with what they were experiencing.

When I met with the group, I immediately set ground rules as to how we would proceed. This obviously was not a time or place to allow people to try and process their emotions; it would have been harmful and unsafe to do so. However, what I did do, was list and normalize all the possible reactions they might be experiencing or could experience in the days, weeks and the months that followed. I then gave out my phone number indicating they were free to call me anytime for whatever reason. I then proceeded with asking several very focused questions such as, *"What one thought stands out the most for you?"* This is a question you are asked to answer at the end of every chapter. The reason for this is that our thoughts drive our behavior and fuel our emotions. The thoughts you identify across all chapters will help to formulate your approach to the stress you're experiencing and the care that may work best for you—what you may need to do differently.

One Question

In these situations, there is one question that brings everyone together, connecting them to the reality that what they are experiencing is the norm and that they are not alone. This specific question is, *"Where are you experiencing this the most in your body?"* Everyone will generally have a physiological reaction they seldom or never experience, as was the case for everyone in this group. Headaches, fatigue, feeling numb or detached, trouble sleeping, jumpy, easily startled, not wanting to talk, intrusive thoughts, difficulty staying focused, finding it hard to think and, for some, finding it difficult to walk past the room where it happened, were a few of the responses; all quite normal.

Their responses generally began with, "I never have but . . . I'm always but . . . Usually I can but . . .". In other words, *how their bodies responded was not a choice.* Also, it's important to consider that, regardless of their level of exposure, all were having spontaneous, physiological reactions that needed their attention. Their reactions reflected hyperarousal, or overly activated responses, and hypoarousal, or shutting down responses. Both of these nervous system generated reactions were in need of different self-care responses. There's more to this story, but let's spend a bit more time on arousal issues triggered by stress.

Mindset: *Stress need not be traumatic to trigger arousal responses; being anxious or stressed is all that is needed (DeMarco, 2024).*

I had been doing a number of trainings over a short period of time. I thought I was doing fine until I opened my overnight bag at the hotel I was staying at and discovered that I had not packed my dress slacks earlier that day, nor had I packed my dress shoes. I couldn't believe I forgot my pants. I took that as a sign that my body had no desire to be in dress slacks or shoes. It needed more of the comfort of tennis shoes and well-worn comfortable jeans and for me to take a break. I ended up buying a cheap pair of slacks at Kmart that I took off immediately after the training and put on those comfy jeans for the long drive home. Obviously, this was not traumatic, not life-threatening, yet it let me know my body was going in one direction, my brain in another, neither in the right direction. The fact is when our body is not doing well neither are our cognitive functions. It let me know I was beginning to function outside my window of tolerance.

Window of Tolerance

Life's demands, relationship issues, workplace stress can certainly trigger arousal reactions that push us outside of our "window of tolerance". The "window of tolerance" description of what happens to our nervous system under stress was developed by Daniel Siegel in 1999 (Wright, 2022). It's a much less technical way of explaining the neurophysiological response to stress, the brain, the autonomic nervous system and the endocrine system. Essentially, when the stress we are exposed to is no longer tolerated by us or we lack insufficient self-care strategies in response to what is stressful for us, our nervous system is thrown out of balance into an activated state of fight or flight or shutting down. In a hyperarousal state we can experience racing thoughts, difficulty concentrating, focusing, sleeping. Anxiety can set in, relaxing is difficult, breathing is shallow, heart rate increases along with blood pressure. We can be easily startled, more aggressive or agitated, impulsive and have difficulty making decisions or making bad ones because of impulsiveness. Hypoarousal triggers opposite reactions. We can experience spaciness and zone out. We may have difficulty concentrating, thinking, making decisions, even talking. Apathy, withdrawing, and dissociating (for protection from feelings and thoughts), numbness and depression are all possible.

The reactions identified by those in the school intervention I provided consisted of both forms of arousal. Each were in need of different self-care responses such as calming practices for hyperarousal and movement for hypoarousal. These variations in responses are another example of why it is important to identify individual reactions in order to apply the appropriate care response. If interested in a more technical and detailed description of all the processes that are activated by stress, search for Harvard Health: *Understanding the Stress Response* (2024).

It's also critical to appreciate that an aroused nervous system will have trouble responding to reason and to language, such as "be calm" (DeMarco, 2024; NICABM, 2025). The nervous system responds to sensory cues like soothing sounds, touch and movement, not talk. The following two YouTube segments are the stories of two highly educated and experienced leaders in the field of stress and what happened to them that taught them so much about regulating the nervous system.

Polyvagal Response

Dr. Stephen Porges is a distinguished behavioral neuroscientist and professor of psychiatry who developed the Polyvagal Theory (Porges & Dana, 2018). He has done so much to help us understand how the vagus nerve helps us with regulation. The vagus nerve has a number of branches, which connects with our brain, lungs, stomach and guts; thus, it's called the polyvagal response. Basically, via abundant research, he discovered that our behavior is tied to our physiology. In other words, *we can only behave in a way that our physiology allows us to behave.* Being a scientist and psychologist Dr. Porges was interested in his own brain, so he made an appointment for an MRI. Listen to what he says about that experience.

Activity One: The MRI Experience

I highly recommend that you view Dr. Porges' personal description of his experience at the following YouTube link. A written summary follows but what he has to say is even more impactful than my summary.

"The Polyvagal Theory: Looking At Trauma From A New Perspective"
https://www.youtube.com/watch?v=MKkDAOW2yd4

Summary: As he is being moved into the tubular scanner, he senses a bit of anxiety and says, "Stop I need a glass of water." After he finishes his water and when they move him further into the scanner his body starts responding with a panic attack. As much as he tries, he can't reason it away. He has to get out and get out of there fast to some place safe. He had no idea his body would respond the way it did. When it did, he needed to act, to *do something different* with his body to reduce that stress. What he learned from this is stated in the following mindset.

Mindset: *Our neuro-biological responses can profoundly change the way we respond. It's sometimes very difficult to think away the effects of stress because our physiology is in need of an experience different than a cognitive one. The reality is different stressors demand different solutions.*

Law Enforcement and Firefighters

Think about this. First responders are trained, through repetition, to enter into the dangerous situations they encounter at a cognitive level, being very observant and making decisions based on the knowledge they have as to what procedures are the safest to initiate, given what they observe. I know this all too well as my son spent 30 years in law enforcement and did well as long as he could regulate his emotional reactions by staying at the cognitive level. However, as happened to Dr. Porges, responders will at some point be exposed to situations that immediately trigger sensory, lower to mid-brain reactions that then shut down those cognitive processes while the stress/survival reaction takes over. When my son's close friend, another officer, was gunned down and killed while in his patrol car, it took time for my son to return to his pre-level of physiological functioning. Trying to think it away was not helpful.

The other aspect that leaves first responders vulnerable to stress is that they remain hyper-alert, their systems are constantly ready for the next danger. In some ways the gas pedal is always on the floor so their systems simply run out of gas unless they refuel at a physiological level. If they don't do this regularly, they become vulnerable to all forms of helper stress—especially compassion fatigue, secondary trauma and post-traumatic stress. They too need the kind of self-care that helps to *regulate or calm* that hyper alert response. This certainly was needed by healthcare workers during COVID due to their over exposure to such distress.

Vital First Step to Relieving Stress

Dr. Peter Levine is the founder of The Somatic Experiencing® method, which is a body-oriented approach to the healing of stress. It has been his life's work, resulting from his multidisciplinary study of stress physiology, psychology, ethology, biology, neuroscience, indigenous healing practices and medical biophysics, together with over 45 years of successful application. Dr. Levine (2011) has stressed for years that "trauma is a physiological phenomenon, rather than a purely psychological one." He wrote, "psychologists, psychiatrists and other helping professionals need to understand the core mechanisms of how to stabilize the body's reactions to traumatic stress on the physical level in order to help trauma victims regulate their sensations and emotions" (Steele & Malchiodi, 2012, pp. 5–6). As stated earlier, when we fail to regularly regulate these stress responses and when exposure to stress is consistent and/or repetitive, we remain in an activated arousal/survivor response that predisposes us to all forms of helper stress. Remember that our stress reactions may not be due to trauma exposure, yet still be in need of care that address these physiological responses.

Activity Two: Calming the Fear

I also recommend that before reading further you listen to Dr. Levine's personal reactions when he was struck head on by a car while walking across the street. My comments will follow that viewing.

"Dr. Peter Levine on working through a personal traumatic experience"
https://www.youtube.com/watch?v=9hP2KJ3UgDI

Summary: You heard how he was unable to process the questions the paramedics were asking him and how dangerously high his blood pressure was until one gesture from a pediatrician who happened to be there, was experienced at a sensory level. This helped regulate his nervous system and slow down his heart rate so he could begin to process things at a cognitive level.

What does this experience tell us? It tells us that the first level of stress reduction ought to be at a physiological/sensory level and only thereafter, if needed, an integrated physiological-cognitive process. Talking about what is happening to us can initially have its limitations. We'll discuss this shortly. First, I want to present two more documented experiences as to the physiology of stress.

Being Human

It doesn't matter how smart we are, how experienced we may be as helpers, stress doesn't really care. Allow me to give you a personal example of how stress can interfere with our thought processes, do damage and in this example ended up costing me $500 (Steele, 2019). Here I am a college educated professional, in my mid-thirties, single and living in a first-floor apartment with a door wall that led to an outdoor patio area. It was just several steps from the kitchen on the other side of a dining room table. One day the pot I was using to cook somehow caught fire. The flames rose over the edge and I had no fire extinguisher handy. I heard myself say, "remain calm." My next thought was something like, "I got this. I'll just take the pot outside to the patio." I grabbed the pot and then walked over to the door wall, but it was locked. Now visualize this. I placed that very hot, flaming pot on the linoleum covered floor to unlock the door wall. When I came back after putting the fire out, I saw what I had done. That's right. I saw the outline of the pot on the linoleum floor. It had melted the linoleum which couldn't be patched. I thought I was thinking clearly under that minor stress. I could not believe what I had done. Besides losing my security deposit, I learned a valuable lesson.

Mindset: *Stress alters the way we think and process information and subsequently how we behave. When that stress piles up, what we think and how we behave only gets worse. Everyone caring for others is vulnerable to several types of stress no matter their knowledge or experience.*

This is not new information. Interestingly the Yerkes-Dodson Law of 1908 (Wikipedia, 2013) concluded that, "performance increases with physiological or mental arousal, but only up to a point. When levels of arousal become too high, performance decreases" (para. 1).

Mindset: *The quality of our performance on any task, whether physical or mental, is related to our level of stress (emotional arousal). If we are feeling either very low (hypo) or very high levels of arousal (hyper), then our performance is likely to be impaired.*

Holy Crap

I remember when I was a consultant to a number of professionals who provided debriefing for survivors of trauma. I always insisted that they call me following the conclusion of their debriefings. Following one of these debriefings, one of the debriefers called, it sounded like he was in his car. When he said he was, I yelled, *"Look at your speedometer now!"* The next thing I heard was *"Holy crap."* My response was, *"Slow it down, take a deep breath and pull off the road as soon as you can so we can talk for a minute."* The details of what he was exposed to in that debriefing triggered his nervous system's arousal response. He was speeding inside but not cognitively aware of how much until he looked at his speedometer. He hadn't followed protocol, which was to take a minimum of 15 minutes after debriefing to just walk around and be mindful of his surroundings in order to help regulate the nervous system's response to the difficult details and emotions that can emerge in efforts to help others in distress. He said he thought he was doing fine. The point is *we are not always consciously aware of the ways stress is impacting us physiologically.*

Mindset: *"A stressful situation, whether something environmental, such as a looming work deadline, or psychological, such as worry about losing a job, can trigger a cascade of stress hormones that produce well-orchestrated physiological changes" (Harvard Health Publishing, 2024). It's unavoidable.*

For this reason, self-care dictates the following mindset.

Mindset: *It is critical that we maintain a daily routine that helps maintain a nervous system balance (remaining in our window of tolerance) in the midst of the distress of others we are trying to help. This is also essential because our peers may also not recognize the arousal reactions we may be experiencing. Dr. Bruce Perry provides a remarkable example of this.*

Heart Rate and Stress: Children of Waco

Dr. Bruce Perry (Supin, 2016, pp. 7–8) gives us a wonderful example of how this works when he describes his experience with the 21 children rescued from the Waco, Texas, Branch Davidian cult standoff. When he arrived, the children were in the custody of the FBI and Child Protective Services. Perry was greeted by a Texas Ranger who wanted no one doing therapy on these children. He offered the Ranger a deal. He told him if he could take the pulse of one of the girls who was sleeping soundly and if it was under 100 he would leave. The normal resting rate for a girl her age is around 80. Her pulse was 160. He and his team stayed for months. The fact is, when stressed our heart rate is elevated; we may show no outward signs yet *the body knows.*

Over time what they observed is that the Waco children had about three hours of therapeutic intervention a day; not one minute of it was formal therapy. What they also witnessed is that children would seek small doses of support throughout the day, an adult or activity that would make them laugh, another who gave good hugs. *Their heart rates began to go down with these small doses of physiological regulators, which became buffers from further symptoms.* We need to follow the wisdom of children.

The children were engaged in sensory activities, movement play, seeking comfort, not talking about what happened. Chapter Nine on self-care practices presents a number of basic sensory ways to regulate our nervous system daily. Movement can certainly be one of those beneficial ways to help us stay within our *window of tolerance* or climb back inside if stress pushes us outside that window—our comfort zone. Let me take you through a brief activity to demonstrate. In fact, this is a good time for an activity to get you up and moving for a minute and also experience the emotional and cognitive shifts that the simplest of movements can cause.

Activity Three: Move to Change (Group/Individual)

As a reader try this yourself. (It can also be used in a group setting if presenting). Record the directions below on your phone then simply hit play and follow the directions, as if you are a participant in a training, and when told to do so, change positions. It takes no more than three minutes. *If presenting,* participants are given the following instructions.

- ❑ First, I want you to get comfortable. We're all going to take three deep breaths and let the air out very slowly . . . Alright take that first deep breath, hold it for a few seconds, alright now exhale very slowly. We'll do this two more times.
- ❑ Now, while sitting with hands on your lap, I want you to take a minute to focus on some stressful experience you are having or recently had (pause briefly). Take a minute to pay attention to where in your body or what part of your body responds the most as you think about this stressor. As I ask questions about what you are experiencing, simply hear your voice answer them as if you are answering for all to hear . . . *Do you feel a particular emotion? Where do you feel it? What is that emotion? What one thought really stands out for you about this stress or stressor?*
- ❑ Now I want you all to stand up with your feet shoulder width apart and your arms folded over your chest. Hold this position for a minute while thinking about that stressor (pause). *How does this position change the way you feel about this stressor? Is that feeling more intense than when you were sitting down or less intense? When you took this pose what thought jumped into your mind about this situation? Is it different, even in the slightest way from what you previously thought? Hold on to this for a minute . . .*
- ❑ Now I simply want you to place your hands behind your back and lower your head—chin to chest if you will . . . Hold this pose for a minute (pause). *Now how does this position change the way you feel about this stressor? Is that feeling more intense than when you were sitting down or less intense? In this pose what thought jumped into your mind about this situation? Is it different from the previous thought? Hold onto this for a minute . . .*
- ❑ Now I want you to sit down and clasp your hands behind your neck and just lean back a little in your chair and hold that pose for a minute

while you think about that stressor (pause). *Now how does this position change the way you feel about this stressor? Is that feeling more intense than when you were sitting down or less intense? In this pose what thought jumped into your mind about this situation? Is it different from the previous thought? Hold onto this for a minute . . .*

- ❑ Now one more posture change. I want you to lean forward and place your elbows on the table and rest your head in the palm of your hands and hold this pose for a minute while thinking about that stressor (pause). *Now how does this position change the way you feel about this stressor? Is that feeling more intense than when you were clasping hands behind your head or less intense? In this new pose what thought jumps into your mind about this situation? Is it different from the previous thought? Hold onto this for a minute . . .*
- ❑ Okay let's all take in a deep breath . . . hold for a few seconds . . . then exhale slowly. Have participants return to their seats.

Once seated, I will ask for a show of hands as to how many experienced a change in the way they felt and thought about that stressor when they took a different pose.

My experience tells me you likely experienced what others have experienced with this activity. The majority of participants will raise their hands indicating that a different pose caused either a shift in feelings and/or thoughts associated with their stressor. What this demonstrates is that even brief movements can help to regulate our reactions to challenging situations.

Now there are always a few who did not experience such a shift. If this was you, that's alright because it takes us back to a *Chapter One* mindset that stated that "no one intervention works for everyone". It's sometimes just a matter of trying different sensory activities to discover what works best for you. Perhaps you needed to move around more, go for a walk or perhaps music would have altered your feelings and thoughts. It's different for each of us. However, what we do know is that even brief moments of changing what our body has been doing can better help regulate our emotions, thoughts and unwanted physiological reactions. More about using the body as a resource will be discussed in *Chapter Nine* when detailing self-care practices.

Physiology First—Talk Later

In earlier years we didn't have neuroscience to support theories on stress. Today the research is quite abundant. Stress triggers predominant processes in the limbic/subcortical and right hemisphere of brain (Perry & Szalavitz, 2006) limiting access to the cortex (upper brain) and left hemisphere

(Levine & Kline, 2008). This minimizes our ability to reason, to think things through, to focus and process information. Cognitive processes can take second place to stress.

Instead of Talking—9/11 Survivors

Researchers at the University at Buffalo and University of California, Irvine, obtained data from a random sample of 2,000 Americans after the September 11, 2001 terrorist attacks. "What they discovered surprised them—participants who chose not to discuss their feelings right after the attacks often fared better over the subsequent two years than those who did" (Kingsbury, 2008, para. 2). Dr. Spencer Eth (van der Kolk, 2015, p. 231) found a similar response in 2002 from 225 who escaped from the Twin Towers. When asked what was the most helpful, they replied, "acupuncture, massage, yoga and Eye Movement Desensitizing Reprocessing (EMDR) in that order." Eth's survey suggests, along with others, that the most helpful interventions are those focused on relieving the physiological symptoms of trauma. When I interviewed educators most exposed to the chaos and disbelief of what happened on 9/11, they also told me what was most helpful to them was the use of the many of the health clubs who opened their doors to educators so they could use the pools, the hot tubs and receive massages (Steele, 2015, pp. 65–69). Over and over, I heard that it was the sensory experiences, like exercise, not talking about it, that was getting them from one day to the next.

Over the years, I have met with many survivors who were directly exposed to a variety of traumatic incidents such as the Gulf War, the bombing of the Federal building in Oklahoma, 9/11 survivors from both New York and Washington DC, hurricanes Katrina and Rita, and far too many traumas involving school shootings and other forms of violence. These survivors had very high levels of exposure to the visuals, the sounds, the smells, the terror and the chaos experienced with these situations. After the first few days, many also reported that talking only intensified the primary reactions they first experienced at those tragic incidents.

If talking wasn't helping what was helpful? I remember one clinician I met saying that a few months after 9/11 area restaurants conducted an informal survey and found that the consumption of mashed potatoes had tripled. What are mashed potatoes? That's right comfort food. A simple but comforting, soothing sensory experience associated with good memories. For some, it might have been chicken noodle soup and for others it was exercising or massages. However, sometimes, when what we are doing for relief is not working, we need to take another look at our stress reactions in order to determine the source triggering these responses.

When It's Not Working

Asking you to complete the assessments in subsequent sessions will help you identify what is problematic, for example, not returning a client's calls. This is a behavioral response. Unfortunately, it doesn't tell us the reaction you are having, or what is being experienced at the subjective level, that may be causing this avoidant behavior rather than doing what needs to be done in a helping role. When this happens, you need to approach stress from a different perspective. We did this briefly, in the second chapter, with the example of not returning calls and determining the source of that behavior by asking what was happening at the time. This in turn allowed us to determine whether the source was related to burnout, compassion fatigue, empathy distress or secondary trauma. This is important to helping you select different solutions for your different reactions. We are going to spend more time on how to do this as part of the assessment process. This is so essential, let me repeat the mindset we established in *Chapter Two.*

Mindset: *It's the subjective ways we are experiencing stress that often matter most in determining the most appropriate self-care strategies.*

Do Not Assume

Over the years, I can't count the number of times I've observed or learned that recommended interventions in response to the stress being experienced were made on the assumption of knowing what was best for others without first exploring what those in stress were actually experiencing in their "subjective world". In other words, how they were now viewing themselves and others, and the world around them as a result of what happened to them. When I was assisting schools across the country with how best to respond to traumatic situations, and ways to help their students, I cautioned them to give students a choice as to what they felt would help them the most, because not all students exposed to the same situation have the same response. This holds true for you as well. You can be exposed to the same stressors as your peers yet have very different reactions. You can also try the same intervention and have different results. Research, for example, shows that mindful practices can sometimes increase or intensify one's stress reaction (King, 2021) rather than calm it.

Worry

One question I suggested to school crisis team members that helps quickly identify student's subjective experience is, "Since this happened, what is your biggest worry?" Many different times I heard some students express great sadness after a non-violent loss or fear that the same might happen to them. On the other hand, there were those students exposed to the same incident whose major concern was wondering if the high school football game scheduled for that Friday night was still going to be played. Some thought this was insensitive. In reality, for those individuals, it was what they needed in order to process the vulnerability they were likely experiencing. For those students, exposing them to interventions specific to trauma could, in fact, trigger reactions they did not initially experience and do more harm than good. Schools that allowed that game to be played, even when delayed for a day or two to promote it as a way to honor and/or support survivors, saw far more positive responses than those who cancelled the game. *Think about this.* A football game activates so many primary, neuro-physiological reactions that can indirectly calm or change those lower brain stress responses in ways that are tolerable. For some it became their "safe place". Of course, there were those who did not "feel" right going to the game but they could choose not to go and spend time with friends in their "safe place" which was more empowering for them. *This holds true for helpers as well.*

Mindset: *Our choice of self-care is most effective when it safely addresses the subjective ways we are experiencing stress.*

The Rest of the Story

This assuming of what's best for others in stress whether it's burnout, compassion fatigue or secondary trauma, takes me back to the final moments of the intervention I was providing for those dealing with that terrible shooting by that six-year-old student. Leadership made assumptions in this situation as to what staff were needing most. Following their responses to the questions asked, we talked about immediate self-care, especially related to their physiological responses. The group was most appreciative for the information about hyper and hypoarousal reactions and what might be helpful to regulate these. Unfortunately, as I was making a final summary of what stood out for me about them and their responses, the principal came in the room and indicated he wanted everyone to stay in the room when finished so he could bring in a photographer to take their picture. It was presented in a way that left many feeling that they had no choice. The room went immediately silent; you could hear the proverbial pin hit the floor. Not a word was uttered. Their bodies froze. I could see the disbelief on their faces. As soon as the principal shut the door behind him, I told the group that I would talk to him and anyone who wanted to leave could do so. They needed a voice to speak for them as well as a choice to do what would be most helpful for them at the time. Many left.

The principal had good intentions but was not at all in touch with the subjective ways these helpers were experiencing what had happened and what they needed. Getting one's photo taken is generally associated with a happy event or an accomplishment of some kind, nothing his staff was experiencing. I did hear from several people later who called to thank me for making it easier for them to leave. The last thing they wanted was a photo reminding them of that unthinkable tragedy. In addition to this, the help provided was minimal because of the size of the group. Those most exposed really needed to be in a group of their own. I certainly did not want to allow them to be talking, in this larger group, about some of the details of what they experienced. Had I allowed this, it would have only activated others and potentially left them worse off than when they came in. However, my initial suggestion of meeting with separate, smaller groups was not acceptable to the leadership at the time.

This is why it is essential for us to appreciate that, if working in organizations serving traumatized individuals, our support is dependent upon leadership not only being trauma-informed but supporting practices that support helper well-being and vulnerability to secondary trauma or post-traumatic stress. This is the reason for spending time in *Chapter Six* outlining what helpers need most if working in an environment helping those in trauma.

Let's return then to how we can get to our subjective experience when what we are doing is not helping to relieve our stress.

Exploring Our Subjective World

How then do you discover the subjective source of what is driving an unwanted stressful response so appropriate self-care can be applied? Years ago, when I stopped trying to be an analyst and approached helping others as a non-knowing helper by giving those in distress opportunities to reveal how they were experiencing their situation subjectively, we determined what would be most helpful actually came from themselves. It's all about being curious. I think you'll appreciate this after completing the following activity related to the subjective way you may be responding to stress in your life.

Activity Four: Identifying Your Subjective Experience

The questions you will be asked to answer in writing may surprise you, as most people have never been asked these specific questions.

For this activity you will need to go to Appendix B-2, My Subjective Experience Worksheet. Complete the activity as best you can. When finished return here.

If presenting, inform participants before they start, that many of them are likely to have never been asked questions like these, yet they do help reveal one's subjective experience which then helps reveal the focus of self-care. Suggest that it will be beneficial to answer these questions because they are designed to help them think differently about their experience because, when we think differently, we get different results.

My experience tells me that your responses to this activity are similar to those of the many responses I've heard from others over the years. Many of you have never been asked some of these questions, or asked those you are helping. Most cite the question, "What is the worst part of the worst part?" helping them isolate one core thought or feeling triggering their reaction that they hadn't thought about or felt before; this makes it easier to determine what needs changing. Some expressed that talking to their stress empowered them while others said it diminished the power of the stress and, for others, naming it did the same. And for others, putting a size to their worry was helpful by encouraging them to consider doing something about it without further delay. Still others said it diminished the intensity when comparing it to other worries, while also helping them realize the need to address the bigger worries. It was different for everyone. All agreed this process was helpful. So, let me just say a word or two about the healing power of curiosity.

Curiosity

The above activity was about being curious. The more curious you are about what stress is like for you, the easier it becomes to determine what will be most important in your efforts to best manage that stress. Being curious allows you, and anyone attempting to help you with a particularly difficult stressor, to have a far better idea as to

- ❏ its intensity,
- ❏ how it may be changing the way you view yourself, your sense of competence, the work you are doing,
- ❏ how it is impacting you at a physiological level, cognitive and emotional level,
- ❏ what triggers its intensity and who or what helps to soothe it,
- ❏ how it's altering your ability to manage in that environment or with the conditions associated with that stress, and
- ❏ how others may or may not be helping.

In other words, curiosity is going to make it easier to identify the focus of those self-care strategies that will matter most to your ongoing effectiveness as a helper and your overall well-being. It's also a wonderful way to help those you are helping. Following are a few examples.

Examples

Q. When do you feel it (stress) the most? If you tell me, you begin feeling it when you are getting ready to go to work, I know there are going to be a number of workplace issues that may or may not be resolvable. Obviously more questions regarding the workplace culture and conditions need to be pursued. On the other hand, if you tell me the stress hits you in the afternoon, I would want to know what you do on your lunch hour, if you take lunch and what you do mid-afternoon to regulate your responses to the stress of the earlier part of the day. Your stress response may be situational or a failure to take morning stress breaks. There could be a number of possibilities that are resolvable.

Q. How does it change what you think about yourself, the work you are doing? If your response to this is that you want to be helpful but are not feeling competent enough to help the clients assigned to you, the obvious need is additional training and/or further education. If your supervisor is not providing the support needed or the workplace provides little incentive to further your education, the focus could be on looking for a workplace that does. If you tell me, you are just more anxious about going to work, we would need to narrow down what thoughts trigger that anxiety such as work expectations, certain clients and/or tasks.

Q. Have you told anyone about the stress you are experiencing? If you have not, that is a problem in itself. Further curiosity is needed to explore the fears about telling someone else. If you tell me you're worried that your peers might become concerned about your competence, I might question in what ways you feel incompetent in order to determine if there are training issues. I might have concerns about the culture of your workplace and absence of supportive colleagues, maybe personal trust issues, or self-compassion difficulties. In either case it gets closer to what may be causing you undue stress. If you reply "yes" to this question, I would ask the next question.

Q. When they found out, what did they say to you? If you tell me they said you needed to suck it up or find another job, you are not the problem. They're right about finding another job, another workplace that is more supportive; they are not right about sucking it up.

Q. What is your biggest worry? If your biggest worry is that you are finding it more difficult to manage your emotional reactions to victim's stories/situations and you tell me that, in comparison with other worries, this is in the middle third of all your worries, I would suggest that we need to further evaluate the possible cause. I would wonder if this is the result of having no client diversity or too much exposure at one time. If this were the case, I would want to check to see if there are other toxic burnout factors taking place in your work environment that are contributing to your exhaustion. I might wonder if you're not getting sufficient supervision to address countertransference issues or being too empathetic and in need of emotional and cognitive regulation practices. I might wonder about your own past history and whether the work is triggering vicarious, unresolved issues. I would also want to evaluate your self-care practices, how frequently you engage in self-care, how specific your care efforts are to what you are experiencing and what you do to regulate your reactions at the time your emotional responses are triggered. Any one of the answers to these questions make it easier to determine the self-care practices that may be most appropriate for you. The assessments, surveys and activities over the next four stages will address all the possibilities listed in this final question.

Note: If one's arousal responses are not regulated, not being tolerated or within that window of tolerance, as in the case of trauma, these questions may be difficult to answer because stress is limiting access to cognitive processes. In these situations, the body needs to be resourced to help establish what Bessel van der Kolk (2015) refers to as "islands of safety", where arousal re-enters the window of tolerance so one's emotions are not limiting the cognitive functions needed to process information. This is an intervention strategy that will be discussed in *Chapter Nine: Self-Care Strategies.*

Approach Points Aligned with Those of Self-Care (Self-care approaches are in parentheses)

1. We've established that stress is first a physiological reaction and, as such, efforts to alleviate and/or manage that stress need to be initially directed at resetting that response at a physiological level via sensory-based activities (It's a necessity, not an indulgence. It's about managing our energy).
2. We've established that stress need not be traumatic for our physiology to be activated. Simply navigating our way through life triggers physiological reactions (It's about managing our energy daily).
3. We've established that under stress, language can be less than helpful and, at times, sensory-based activities are more beneficial (Utilizing effective effort to determine what works best for us personally).
4. We've established that the physiology of stress alters the way we cognitively process what is happening to us, the decisions we make, our focus

and concentration and only improves when our physiological reactions are regulated (It's about managing our energy, self-preservation, self-protection).

5. We've established that stress is a subjective experience and, as such, triggers various sensations, feelings and thoughts that make our response unique from others exposed to the same stress (It's personal).
6. We've learned that identifying the subjective source of our reactions via being curious, helps to identify what care response may matter most in efforts to remain resilient in the face of that stress (Getting at the source of our reactions).
7. We've established that it's essential to our wellness, well-being, and effectiveness to function within one's *window of tolerance* and when pulled outside that window, at any given time, to know how to climb back in (It's about necessity, self-preservation, managing our energy, sustainability, saying *yes* to what matters most to us).
8. We've established that our self-care efforts must be inclusive of those that help regulate and, as needed, restore physiology functioning within one's window of tolerance. (It's about managing our energy. It's a necessity, not an indulgence).
9. We've established that there are multiple ways to change or regulate the physiological reactions to stress (It's about advocating for what helps best maintain our well-being).
10. We've established that, as helpers, daily attention to our physiology must be a core component of self-care for those efforts to be effective in preventing and, as needed, regulating and recovering from those unwanted reactions to the stress of helping (It's a necessity. It's about self-preservation. It's about managing our energy to be at our best doing what matters most to us.).

My Final Questions

Go to Appendix B-1 & B-1.2, My Final Questions. Record your answers for the following two questions.

1. Of all that you read or experienced in this chapter what one thought stands out the most for you?
2. Of the mindsets established in this chapter which one stands out the most for you?

My experience has been that participants select a variety of different mindsets that are most meaningful to them. Thoughts tend to be "I need to move more,

I never thought about the physiology of stress as it was explained, I need to learn more about that window of tolerance, the worry question is great, I like the idea of being a non-knowing helper, it kind of takes the pressure of supposedly knowing what's best for folks."

Summary

In the next stage, you'll be evaluating your workplace for those burnout practices that harm, versus those that support what you do while helping you flourish and thrive in your workplace. This stage will also include factors associated with secondary trauma and post-traumatic stress. Following the upcoming Second Stage, you'll be evaluating factors associated with self-compassion, compassion satisfaction, compassion fatigue and empathy distress. These and other outcomes in subsequent chapters will then isolate those areas that are in need of your care. The final stage identifies specific care strategies and multiple resources that allow you to then explore which strategies may help you the most. Remember, there is no quick fix, no one practice that's best for everyone. Consider the final stage as having collected the information, tools and resources needed for your personal, unapologetic self-care focus and taking the action needed to support your well-being as a helper because you deserve it, as do all those you are helping.

References

DeMarco, M. (2024, January 14). *What Happens When Your Stress Exceeds Your Window of Tolerance.* Retrieved August 10, 2025 from https://www.psychologytoday.com/gb/blog/soul-console/202401/unraveling-your-stress-may-exceed-your-window-of-tolerance

Harvard Health Publishing (2024, April 3). *Understanding the Stress Response.* Retrieved September 2, 2025 from https://www.health.harvard.edu/staying-healthy/understanding-the-stress-response

King, K. (2021, August 9). *The Limits of Mindfulness: For the Greatest Benefit Understand the Risks Clearly.* Retrieved May 17, 2025 from https://www.psychologytoday.com/gb/blog/lifespan-perspectives/202108/the-limits-mindfulness

Kingsbury, K. (2008, June 5). *Talking Out Trauma: Not Always a Help.* Retrieved August 31, 2018 from https://time.com/archive/6932622/talking-out-trauma-not-always-a-help/

Levine, P., & Kline, M. (2008). *Trauma Proofing Your Kids.* Berkeley, CA, North Atlantic Books.

Levine P. (2011). *In An Unspoken Voice: How the Body Releases Trauma and Restores Goodness.* CA, North Atlantic Books.

NICABM (2025). *How Can You Help Your Clients Understand Their Window of Tolerance?* Retrieved August 10, 2025 from https://www.nicabm.com/trauma-how-to-help-your-clients-understand-their-window-of-tolerance/

Perry B., & Szalavitz, M. (2006). *The Boy Who Was Raised as a Dog: And Other Stories from a Child Psychiatrist's Notebook—What Traumatized Children Can Teach Us About Loss, Love, and Healing.* NY. Basic Books.

Porges S., & Dana D. (2018*). Clinical Applications of the Polyvagal Theory: The Emergence of Polyvagal-Informed Therapies.* NY, WW Norton & Company.

Steele W., & Malchiodi C. (2012). *Trauma-Informed Practices with Children and Adolescents.* NY, Routledge.

Steele, W. (2015). Play Therapy for Children Experiencing Grief and Traumatic Loss. In D. Crenshaw & A. Stewart (Eds.) *Play Therapy: A Comprehensive Guide to Theory and Practice.* (pp. 304–320). NY, Guilford Press.

Steele, W. (2019) *Reducing Compassion Fatigue, Secondary Traumatic Stress and Burnout: A Trauma Sensitive Workbook.* NY, Routledge.

Supin, J. (2016, November). *The Long Shadow: Bruce Perry On the Lingering Effects of Childhood Trauma.* Retrieved May 13, 2026 from https://www.thesunmagazine.org/articles/28171-the-long-shadow

van der Kolk, B. (2015). *The Body Keeps the Score: Brasin, Mind and Body in the Healing of Trauma.* New York, Penguin Books.

Wikipedia. (2013). *Yerkes-Dodson Law.* Retrieved April 7, 2025 from https://en.wikipedia.org/wiki/Yerkes%E2%80%93Dodson_law

STAGE TWO

The Environment Matters

We Flourish When Environments Meet Our Needs

CHAPTER 4

Toxic Cultures and Burnout

Theme

Helpers can experience empathy distress, compassion fatigue and/or secondary trauma without experiencing burnout. On the other hand, burnout leaves helpers more vulnerable to compassion fatigue, secondary trauma and/or empathy distress. This chapter is specific to burnout and helping you determine those toxic workplace practices leading to burnout. In the next chapter you'll be able to identify practices that support a flourishing culture, your wellness and well-being. By comparing possible burnout factors with the practices of flourishing cultures, you will be able to better determine the negative or positive impact your current workplace is having on your well-being and what you either need to continue doing or do differently.

It's Not Always You

Mindset: *The stress I am experiencing as a helper is not always because of me but because of the practices and policies of my workplace.*

Toxic workplace cultures consist of practices and conditions that are stressful and lead to burnout. Such practices are the result of leadership failures to

DOI: 10.4324/9781003673699-6

focus on the wellness and well-being of its employees and more on quotas. These cultures have high levels of burnout. Helpers in these environments are at risk for, not only burnout, but also compassion fatigue, low levels of wellness, well-being, helper effectiveness and shortened sustainability. Sleek (2024) reported that toxic workplaces leave employees sick, scared and looking for an exit. Mayer (2025) reported that 67% of employees feel their workplace is toxic and 74% reported that their mental health was poor as a result. Mayer goes on to report that 68% indicate that managers and supervisors care more about meeting objectives than how employees are treated.

In a Forbes article, MacArthur (2024) refers to the toxic workplace as "The Silent Killer". For the past 40 years, 501(c) Services (2025) has worked with non-profits to "support sustainable workplaces". It prefers to replace the term "toxic" with the term, "cultural misalignment" yet agrees that such misalignments lead to employee stress and high turnover. Once again, it's not the terminology that matters as much as what your workplace culture is doing to you, or for you, and your reactions to those practices. For our purpose, we'll continue with the term "toxic". The reality is that workplaces are often a combination of toxic practices and practices that support well-being. This combination means that, to determine the most effective self-care for you personally, you must first evaluate the degree to which those toxic practices may be diminishing your effectiveness, wellness, sustainability and well-being. These outcomes then need to be compared to the strength of those practices in your workplace that allow you to flourish and experience a sense of self-fulfillment, purpose, compassion satisfaction, not fatigue.

The "S" Factor

"S" stands for satisfaction. What's interesting is that compassion fatigue is actually measured by evaluating our level of compassion satisfaction. Research shows that the higher the satisfaction the lower the stress or fatigue (CoffeePals, 2025; Scott, 2020). Most helping professionals do not need to complete an assessment tool to determine if they are stressed out or fatigued. In fact, assessment results alone could be misleading. Just because the practices of a workplace are rated as toxic and stress inducing, does not mean they are for you personally. This is the reason for completing several assessments and surveys to best determine your self-care needs. *Remember that compassion fatigue can exist without burnout as each has its own characteristics and sources (Celia, 2019).*

For over 20 years, I traveled regularly across the country to provide trauma related training. All the issues related to flying, long lines at the airport, delays, cancellations, the stress of turbulent flights, never knowing who will be sitting next to me in a box that provided limited movement were all stressful. Then there were the stressors related to getting to and from hotels, different beds, room conditions and, added to these stressors, were the conditions of the training environments themselves. Try using slides in an environment that allowed the sun to shine in but on the screen being used for power point; it was a washout. Sound systems, limited technology, malfunctioning technology and seating arrangements, always meant making changes.

RFI

I remember being at a school site and presenting in their auditorium. Suddenly, thirty minutes into the presentation another voice was coming out of the speakers. Of course, I was stopped mid-stream. Everyone in the audience kind of chuckled and then told me that the broadcast station next door would occasionally cut into their sound system; I kid you not. What made it more stressful was that the interruption was not predictable. This happened several times throughout the day. It's called RFI, Radio Frequency Interruption and, in this case, caused by the school's sound system not being adequately filtered. A bit stressful for sure until I started new topics with, *I've got another news flash for you* and, at other times, *This just in.*

When I look back now, all those stressful conditions strengthened my adaptability. At least a half dozen times in different locations my trainings were interrupted by fire drills. Once during a training in Oklahoma, we had to shelter because of approaching tornadoes. And, experiencing all these work-related stressors and conditions before even beginning a training session, and sometimes in the midst of presenting, I never lost my energy or enthusiasm, never fatigued because of the "S" Factor. The satisfaction experienced from helping other helpers was far greater than all the "little" inconveniences.

Trauma Survivors

On a more serious note, as I was writing this work numerous memories of trauma survivors I met and helped arose. I remember two teens who were sitting on their porch with another friend when a car drove by, shot several rounds hitting their friend in the head while he sat between them. He died between them. I remember the wife in Kuwait whose husband was brutally tortured and killed during the Gulf War and seeing a picture of his tortured body. There were Tommy and Elizabeth whose older sister was brutally murdered by a child serial killer. I remember the notes given to me by parents whose children had taken their own lives. I remember time I spent with Parents of Murdered

Children and hearing, "When you lose a parent, you lose a part of your past but when you lose a child, you lose your future." I remember the many stories of witnesses, surviving victims and traumatized helpers.

Despite all I was exposed to directly and indirectly, they never became intrusive memories. This was due in part to always approaching survivors with a great deal of curiosity as to what their experience was like for them at a subjective level. This was briefly addressed in the previous chapter. An approach like this allowed me to remain empathetic without becoming overwhelmed by the details of their experiences—a form of psychological detachment. What also protected me was the satisfaction derived from seeing the positive changes these victims were making because of the interventions they were provided. The work I was doing was also fulfilling a personal purpose that was much larger than myself. I was blessed in that I learned the hard way, and with help, to appreciate the importance of self-satisfaction via a lot of self-care. These efforts not only helped to shape my purpose as a helper but fueled my passion to fulfill that purpose.

Mindset: *Put simply, a purpose that is fulfilled (satisfied) leads to less stress (Sutin et al., 2023).*

Rest of the Story

The other blessing that made that possible was the workplace environment. I was allowed a great deal of flexibility when it came to working hours. What leadership expected from me was always very clear; how I went about it was, for the most part, up to me. In addition, I was provided the resources needed to develop and publish specific "tools" for helpers to support the use of skills they were learning. My support staff were skilled and supportive and accomplishments were recognized and rewarded. I was also constantly connected to and engaged with other helpers across the country. All of these factors reflected a flourishing workplace culture where wellness, well-being, fulfillment and satisfaction, left little room for toxic stress to survive.

The practices of a flourishing culture are detailed in the next chapter, where you will also have the opportunity to evaluate the existence of those flourishing practices in your current environment and then have the opportunity to reflect on the combined outcomes of toxic burnout practices you may be experiencing with those of flourishing environments. This will be done within the framework of the satisfaction you are or are not experiencing in your current environment, given the practices of that environment. The overall process will better help determine what areas need your self-care. For now, let's focus on identifying possible toxic practices and your reactions that may be causing you stress.

Evaluation

Follow the instructions below to evaluate those toxic practices that may currently exist in your workplace environment.

Activity One: Chapter Four—Toxic Workplace Survey

Go to *Appendix A-1* and complete the Toxic Workplace Stress Survey. Record your score on the Stage Two Outcomes Worksheet in *Appendix B-3a*. When finished return here for comments.

If presenting, ask for feedback from participants once they have completed this activity. Ask them what surprised them the most about the survey itself. Being curious, also ask what practice they identified as the most difficult to manage. Their answers, while in a group setting, will help reinforce that they are not alone regarding those issues in their work environments they may have little control over. This process can also help develop a better realization as to stress factors not previously considered toxic and the subsequent need to rethink responses to these stressors.

However

Earlier we spoke about the power of fulfilling a purpose and its protection against burnout. However, even if your purpose, while working under toxic conditions, is being served the toxicity will still have an impact on your wellness and eventually your well-being. The first place it will impact is your nervous system, which is as keen as a dog's ability to hear what's coming before us humans. Our nervous system will be responding and absorbing the negative sensory aspects of those staff conflicts, complaining, disengagement, bullying and other ongoing negative stressors. It will increase the arousal stress response. The American Institute of Stress (AIS, 2023) reports that even resilience training alone "cannot combat the detrimental effects of a toxic work culture." In fact, under these conditions, it's possible to develop "toxic resilience", or pushing through all the toxicity despite experiencing exhaustion, and other negative impacts, while trying to fulfill your purpose for working there. The more appropriate term according to Lee (2024, para. 4) is *maladaptive resilience* which is captured in the phrase "That's just the way things are". In addition, if satisfaction is limited in your personal life, those toxic practices take on more intensity. At some point having your purpose satisfied will not be enough. At best, *working in a toxic environment in order to fulfill a specific purpose needs to be a short-term goal.* All this will become clearer in the next chapter when you have the opportunity to identify those practices that enrich, not deplete your professional and personal satisfaction and well-being.

Approach Points Aligned with Those of Self-Care (Self-care approaches are in parentheses)

- ❑ To determine the most effective self-care for you personally, you must first evaluate the degree to which those toxic practices may be diminishing your effectiveness, wellness, sustainability and well-being (It's about applying effective effort).
- ❑ Put simply, a purpose that is fulfilled (satisfied) leads to less stress (It's saying *yes* to what matters most to you).
- ❑ Working in a toxic environment in order to fulfill a specific purpose needs to be a short-term goal (It's about managing your energy and saying *yes* to wellness and well-being).

If presenting, repeat the process established in previous chapters.

My experience has been that many do not realize the level of toxicity in their workplace and that there were practices they had not thought about as being toxic. They also found it interesting, as well as disturbing, that resilience alone cannot protect against burnout and can lead to maladaptive resilience. It's disturbing because, for some, it forces them to accept that they are in a no-win situation while others realize how important self-care is under these conditions. For some, this realization becomes a motivator to do more about their self-care. I do indicate that most workplaces involve both toxic and flourishing practices. I follow by indicating that flourishing practices can sometimes offset the negative effects of toxic practices, and that this is why it's important to identify those flourishing practices that may exist in order to do a comparison to best determine what you need to consider regarding your self-care.

Summary

In the next chapter we examine wellness, well-being, practices of flourishing cultures including engagement, the single most researched and strongest predictor of workplace well-being. Examining the practices of flourishing cultures provides an opportunity to evaluate what may be missing in your workplace that would otherwise benefit your well-being and help minimize the stress you experience. In addition, for some of you, these factors are key points to explore should you be thinking about looking for another workplace.

References

AIS. (2023, September 8). *Battling Burnout: Resilience Can't Fix a Toxic Workplace*. Retrieved July 20, 2025 from https://www.stress.org/news/battling-burnout-resilience-cant-fix-a-toxic-workplace/

Celia, F. (2019, October 22). *Compassion Fatigue: A Different Kind of Burnout*. Retrieved August 1, 2025 from https://physicians.dukehealth.org/articles/compassion-fatigue-different-kind-burnout

CoffeePals. (2025, June 18). *How To Fight Burnout with Workplace Satisfaction Strategies*. Retrieved July 12, 2025 from https://www.coffeepals.com/blog/addressing-burnout-how-workplace-satisfaction-can-combat-employee-stress

Lee, B. Y. (2024, January 19). *How Do You Prevent Maladaptive Resilience?* Retrieved July 20, 2025 from https://www.psychologytoday.com/gb/blog/a-funny-bone-to-pick/202312/how-do-you-prevent-maladaptive-resilience

MacArthur, H. (2024, October 29). *Toxic Workplace: The Silent Career Killer*. Retrieved January 20, 2025 from https://www.forbes.com/sites/hvmacarthur/2024/10/29/toxic-workplaces-the-silent-career-killer/

Mayer, K. (2025, February 10). *It's Likely You Have a Toxic Workplace. Now What?* Retrieved May 7, 2025 from https://www.shrm.org/topics-tools/flagships/all-things-work/you-likely-have-a-toxic-workplace-now-what

Scott, E. (2020, December 2). *Link Between Happiness and Stress Relief*. Retrieved July 2, 2025 from https://www.verywellmind.com/links-between-happiness-and-stress-relief

Sleek, S. (2024, June 7). Toxic Workplaces Leave Employees Sick, Scared and Looking for an Exit: Here's How to Combat Unhealthy Conditions. Retrieved May 7, 2025 from https://www.apa.org/topics/healthy-workplaces/toxic-workplace

Sutin, A. R., Luchetti, M., Stephan, Y., Sesker, A., & Terracciano, A. (2023). Purpose in life and stress: An individual-participant meta-analysis of 16 samples. *Journal of Affective Disorders*, 15: 378–385. https://doi.org/10.1016/j.jad.2023.10.149

501(c) Services. (2025, April 15). *Why Toxic Environments Thrive*. Retrieved May 5, 2025 from https://501c.com/why-toxic-work-environments-thrive

CHAPTER 5

Flourishing or Toxic?

Self-Care Deserving

Theme

The average person spends 90,000 hours, or one-third of their time, at work (Harvard Division of Continuing Education, 2025). Approaching self-care, as presented in the first chapter, supports that you are deserving of working in a non-toxic workplace, a workplace that provides you with opportunities to flourish. This chapter addresses the major practices that support a flourishing environment. It provides the opportunity to identify those practices that protect against burnout. You'll then be able to compare these practices with the burnout practices in your environment to better determine where to focus your self-care strategies.

A Flourishing Environment

A flourishing environment is one that will provide far more satisfaction than stress (Solano, 2025). Research shows us that "Flourishing workplace interventions (practices) not only increase happiness at work, but also reduces stress and emotional exhaustion" (Young, 2023, para. 1). In this era of "The Great Exhaustion" (Ballesteros, 2024) a flourishing environment is a priority.

DOI: 10.4324/9781003673699-7

A flourishing environment produces employees "who manifest enhanced work engagement" (Imran et al., 2020). This is very important because high levels of engagement can significantly increase well-being. Aldana's research (2025) found that high levels of engagement increased well-being by 66% and decreased absenteeism by 88%, meaning greater workplace satisfaction and less stress. Let's then look more closely at the practices supporting engagement.

Engagement

Engagement and well-being are inter-connected yet very different. According to the Engagement Multiplier (2025) engagement is about working together to support a common purpose, whereas well-being is about reducing stress. The "reducing stress" examples they cite are from Arianna Huffington's organization, Thrive Global, which is focused on improving health and productivity. Paid days for staff to volunteer in the community, meditation, yoga classes, taking part in the Virgin Pulse wellness program and matching a portion of staff's charitable contributions are only a few of the examples mentioned. The Virgin Pulse app, for example, is used as frequently as Facebook. Its "users show 50% sustained engagement, 52% stress reduction and 40% lower turnover rates" (Virgin Pulse, 2023). Research also indicates that high engagement employees have higher psychological well-being and experience personal sense of accomplishment, while lower engagement groups show higher emotional exhaustion and depersonalization (Shuck & Reio, 2013). Gomez & Chavez (2023) also showed that engagement is a predictor of well-being. Consider low engagement environments as toxic environments that produce high levels of stress while higher engagement levels improve well-being and lower stress, with one exception.

The Exception

You can be highly engaged and in an environment that supports engagement practices yet be experiencing high stress if you are also experiencing low well-being. In other words, low well-being will limit the stress benefits of engagement (Rasool et al., 2021). In fact, "those with low well-being in high engagement cultures have a 61% higher likelihood of burnout" (Harter & Witters, 2025), which is inclusive of physical, emotional and mental exhaustion. Research speaks to the importance of our well-being as a protector against the negative effects of helper stress. This raises the question of what constitutes well-being. Before defining well-being and reviewing several essentials necessary for higher levels of well-being, engagement needs a closer look as it is not always understood.

The Engaged Helper

Gallup, a world leader in engagement practices, defines engaged employees as "those who are involved in, enthusiastic about and committed to their workplace" (Gallup Daily, 2017). Engagement Multipliers define it as the "ability of the employee to be present, focused, and engaged while feeling connected to the organization's purpose" (2025). Solano (2025) states that engaged employees are motivated, inspired and feel their work matters. If these "fit" you, then you're highly engaged but let's give you the opportunity to take a closer look. The Self-Engagement Survey you'll complete is very brief but reflective of multiple indicators of engagement presented by several researchers.

Activity One: Go to Appendix A-2 Self-Engagement Survey. Record your score on the Stage Two Outcomes Worksheet in Appendix B-3a. When finished return here for a brief discussion.

If presenting, simply ask participants to share what they found to be the *somewhat* and *rare* responses. Following this, ask what they found to be the positive factors. Sharing these in a group format will likely reveal that there are some weak areas that are common across the group while strong areas will have more limited response. Occasionally, you may find that a fair number of participants experience high engagement. Encourage conversation with these participants. Suggest to others in the group to ask these individuals what practices they find most beneficial.

It is also necessary to reflect that they may want to be engaged, but are in an environment that makes this difficult because of leadership's failure to support practices leading to engagement.

My experience has been that this issue is frequently scored in the *somewhat* and *rarely* range on questions 2, 3, 7 and 8 on the *Self-Engagement Survey.* The reality is, that initiating and sustaining engagement practices in the workplace is largely dependent on leadership. This invites asking what kind of leadership promotes engagement?

Workplace Engagement Practices

Your current level of engagement is generally the result of how well leadership engages in practices to engage you. *Dare to Lead* is a book about acknowledging the responsibility today's leaders have toward those they are leading. It's about the courage it takes to lead in an ever-changing world and, within our focus, a very stressful one. *It's about daring to actively care for and be connected to the people leaders are leading.* As the author, Dr. Bene Brown writes, *"care and connection are irreducible requirements for wholehearted, productive (engaging) relationships between leaders and team (staff) members"* (Brown, 2018, p. 12). In human services, mental health and other organizations responding to those in distress, the level of engagement employees experience with their managers and/or supervisors is also predictive of retention and clinical efficacy with clients (Mental Health America, 2017). Leaders who support organizational and helper well-being, support policies and practices associated with high levels of engagement, which helps minimize the daily dose of stress helpers experience.

Mindset: *The more engaged I am, the more passionate I am about what I do with those I am helping and the more committed I am to my organization.*

Let's examine how well your leadership is promoting your engagement by checking the practices they do or do not engage in as leaders. The next survey lists all the ways employees become engaged with the help of leadership, inclusive of managers and supervisors.

Activity Two: Go to Appendix A-3 Employees Will Engage When Worksheet. Record your score on the Stage Two Outcomes Worksheet in Appendix B-3a. Return here when finished.

If presenting, ask what surprised them the most about their response to this survey and then follow with asking for their questions. When answering keep focused on the relationship between engagement and well-being, indicating that you'll be covering well-being next.

My experience has been that some participants will indicate that they previously associated the absence of some of these practices as factors of burnout. They are correct. I would also add that their absence is likely also associated with lower levels of workplace well-being. Someone will suggest that their workplace provides excellent benefits to support their health but does not utilize a number of these engagement practices. I would refer to the Stage One discussion about the power of perception regarding how stress is experienced. I would ask that person, using a scale of 1–10, how satisfied they are in their workplace. I would suggest that when we feel satisfied, we are and whatever stress does exist is likely minimal. If fairly satisfied, I would reflect that their personal needs are being met to their satisfaction, and therefore their stress level is likely manageable yet needs to be periodically evaluated as conditions change.

I would also suggest to the group that they have a lot to reflect on and absorb, especially given the assessments they've completed up to this point. Assure them, that when they evaluate all these factors and the additional ones to come, they will be able to determine what matters most to them as helpers. I would suggest that when employees feel supported, connected to one another inclusive of leadership (engaged), they are more likely to remain loyal, perform at their best, experience a sense of fulfillment, satisfaction and well-being (Dewar, 2025). This takes us to defining well-being and addressing two very essential needs for well-being to thrive.

Well-Being

The interchangeable use of the terms "wellness", "well-being" and "holistic wellness" can be confusing. Furthermore, measuring well-being can be difficult because of its many varied definitions. Jarden & Roache (2023) indicate that the definition of well-being varies from one profession to another. What one includes, others do not, yet abundant research speaks to the importance and inter-relationship between engagement and well-being in the workplace (Gomez & Chavez, 2023). At the same time, most do report and agree that engagement and well-being are the essence of a flourishing, thriving workplace environment. Let's do a brief review of a few of the ways well-being can be approached.

How Helpers Experience Well-Being

The New York Times bestseller *Wellbeing: The Five Essential Elements* (Rath & Harter, 2010) defined the concept of well-being in the workplace to include physical, community, financial and social well-being. Social well-being is inclusive of relational, emotional, psychological and spiritual well-being. The primary difference between wellness and well-being is that wellness generally refers to the pursuit of activities and lifestyles that create overall health, whereas well-being goes beyond health to encompass a *state of being* such as positiveness, self-fulfillment, happiness, having a purpose (Take Care, 2025). In a broader sense well-being involves a sense of satisfaction with the different components of our lives—physical, financial, mental, emotional, social and spiritual well-being (Muldoon, 2022). Most assessments of well-being focus on satisfaction. Although satisfaction is subjective, we can say *if we feel satisfied, we are and life is well.*

The Big Two

The two additional workplace practices, in addition to engagement, that reflect a culture supportive of helper well-being include opportunities for self-fulfillment and value alignment.

Self-Fulfillment

Mindset: *When my workplace gives me the opportunity to grow and contribute to society and my community in a meaningful way, I experience a greater sense of fulfillment.*

According to the company O.C. Tanner (2023), 83% of employees say that personal fulfillment (finding meaning and purpose) in everyday work is the single greatest contributor to having a positive work experience. The article goes on to point out that being able to accomplish what matters most to us leads to a 700% likelihood of experiencing self-fulfillment. Fulfillment has been defined as "a sense that your work matters, contributes to your growth and connects you with others" (Herbert, 2025, para. 1). If you rated self-engagement as fairly high, it's very likely that you're experiencing a sense of fulfillment while being engaged with others.

Solomon (2024) would reinforce the importance of the type of connections we have in the workplace. He would ask, "Do they support you and bring you joy even in the hard times?" He points out that the "Harvard Study of Adult Development—one of the longest running studies on happiness—found that good relationships are the single strongest predictor of happiness", or as his friend reminded him, "It doesn't matter if you're saving the world, if you're doing it with a bunch of jerks." In other words, *self-fulfillment is not just the result of accomplishing what matters to us, the effort must be shared with others*. Furthermore, research shows that living in alignment with our core values leads to numerous benefits inclusive of "experiencing greater levels of happiness and fulfillment" (Urell, 2024). Since value alignment is a definite path to well-being and self-fulfillment in the workplace, let's spend a little more time exploring its importance to mediating stress.

Value Alignment

Value alignment is a two-sided effort. If I decide to work for an organization whose values do not align with mine, that is on me. If I join an organization whose stated values align with mine but that organization fails to enforce practices that support those stated values, that's on them. No one wins when values are not in alignment; such an environment is likely toxic with high levels of burnout.

Mindset: *When my values align with my organization's values and practices I do well; when they do not, my well-being suffers.*

Evans (2024) reports that value alignment results in enhanced job performance, emotional well-being, increased motivation and greater loyalty to the organization. These outcomes definitely facilitate personal and professional growth. Years ago, Sheldon & Eliot's research (1999) showed that "individuals who live in accordance with their values, experience higher levels of well-being and life satisfaction. The classic book, *Good to Great* (Collins, 2001) also reinforced, via abundant research, that an organization's core values help its employees move from good to great, to flourish, endure and sustain that effort over time. According to Torres et al. (2022) values are a reflection of our culture and who we are. Values enable and empower us to establish priorities and make decisions we can live by. When workplace values are unified and all engage in the practices supporting those values, well-being and self-fulfillment are very high.

A wonderful example of a unified theme of shared values is the story conveyed to me about the deadly attack and massacre at Virginia Tech. In April of 2007, Seung-Hui Cho, a senior American student at Virginia Tech, killed 52 students in the deadliest rampage in US history at that time. Weeks later, a young Korean lady was going door to door in her apartment complex apologizing for what he had done (Steele, 2015). Koreans have a very collective, unified value approach to culture (Yuh, 2016) that values the following, "If one of us has injured you, we have all injured you." This is the essence of a healthy workplace, one that supports the collective well-being of its employees and community.

Misalignment

So, what about a workplace that values what you value but whose practices do not support that value or hold its employees accountable when their behaviors conflict with these values? Neuroscience shows that "misalignment of values and action (workplace practices) can lead to chronic stress and burnout" (Brain First Institute, 2024).

Moral Distress—Moral Injury

Employees put in the position of engaging in practices that go against their own values, or who witness the behaviors of others that conflict with that employee's value, experience moral distress or moral injury. If you checked/circled #s 27 or 37 on the Toxic Environment Survey from the previous chapter (Are you asked to do what goes against what you value?) you are not a good fit with that environment, and the longer you stay the greater the moral distress and psychological injury you may experience because of the moral dilemma and distress this creates for you.

Moral distress is the result of witnessing some action that goes against our moral code or being unable to do anything about a moral conflict we witness. It is more likely to take place in toxic cultures. Moral injury is much more intense and stressful and its reactions are internalized. Moral injury happens when we directly do something that violates our moral code, or fail to prevent others from violating what we consider morally wrong. Many combat veterans, for example, experience moral injury along with law enforcement officers because of what they may do or witness colleagues do in the midst of potentially dangerous or highly stressful situations. It is a reaction that has also been reported more frequently during the COVID pandemic and what took place in overcrowded facilities in the midst of life and death decisions.

Moral injury victims often suffer deeply and in silence because of the guilt, shame and sense of betrayal they experience (Weisleder, 2023). Value alignment therefore is essential to well-being. Neuroscience tells us that when we act in accordance with our values dopamine is released. Dopamine helps us feel pleasure (not stress). The fact is "we are neurologically wired to seek satisfaction and pleasure by staying true to our values" (Value Graphics, 2023).

Let's Compare

What might be helpful at this point is to briefly reflect on the rating you arrived at in the previous chapter, on toxic workplace practices, and compare that rating with those for self-engagement and leadership engagement. Simply record your rating for each below. Brief comments will follow.

Toxic Workplace
Toxic ______, Concerning ______, Minimal ______
Self-Engagement
Rarely ______, Somewhat ______, Very Engaged ______
Leadership Engagement
Little ______, Somewhat ______, Very Engaged ______

Reflect: Consider engagement as a strong indicator of personal satisfaction, being in an environment concerned about your well-being, as well as providing you with opportunities for growth and self-fulfillment. When engagement levels are high, toxic practices are likely minimal. When engagement levels are *somewhat, rarely* or *little,* organizational support for your well-being is likely limited, as are opportunities for growth and experiencing a sense of fulfillment. This condition is also highly associated with toxic practices and burnout.

When toxic practices are minimal, engagement is generally high. However, if there is low toxicity and only a *somewhat* level of engagement, opportunities for growth and fulfillment are likely being compromised along with your overall well-being. If this is the case, you need to ask yourself how satisfied you are with your workplace's limited opportunities and well-being support. If satisfied with what you are accomplishing, how you are accomplishing it and where you are accomplishing it, wonderful. If at some point this changes it's likely because toxic practices have increased, engagement has decreased and you are no longer feeling fulfilled or perhaps are even fatigued.

Evaluating Burnout

Burnout Assessment: Why This Tool?

The assessment tool you are being asked to complete was selected because a) when burnout is high, compassion fatigue for helpers is more likely, and b) because it also focuses on stress related factors in our personal lives, which either contributes to or helps reduce burnout and fatigue in the workplace. All the different areas on this tool will be explored throughout this work. The tool captures many of the factors associated with burnout, including workload, control, reward, community, fairness and values, in addition to the personal well-being areas of physical, mental, emotional, spiritual and relational well-being. The tool is quite comprehensive and, at the same time, helps identify strengths and sources of resilience. I especially like the scoring system. It captures the overall level of burnout, the specific categories showing the highest and lowest levels of stress and individual reactions indicating a potentially "at risk" issue that if neglected could become much larger. The concern regarding single "at risk" stressors relate to the mindset established in *Chapter Two* that it only takes one specific stressor, such as empathetic distress, *to decrease our effectiveness, erode our sense of well-being and challenge our thoughts about self, what we do and who we help.*

Go to Appendix A-4: Burnout Assessment. Complete and record your scores In Appendix A-3a for Workplace Scores and B-3b for Personal Well-Being areas. When finished, return here for a brief discussion.

If you are a presenter/trainer and wish to use this tool, always remind participants before they begin that you will never ask about their personal scores related to any of the assessments they'll be completing. What you will ask about are their reactions to the tool itself, what categories or questions they found most helpful, questions they've never been asked before and what they think of scoring methods. This is a way to keep attendees engaged and curious as to similar and different responses from those in the group. At times their response will feel validated and at other times they will rethink their responses or even disagree.

Do indicate the importance of evaluating for burnout because higher levels of burnout lead to a higher likelihood of experiencing compassion fatigue, which leads to a host of other physical, emotional, mental and relational stress reactions. Also indicate that their results will become far more meaningful once they are compared with those of other assessments and surveys yet to be completed. For example, the meaning of outcomes for self-compassion, compassion satisfaction/fatigue, empathy distress, secondary trauma or post-traumatic stress are influenced by individual outcomes of each area measured. The one area on this tool likely to raise the most questions and feedback is spiritual intelligence.

It's Not What You Think

Of all the questions you as readers might have about this tool, I would not be surprised if the majority of comments are about Spiritual Intelligence (SI). SI is not a category or term frequently seen on stress tools. Personally, I am glad to see it but it does need a brief explanation. SI is not about faith or religion. SI is about how we view and respond to life and how we go about achieving one that is purposeful and meaningful. It's about our approach to life in ways that embrace resilience and the emotional/cognitive regulation necessary to avoid or effectively recover from the negative impact of empathetic distress, compassion fatigue or secondary trauma.

Spiritual intelligence is like a super vitamin when it comes to well-being, resilience, self-fulfillment and its preventative factors against the downsides of helper stress (Griffiths, 2025). It's so important that you'll be asked to complete the formal, more extensive, well researched Spiritual Intelligence Self-Report Inventory (SISRI) assessment tool when we talk about self-care. It's included as a self-care strategy because some of its practices reflect the Western version of the Mind, Body, Spirit practices of Eastern cultures. Let's then do a quick review of the *approach points* in this chapter that align with those of self-care.

Approach Points Aligned with Those of Self-Care (Self-care approaches are in parentheses)

- ❑ When my workplace gives me the opportunity to grow and contribute to society and its community in a meaningful way, I experience a greater sense of fulfillment (It's a way of approaching life and maintaining my well-being, sustainability, saying *yes* to myself, a management of my energy).
- ❑ Spiritual intelligence is about how we view and respond to life and how we go about achieving one that is purposeful and meaningful (It's a way of approaching life and maintaining well-being).
- ❑ When my values align with my organization's values and practices I do well; when they do not, my well-being suffers (When my approach to self-care aligns with my approach to stress, I do well).
- ❑ The more engaged I am, the more passionate I am about what I do with those I am helping and the more committed I am to my organization (It's about managing energy, sustainability, saying *yes* to myself, *yes* to *eustress*, wellness and well-being).

My Final Questions

Go to Appendix B-1 & B-1.2, My Final Questions. Record your answers for the following two questions.

1. Of all that you read or experienced in this chapter what one thought stands out the most for you?
2. Of the mindsets established in this chapter which one stands out the most for you?

If presenting, be curious as to their responses to each of these final questions. Provide time for them to reflect and answer. There is no need to process.

My experience has been that participants from helping non-profit organizations struggle the most with limited leadership engagement practices and well-being support, other than healthcare related benefits. This makes perfect sense as the prevalence of stress among helpers is high. If they have questions regarding their assessment outcomes, I would reiterate that these are reference points as to what may or may not need self-care attention and that additional assessments are necessary before analyzing outcomes. The key is to ask themselves how satisfied they are with their current conditions, the stress they are experiencing and the ways they are responding to that stress. I would remind them how stress is a friend letting us know, at times that *doing differently* is needed. Also mention that all assessment outcomes will be discussed in Stage Four.

Summary

You have learned a great deal up to this point. Later we'll help you put this all together to personalize your self-care plan. Before we get there, *we need to address the higher risk for experiencing secondary trauma or post-traumatic stress when working for organizations that are responding to, or helping those, experiencing trauma in their lives. As their stories, their situations or conditions can be quite traumatic for helpers as well.* These environments demand additional practices to support their helpers, specific to secondary stress and post-traumatic stress, because of the trauma survivors and/or conditions they are responding to.

In reality, many helping organizations are seeing many more trauma victims despite trauma victims not being the primary population they serve. When this is the case, helpers serving these individuals should be well trained in trauma specific strategies and most importantly should have access to a supervisor who has core competencies for dealing with trauma. This is essential to the well-being of all involved—helpers and those they are helping. This will be made clear in the following chapter and conclude our review of workplace cultures. Following this we'll then look at compassion fatigue, self-compassion, compassion satisfaction, empathetic distress, cognitive and emotional regulation and additional practices. Once these elements are evaluated, you'll be ready to approach your self-care planning.

References

Aldana, S. (2025, February 5). *Employee Engagement Statistics: 25+ Critical Insights for 2025.* Retrieved May 20, 2025 from https://www.wellsteps.com/blog/2024/05/30/employee-engagement-statistics/

Ballesteros, E. (2024, February 13). *We're More Exhausted Than Ever.* Retrieved July 5, 2025 from https://time.com/6694092/exhaustion-increasing-causes-essay/

Brain First Institute. (2024, August 29). *Aligning with Values: The Neuroscience of Values-Based Actions.* Retrieved July 8, 2025 from https://www.brainfirstinstitute.com/blog/aligning-with-values-the-neuroscience-of-values-based-actions

Brown, B. (2018). *Dare to Lead: Brave Work, Tough Conversations Whole Hearts.* NY, Random House.

Collins, J. (2001). *Good to Great.* London, Random House Business Books.

Dewar, K. (2025, January 7). *20 Benefits of Employee Engagement: Why It's So Important.* Retrieved July 5, 2025 from https://www.achievers.com/blog/benefits-employee-engagement-why-important/

Evans, M. (2024, July 25). *The Importance of a Workplace That Aligns with Personal Values.* Retrieved May 20, 2025 from https://www.forbes.com/councils/forbesbusinesscouncil/2024/07/25/the-importance-of-a-workplace-that-aligns-with-personal-values/

Engagement Multiplier. (2025). *Employee Engagement vs Employee Well-Being.* Retrieved July 5, 2025 from https://www.engagementmutiplier.com

Gallup Daily. (2017). *Gallup Daily: U.S. Employee Engagement.* Retrieved May 5, 2026 from https://news.gallup.com/poll/180404/gallup-daily-employee-engagement.aspx

Gomez, M.D.C., & Chavez, C. C. (2023, August). Thriving in the new normal: Exploring the link between employee well-being and work engagement. *British Journal of Multidisciplinary and Advanced Studies,* 4(44): 44–51.

Griffiths, R. (2025). *Top Ten Features of Spiritual Intelligence.* Retrieved August 8, 2025 from https://sqi.co/top-ten-features-spiritual-intelligence/

Harter, J., & Witters, D. (2025). *The Link Between Employee Engagement and Well-Being.* Retrieved July 5, 2025 from https://www.futureofbusinessandtech.

com/employee-well-being/the-link-between-employee-engagement-and-well-being/

Harvard Division of Continuing Education (2025, February 24). *Why Workplace Culture Matters.* Retrieved July 5, 2025 from https://professional.dce.harvard.edu/blog/why-workplace-culture-matters/

Herbert, N. (2025, July 21). *Employee Fulfillment: Where Purpose and Belonging Come Together.* Retrieved July 8, 2025 from https://chronus.com/blog/employee-fulfillment

Imran, M. Y., Elahi, N. S., Abid, G., Asfaq, F., & Ilyas, S. (2020). Impact of personal organizational support on work engagement: medicating mechanisms of thriving and flourishing. *Journal of Open Innovations Technology, Market and Complexity,* 6(3): 1–18.

Jarden, A., & Roache, A. (2023). What is Well-being. *Int J Res Public Health,* 20(6): 5006. https://doi.org/10.3390/ijerph20065006

Mental Health America (2017, October 18). *Mind The Workplace: Workplace Wellness Report.* Retrieved August 15, 2018 from https://mhanational.org/research/mind-the-workplace-workplace-wellness-report/

Muldoon, C. (2022, August 23). *Wellness VS Well-Being: What is the difference?* Retrieved July 5, 2025 from https://www.webmdhealthservices.com/blog/wellness-vs-well-being-whats-the-difference/

O.C. Tanner. (2023). *Part 3: Fostering Fulfillment at Work to Elevate the Employee Experience.* Retrieved July 9, 2025 from https://www.octanner.com/webinars/3-part-series-strengthening-workplace-community-with-the-2023-global-culture-report-3

Rasool, S., F., Wang, M., Tang. M., Saaed, A., & Igbol, J. (2021, February 26). How Toxic workplace environment effects the employee engagement: The mediating role of organizational support and well-being. *Int J. Environ Res Public Health,* 18(5): 2294 https://doi.org/10.3390/ijerph18052294

Rath, T., & Harter, J. (2010). *Wellbeing: The Five Essential Elements.* NY, Gallup Press.

Sheldon, K. M., & Eliot, A. J. (1999). Goal striving, need satisfaction, and longitudinal well-being: The self-concordance model. *Journal of Personality and Social Psychology,* 76(3), 482–497.

Shuck, B., & Reio Jr., T. G. (2013). Employee engagement and well-being: A moderation model and implication for practice. *Journal of Leadership and Organization Studies,* 21(1): 43–58.

Solano, E. (2025). *Flourishing In the Workplace: Cultivating a Positive Culture.* Retrieved July 5, 2025 from https://ilha.org/flourishing-in-the-workplace-cutivating-a-positive-workplace-culuture

Solomon, E. (2024, November 3). *The Secret to True Fulfillment. Finding Real Fulfillment: Why You Need to Start with "Who".* Retrieved July 8, 2025 from https://www.psychologytoday.com/us/blog/story-over-spreadsheet/202411/the-secret-to-true-fulfillment

Steele, W. (2015). *Trauma in Schools and Communities: Lessons Learned from Survivors and Responders.* NY, Routledge.

Urell, S. (2024, May 7). *Living in Value Alignment: A Path to Fulfillment.* Retrieved July 8, 2025 from https://www.beginboundless.com/post/living-in-value-alignment-a-path-to-fulfillment

Take Care (2025). *Wellness and Well-being: What's the Difference?* Retrieved July 25, 2025 from https://takecare.org/resources/wellness-vs-well-being-whats-the-difference/

Torres, C. V., Neiva, E. R., & Glazer, S. (2022). Values in Organizations: Theory Measurement, and Theoretical Reflections. In M. O. Macambira, H. Mendonça, & M. Paz (Eds.), *Assessing Organizational Behaviors: A Critical Analysis of Measuring Instruments.* (pp. 191–221). Cham, Switzerland, Springer Nature.

Value Graphics (2023, August 28). *The Neuroscience of Values Alignment and Business Strategy.* Retrieved January 7, 2026 from https://valuegraphics.com/blog/the-neuroscience-of-values-alignment-a-business-strategy-for-a-values-driven-world

Virgin Pulse. (2023, May 16). *Pulse Takes Well-Being to the Next Level with New AI—Powered Homebase for Health Enhancement.* Retrieved May 20, 2025 from https://www.prnewswire.com/news-releases/virgin-pulse-takes-personalized-wellbeing-to-the-next-level-with-new-ai-powered-homebase-for-health-enhancements-301825184.html

Weisleder, P. (2023). Moral distress, moral injury and burnout: Clinicians; resilience and adaptability are not the solution. *Ann Child Neurol Soc,* 1: 262–266. https://doi.org/10.1002/cns3.20048

Young, A. M. (2023, February 16). *What Flourishing Is and Why It Matters: How the Science of Flourishing Can Address the Silent Suffering at Work.* Retrieved July 5, 2025 from https://www.psychologytoday.com/gb/blog/202302/what-flourishing-is-and-why-it-matters

Yuh, J. (2016, September 6). *Culture: South Korea, A Collective Society in Confucianism.* Retrieved May 5, 2025 from https://sites.psu.edu/global/2016/09/06/blog-entry-culture-south-korea-a-collectivist-society-in-confucianism/

CHAPTER 6

Secondary Trauma, Post-Traumatic Stress

Culture and Well-Being

Theme

In Stage One it was reported that there was a 42% increase of secondary trauma, and a similar increase in post-traumatic stress, following the COVID epidemic among social workers. This chapter reviews the reactions associated with each and provides the opportunity to evaluate for the reactions you may be experiencing. If working in an environment servicing those in trauma, you should expect that leadership is appropriately informed about your vulnerability to either secondary trauma or post-traumatic stress simply because of your exposure to those in distress. At best, you ought to have access to supervision that meets standard secondary trauma core competence. This really is all about how well your leadership is not only trauma-informed but interested in your well-being by providing the necessary trauma-informed support. Given that most organizations serve various numbers of trauma victims, the absence of secondary trauma-informed practices and supervisors who do not meet core competencies can be considered toxic for helpers.

Secondary Traumatic Stress (STS)

Secondary trauma reactions are those also found in post-traumatic stress but they do not meet the full requirements to be classified as post-traumatic stress.

DOI: 10.4324/9781003673699-8

Do keep in mind that PTSD is a formal diagnostic category, whereas secondary trauma is not a diagnostic category yet contains a few of the reactions associated with post-traumatic stress. The criteria for STS consist of symptoms of intrusion, avoidance, arousal and alteration in cognition and mood. Unlike post-traumatic stress, there is no specific number of symptoms required to experience secondary trauma.

Mindset: *Secondary trauma is not a pathological condition; it is not at all an uncommon response to helping those in trauma and distress.*

Secondary trauma is the result of indirect exposure experienced via a client's story or what was witnessed when responding to a situation that was traumatic. It can also result from hearing about the trauma of a close family member or friend. In other words, you were not directly victimized. It can have a sudden onset, for example listening to one client's experience, or it can develop over multiple exposures.

Mindset: *Any one STS reaction can significantly reduce helping effectiveness. If left unattended it also increases the risk for compassion fatigue and post-traumatic stress especially when also dealing with burnout conditions.*

Mitigating and/or preventing secondary trauma is dependent upon three conditions that include being

1. in a flourishing culture, as burnout factors increase one's vulnerability to secondary trauma,
2. provided with supervision that meets secondary trauma core competencies,
3. in an organization that has established secondary trauma organizational policies and practices to support the well-being of its helpers.

Activity One: STS Evaluation

Let's first establish what secondary reactions you may be experiencing, if any.

Go to Appendix A-5 STS Reactions. Identify reactions being experienced. Record your outcomes on the Stage Two Outcomes Worksheet in Appendix B-3a. When finished return here for a brief note.

Note: If you are not currently experiencing any reactions that's wonderful. However, it is important from a preventative position to be supervised by a person you trust and who meets core competency as a secondary trauma-informed supervisor. Please review the following section regarding supervision as it is critically important for well-being regardless of the reactions you may or may not be experiencing.

If you are experiencing any of these secondary trauma reactions, these can usually be resolved via a competent trauma-informed supervisor. However, even when supervisors have the skills to be helpful, the outcome is determined by your perceptions and trust of that supervisor and the supervisory process itself. The supervisory process is the single most common predictor of employee satisfaction, engagement, well-being and reason for staying or leaving the workplace (Sewell et al., 2024). We'll address core competencies first then the supervisory relationship. As a helper or supervisor, the level of secondary trauma supervisor core competency can be evaluated by completing the following activity.

Activity Two: STS Core Competencies

Note: Helpers complete this checklist regarding your current supervisor. *Supervisors complete this checklist* to determine your STS competency.

Go to Appendix A-6 NCTSN Core Competencies for Secondary Trauma-Informed Supervisors.

Record your outcomes on the Stage Two Outcomes Worksheet in Appendix B-3a. Return here when completed.

If presenting, ask each group separately for their reactions.

My experience with direct care helpers is that they often feel their supervisors are not STS competent after taking the survey. If this is the case, they may need to seek help outside their agency if they are experiencing reactions. The additional issue related to the absence of secondary trauma support, by way of supervision, is that staff may also become less engaged and more vulnerable to compassion fatigue. Either way, well-being is sacrificed.

My experience with supervisors is that many are not aware of these core competencies and were never asked about them when hired. This is even the case when supervisors are trauma-informed. Because of the growing incidence of secondary trauma among helpers, these competencies were established in 2018, just over seven years ago as of this 2025 writing. COVID, of course, further increased the incidence.

Why This Emphasis on Supervisory Support?

Sewell et al. (2024) research outcomes support the following mindset.

Mindset: *The strength of supervisory relationship predicts practitioner wellness, compassion satisfaction, minimizes the amount of burnout, secondary traumatic stress and moral distress.*

Gil & Weinberg (2015) found that social workers who reported a lack of supervision experienced higher rates of PTSD, which is inclusive of STS reactions. I would propose that many of the PTSD cases began with secondary trauma and led to PTSD. Weiss-Dagan et al. (2016) did find that when supervision was rated effective, secondary trauma levels were lower.

Perceptions

Kulkarni et al. (2013) and Segal (2025) consider it to be extremely important that staff perceptions—or the subjective ways they experience the workplace culture, policies and practices, leadership and ultimately supervision—are consistently evaluated so that necessary adjustments can be made to support staff performance, engagement, satisfaction and retention. Eisenberger (2002) and Mikkelson et al. (2024) found that positive perceptions of supervision were also associated with positive perceptions of the organization and were also associated with lower stress.

Supervisees Determine Effectiveness

Let's assume the supervisors in your workplace are trauma competent. This does not mean that the relationship between supervisee and supervisor will automatically be beneficial. As stated above, perceptions matter greatly. There has always been anxiety related to supervision. Being a competent supervisor means being aware of the anxieties supervisees bring to supervision, being able to alleviate them and create a safe and beneficial supervisory process. I bring this up because at the core of all trauma-informed principles and practices is safety—doing no harm.

Note: All helpers, supervisees and supervisors can benefit from reading through the remainder of this chapter. It provides ways for supervisors to establish the supervisory process as safe and that one builds trust by demonstrating awareness of the common concerns helpers have about supervision. For helpers entering into supervision, it presents what to look for and what lets you know that the supervisor is sensitive to the concerns you have about the supervisory relationship.

Mindset: *Ultimately the effectiveness of the supervisory relationship, and what the supervisor is hoping to accomplish, is based on how you, the supervisee, experience that relationship.*

Activity Three: Ten Most Common Supervisee Anxiety-Based Thoughts About Supervisors

The following activity cites concerns expressed by many helpers regarding supervisors or managers. Simply circle those thoughts that reflect those you may have about starting with a new supervisor.

1. You are assigned to me as my supervisor. Even though I may have had a good supervisory relationship in the past, I still have no choice in this, so yes, that makes me a bit anxious.

2. You'll be watching me, evaluating my performance, so yes, I'm definitely a bit nervous about how you will react, what you are going to think about me and about my work.
3. Even though I've already heard some good things about you, there may be something about me that hits you the wrong way, so yes, I'll be tentative.
4. There may be something about the way you present yourself, your demeanor, your tone of voice that reminds me of someone in my past that made my life difficult or even hurt me, so yes, I'm anxious and may be somewhat protective in my responses to you initially.
5. Maybe my idea of supervision is not the way you think about supervision, so not knowing that makes me concerned.
6. What if I really need this job and it turns out I have a hard time with you, then what, so yes, that makes me anxious.
7. What kind of relationship is this going to be; will it be helpful, encouraging, a really good learning experience or just the opposite?
8. I know, because my colleagues have also experienced this, that even if I am quite competent, a lousy supervisor can make life very stressful, so yes, I am going to be cautious.
9. I don't know if you are simply going to talk to me about my record keeping and notes rather than provide support for my reactions to what I've been exposed to, so yes, I will be hesitant about talking about those responses.
10. My worst experience was when I was micromanaged. I was never left on my own, so yes, I'll be very cautious about what I communicate especially problems or conflicts that arise.

If presenting: This listing could be used as a handout or put on power point, followed by asking participants for a show of hands after each question as to how many have had these thoughts.

My experience over the years is that concerns about supervision cited in the activity remain the same today as they were years ago, and that trust and safety remain the essential and critical components necessary for supervision to be a beneficial learning experience versus a conflictual or useless one.

Why This Anxiety About Supervision?

Supervisees enter into the supervisory process vulnerable because of any one of the unknowns cited above. Apostol et al. (2025) reported that 60% of supervisees do not communicate personal issues with their supervisor and that 44% do not disclose clinical (intervention) mistakes. Furthermore, 90%

of supervisees do not disclose negative reactions to their supervisor. These responses are fear based. Let's face it; there is a power imbalance in the supervisory relationship. Supervisees enter the relationship with anxieties that must be addressed immediately to help alleviate at least some of their fears. This is best done by structuring the supervisory process (Paru, 2022). Cook et al. (2019, p. 121) reported the following common response from supervisees, "I'm pretty confused about what supervision is supposed to be like . . . If it were explained a little better in the beginning and expectations were set for supervision that would be more helpful."

Mindset: *To reduce your anxiety and start the process of developing a supervisory relationship into an effective, collaborative, supportive and developmentally enriching one, you, the supervisee, must first be made to feel safe with the relationship and the process by having the supervisor address your anxieties.*

Establishing the Safety of Supervision

As an informed supervisor (this applies to all supervisors), the question that needs addressing is, "How do I present myself as someone who is safe?" I am going to answer this by focusing on what trauma-informed supervisors ought to acknowledge in order to initiate an alliance that begins with a focus on it being a safe one. This is a process that communicates that you, the supervisor, are "in sync" with the concerns of the supervisee. When a supervisee experiences that you know some of what they are experiencing and thinking, they begin to feel safe enough to become more emotionally present and vulnerable. For supervisors, these examples become a template for positioning yourselves as sensitive to the needs and fears of supervisees. It also structures the relationship in a way that will make it safer for supervisees to become more comfortable in engaging in self-reflection, especially in the area of secondary trauma and self-care.

Activity Four: Six Focus Points for Structuring Supervision and Addressing Supervisee Anxiety About Supervision

If presenting: Read all the following statements to both supervisors and helpers. When finished, ask what they felt happening to them as you read and what their overall reaction was to listening to these. You might read these first so you have a good sense as to what they accomplish. My experience as to how participants responded to this activity will follow.

Note: *At the beginning of each statement, the italicized term identifies the purpose and role of a supervisor. As readers, it would be beneficial to read these aloud to enhance the sensory experience that participants in trainings respond to.*

1. *Structuring the Process.* There are several aspects about supervision I want to address that hopefully answer some of your questions and concerns. First of all, I'm sure you're wondering how supervision will work out; if it will be a helpful experience, a positive one that gives you the support you'll need, especially when confronted with challenging situations with clients, your peers or the demands of the job. Those are my concerns as well.
2. *Teacher/Educator.* I have three primary responsibilities as your supervisor. One is as a teacher/educator. There will be a lot of procedures to learn especially in these first few months. You'll need my support. There will likely be a few areas we need to problem-solve together as well. If there are issues for which I do not have the answers, I will let you know and then go to my supporters for possible solutions. Learning all you can about how trauma impacts all of us is critical to your effectiveness as a helper. This will take time but I certainly will help you with this. In fact, in our first few sessions, I want to make sure you are aware of the stressors you will face and the reactions you might experience. These stressors, for the most part, will be very normal for the work you do. In some cases, they may become problematic, if we don't work together to develop ways to manage them. In this regard your self-care is very important to your overall well-being, as well as to the quality of your interactions with those you are helping. As a teacher, I also believe that it is important to make this a somewhat predictable process so, at the beginning of every session, I will be asking you what positive experiences you've enjoyed. At the end of the session, I'll ask you of all that we covered, talked about, read or viewed, what stood out the most for you and how this might change or reinforce the way you are interacting or approaching different issues. And, before we end the session, we will agree on what we'll pursue in the next session.
3. *Administrative Role.* I also have an administrative responsibility to help you complete mandatory tasks that neither of us have a choice about, such as record keeping, paper work, certain behaviors related to policies and procedures. Some requirements simply are not negotiable. However, should there be problems, it is my responsibility to bring your attention to the problem and then, together, agree on ways we can fix and/or resolve the issue. I approach problems as an

opportunity to learn, to develop new coping skills, to strengthen resilience. Hopefully, you approach them in the same way. In this regard, if a problem has occurred or a conflict has emerged, and they will, just please let me know immediately so we can work at resolving them before they get out of hand. This will make it easier on both of us.

4. *Supervisor Support.* Finally, I have the responsibility to provide or direct you to whatever support you may need to do the work you will be doing as effectively as possible. If there is something I cannot help you with, I will do my best to connect you to those who can. If there are resources you feel will be helpful to you and the work you're doing, I will do my best to make those accessible. This is important because we have an ethical responsibility to provide our clients with the best possible service. Hopefully, you will feel comfortable enough to let me know if you are experiencing personal stress so I can help connect you with an outside resource, if needed. Your self-care and well-being are important.
5. *Supervisee Responsibility.* Obviously, trusting this relationship will take a little time. You'll need to get a feel for what I think, how I feel about and respond to different issues. That's okay. However, you also have some responsibilities. You need to let me know when you don't understand something, so hopefully I can find a different way to explain it. If what I am asking you to do or talk about makes you uncomfortable, please let me know. There are any number of ways to approach issues. Hopefully, you'll feel comfortable to discuss any conflicts you might experience, so we can work together to arrive at a solution that works best for both of us.
6. *Supervisor Availability.* I'm not going to micromanage you; that's not how you learn. You need some space to explore different ways to be as effective as you can. At the same time, if you want more direction, just ask. In this regard, especially in your first few months, I will respond as quickly and as often as needed to your questions, concerns and efforts to adjust to the various aspects of your job. If I can't get back to you right away, I'll try to send a quick text to you to let you know this. When you do try to contact me, please just leave a voice mail or text me and briefly describe the issue and if it is an emergency. If it is an emergency and I can't get back to you, I'll get you connected to one of my peers, as we work as a team.

I know I've given you plenty to think about but I'm curious about a few things. I'm kind of curious about your overall experience so far. What's been the most positive experience for you? . . . Okay. Let's set up a time for our next visit. I'll let you decide what you want to cover but we'll also begin to identify short-term goals so you're clear about what is expected of you. Please contact me before then if you need to. It doesn't have to be an emergency; it can be a question about record keeping, a procedure, a policy. It doesn't matter.

If presenting and supervisors are in attendance ask them for their reactions to this process and then ask those that are helpers for their reactions.

My experience with supervisors is that many are not this structured when introducing the supervisory process. Many have never been trained to be supervisors and have just been promoted to the position because of their longevity in direct care. Supervision is different than providing direct care and that is often where supervision becomes not the best of practices, nor helpful. Of course, there are always exceptions. When we add secondary trauma to what helpers are exposed to, structuring the supervisory relationship leads to a better sense of safety for all involved. Remember safety is at the core of being trauma-informed.

My experience with helpers and their responses to these structured statements has generally been,

- ❑ "It seemed a bit long and yet I could feel my body just calm down and relax; it made me comfortable with you."
- ❑ "I appreciated the amount of time spent on what you felt was most important about the process. It let me know you take this seriously."
- ❑ "It really touched on the concerns I've had (as a supervisee). It made me feel you were able to tap into my concerns, which made me feel like you would be supportive and helpful."

Almost everyone cites one specific point that either put them at ease or gave them a sense that this was going to be a positive experience. Examples that I liked include,

- ❑ the way you described how each session would start and end,
- ❑ what you said about how you approach accountability,
- ❑ that you would not be micromanaging,
- ❑ the way you described your role, and
- ❑ the fact that it would take time to trust you.

In essence, helpers agree this process would alleviate many of their anxieties by knowing what to expect.

Fourteen Practices for Establishing the Supervisory Relationship as Safe, Effective and Supportive

There are several other important practices that help to make the supervisory process safe and effectively supportive of helpers. As you read about these, ask yourself if this is what you have experienced as a helper or what you do as a supervisor. *These fourteen practices encourage engagement, which we know is essential to well-being, resilience and your sustained effectiveness as a helper.*

- ❑ **Always provide choice.** Supervisees must have the choice to say *yes* or *no* to what you are asking them to talk about or do, such as self-reflect. There may be some days when self-reflection creates too much anxiety to be helpful. Even in addressing the tasks and behaviors that are not negotiable, there need to be choices available as to how they can resolve issues in the designated time frame. Choice gives us a sense of empowerment, which supports a sense of safety.
- ❑ **Be curious rather than analytical or judgmental.** Rather than asking, "Why did you do this?" ask, "What happened?" Curiosity is the cornerstone of empathy. Being curious says, "You matter, what you are experiencing matters to me." Curiosity is also essential for successful self-reflection. Self-reflection is a core competency and matters greatly when attempting to help others with the stress they are experiencing.
- ❑ **Ask open-ended questions.** Olafson & Kenniston (2008) and Easton (2025) indicate that open ended questions are far more productive and allow even the most reluctant to respond more fully to questions (p. 77). Instead of asking, "How did that session with that difficult client go?" ask instead questions like, "What was the best part of that session, what was the worst part, what stands out the most about . . .?"
- ❑ **Teach and engage supervisees in self-regulation practices** especially when addressing or confronting difficult challenges with trauma clients and/or situations. This is a core competency requirement of secondary trauma supervision and applies to responding productively to all forms of stress and a preventative way to avoid supervisee arousal beyond their *window of tolerance.*
- ❑ **Utilize multidimensional learning styles.** Although little is written about this from a supervisory perspective, supervision is a learning experience and as such supervisors need to engage in multiple learning styles. Multidimensional approaches that include auditory, kinesthetic

and visual approaches significantly enhance the learning experience. Research shows that learning improves when multiple learning styles are used (Bozarth, 2018).

- ❑ **Initiate informal brief connections.** Luest (2018) documents that having a connection to another strengthens our resilience. Cheever & Hardin (1999) and Schwartz & Shirra (2018) also found that *those who have a connection with another or others, did better following exposure to trauma than those who did not have a significant connection to at least one other person.* Supervisors have the ability to enhance the effectiveness of their supervisory relationship and the resilience of their supervisees by briefly connecting with them outside of the formal supervisory session. There are a number of ways to accomplish this.
- ❑ **A brief text**: "Just thinking about you. If you have any questions just let me know".
- ❑ **An email** with a brief note—"Saw this and thought you might be interested." —and an attached article.
- ❑ **Making "purposeful rounds.** By this I mean taking a minute for a face-to-face contact with the intent of addressing one of the four universal needs I addressed when talking about engagement (belonging, mastery, independence and generosity). When employees feel valued, they do better than those who do not.
- ❑ **Saying you matter, matters.** Once you identify their interests, it is so easy to connect. For example, "Did you watch that game last night? "Have you read . . . latest novel; I think you'll like it." "I came across this app and thought you might want to grab it." These are very simple ways to say, "You matter." Those who report feeling valued by their employer are significantly more likely to be motivated to do their very best (Hoff, 2025; Hall et al., 2024).
- ❑ **Modeling self-care.** It is equally important that supervisors model self-care practices in the work place. For example, how you protect and use your lunch hour says a lot to others about your commitment to self-care. It's hard to take anyone seriously who is not engaging in what they are presenting as necessary.
- ❑ **Remain accountable.** Establish clear measurable benchmarks to evaluate supervisee progress. Review these regularly to track progress and/or refocus efforts. Without accountability there is no progress or responsibility. This is an area of weakness for some supervisors who have a difficult time moving from their role as "supporter" to that of "administrator". Unfortunately, failure to hold supervisees accountable and confront conflicts and problems, when they first emerge, condones that behavior.

- ❑ **Continuous performance.** Organizations are now moving away from annual and quarterly reviews. The research clearly shows these are not helpful (Dickson, 2018). (*The Dickson source cited is an excellent resource filled with research, I encourage leaders and supervisors to read.*) The solution many are turning to, with great success, is having regular conversations about current performance referred to as "continuous performance management" (Dublino, 2025). This means having regular conversations, even daily, until issues are resolved, which supports what was just said about the importance of brief connections. It's really about staying focused on those daily activities and interactions that present an opportunity for a "teachable moment" (Chandler, 2016).
- ❑ **Read.** No single book or document can cover all the issues around supervision. No one person is an absolute expert. As part of your professional development, take one day to spend just 15–30 minutes to surf the internet. One search can yield multiple topics to pursue. Having an article every now and then to discuss in the supervisory process is another way to connect to supervisees, as well as to reinforce that there are several ways to think about and approach helping others.
- ❑ **View.** Given that we have become a very visual society, bringing YouTube segments into the supervisory process can also be very beneficial to the learning process, especially around topics of trauma and self-care. Using third party references to communicate what you believe is important and will encourage others to listen and hopefully pursue what you believe is important.
- ❑ **Do not go it alone.** Most will agree that managers are not trained to assist supervisors with their stress and risk for trauma. Often management is about meeting contract requirements, licensing and other liability issues especially around client services. Support to assist supervisors with secondary trauma is often limited (Collins-Camargo & Millar, 2012). This is understandable yet leaves supervisors to fend for their own well-being, self-care and professional development. It is important for supervisors to meet regularly for peer support. Being part of a trauma-sensitive supervisor learning community provides a rich cross section of expertise, experiences and support often not afforded supervisors within their own organizations.

When all this is done within an organization that supports preventative secondary trauma policies and practices, the incidence will be much lower and resolved more quickly. What then are those secondary trauma policies?

STS-Informed Organizations

Mindset: *If you are assisting those in trauma, you want to be working in an organizational culture that demonstrates it understands the stressful impact of the work you are doing by providing you with the appropriate support.*

The best way to determine the level of STS support being provided, or not, by your workplace is to complete the Secondary Traumatic Stress Informed-Organization Assessment (STSI-OA). This was developed by the members of the National Child Traumatic Stress Network (NCTSN). The STSI-OA can be used at any level. What applies to those serving children also applies to those serving adults.

Activity Five: STSI-OA

Go to *Appendix A-7 and complete the Secondary Traumatic Stress Informed-Organization Assessment. Record your score on the Stage Two Outcomes Worksheet in Appendix B-3a. When completed return here for further comments.*

Leadership and the STSI-OA

This tool should be completed by leadership. It will generate a good deal of discussion.

My experience with leadership has been that not all trauma-informed agencies are aware of these standards, nor of the Supervisor Core Competencies. The response of leadership completing or reviewing both the organizational assessment and the supervisory competency assessment will provide a strong indication as to their willingness to support the well-being of their direct care helpers. Those that support being trauma-informed will engage in following up with establishing such practices and help their supervisors obtain or improve supervisory core competencies.

If presenting, ask participants what stands out the most for them after completing this assessment. Their comments are likely similar to my experiences listed below. Presenters can use my final comments below and add their responses to what participants have to say if they differ.

My experiences with some of the most common responses from those providing direct care are,

- ❑ "I was surprised by how much I was uncertain about or didn't know if these practices exist in my agency."
- ❑ "My place focuses on physical safety but nothing about psychological safety."
- ❑ "They might give me a day off but I have to pay for training."
- ❑ "I never heard anything about STS in my hiring interview."
- ❑ "I rarely hear anything about STS from leadership."
- ❑ "I don't think there is any formal peer support practice available if one of us is having a high level of exposure."
- ❑ "There's not a great deal being done around trauma at my place."
- ❑ "My place is doing pretty well."

You may need to respond to questions about what constitutes psychological safety. Be prepared to answer that question. Psychological safety does not exist in toxic environments; it exists in flourishing environments where engagement levels are high. It is about feeling safe to speak up and express concerns without fear of being judged, criticized or humiliated. Psychological safety also refers to feeling valued, that peers support one another, that all are treated with fairness and respect and encouraged to openly address tough issues and make suggestions (APA, 2023). These issues are evaluated on the BO Assessment completed earlier so you might want to go back and review your results.

My general comments to direct care staff in non-trauma-informed agencies would generally include the following, "You have a number of options. You and your colleagues can approach leadership and ask for more training around trauma. If leadership has not reviewed the STSI-OA, you could present them with the assessment you just completed and see how they respond to complying with its mandate. You could learn more on your own or ask friends, who work in other trauma serving settings, what their organizations do for them. If the stressors you are experiencing are problematic and wearing you down, you could explore working at other organizations whose trauma culture is more supportive and/or seek outside help for those stressors.

Conclude by reiterating that the fewer the trauma-informed organizational practices, the greater the vulnerability for experiencing secondary trauma. This may not mean you are working in a toxic culture, only that leadership is not informed about the types of practices they need to establish to support your vulnerability to secondary trauma. If once informed and nothing changes, and you wish to remain in that agency, you may need to look for outside help with STS and, when ready or needed, think about looking for a workplace that does provides STS support. Mitigating secondary trauma is best accomplished when trauma competent supervisors are working within a trauma-informed organization. However, when working as first responders, with direct exposure to traumatized individuals and/or incidents, helpers are also more vulnerable to PTSD. Let's give you a few minutes to review and, if desired, complete the PTSD evaluation.

PTSD Evaluation

The causes of PTSD differ from secondary trauma yet include its reactions. *PTSD is the result of direct exposure to a traumatic incident happening to yourself, or directly witnessing trauma happening to others.* Learning of what happened to a close family member or friend also qualifies. Unlike secondary trauma, which most often has a sudden onset from a single exposure, PTSD criteria dictate exposure to multiple aversive incidents and/or details of traumatic incidents such as abuse. Its reactions must also be experienced for one month or more. Additional criteria are listed on the evaluation form you may want to look at and complete.

Activity Six: Recording your Outcomes.

Go to Appendix A-8 PTSD Survey and complete. Record your outcome on the Stage Two Outcomes Worksheet in Appendix B-3a.

Note: Should you be experiencing a number of the PTSD reactions I would recommend meeting with a trauma-informed, clinical professional to make a formal diagnosis. If one is made, there are a number of excellent interventions available that will be reviewed under self-care in *Chapter Nine.*

Approach Points Aligned with Those of Self-Care (Self-care approaches are in parentheses)

- ❏ If helping those who are traumatized, it is essential to your well-being and effectiveness to be in an organization that support secondary trauma-informed practices, including supervisors who meet established core secondary trauma competencies (It's about advocating for your well-being, sustainability and managing your energies).
- ❏ It is important from a preventative position to be in supervision with a supervisor you trust and who meets core competency as a secondary trauma-informed supervisor (It's about advocating for your well-being because you are worthy of it; it's about sustainability).

- ❑ Ultimately the effectiveness of the supervisory relationship and, what the supervisor is hoping to accomplish, is based on how you, the supervisee, experience that relationship (It's personal).

My Final Questions

Go to Appendix B-1 & B-1.2 My Final Questions and record your responses to the two following questions. Return here for a brief discussion.

1. Of all that you read or experienced in this chapter what one thought stands out the most for you?
2. Of the mindsets established in this segment which one stands out the most for you?

If presenting, repeat process from previous segments.

My experience with responses to the final questions is that the majority are related to the factors of supervision presented in this segment. Trust is the biggest issue especially for helpers experiencing secondary trauma. The concern is that supervision may cross the line and become therapy. This is a legitimate concern and unfortunately does happen. To answer that concern, I suggest that supervision for secondary trauma would be about normalizing responses, providing several reading resources and suggestions regarding nervous system regulation strategies. If that supervisor wants to explore previous life experiences that might be leaving a helper vulnerable to trauma, then the ethical line between supervision and therapy is about to be crossed.

Summary: It's All About Compassion, Empathy

Burnout, culture, engagement, wellness, fulfillment, well-being, secondary trauma, PTSD and supervision all play a key role in the ways we manage to maintain our emotional well-being and our sustained effectiveness as helpers in the face of repeated exposure to the distress of those we serve. When self-compassion and compassion satisfaction levels are strong, compassion does not fatigue, nor does empathy distress. In the next stage, you have the opportunity to evaluate self-compassion, compassion satisfaction, compassion fatigue and empathy distress. The combined results from all assessments will then be used to help identify needed areas of self-care in *Chapter Eight.*

References

APA. (2012, March 8). *APA Survey Finds Feeling Valued at Work Linked to Well-Being and Performance.* Retrieved November 10, 2018 from https://www.apa.org/news/press/releases/2012/03/well-being

APA. (2023, December 4). *What is Psychological Safety in the Workplace?* Retrieved June 6, 2025 from https://www.apa.org/topics/healthy-workplaces/psychological-safety

Apostol, A.F., Turner, K., Hoshi, R., & Padduck, A. (2025, March 26). Contributory factors of self-disclosure in clinical supervision: A meta-ethnography. Clin. *Psychol. Psychotherapy,* 32(2): e70068. https://doi.org/10.1002/cpp.70068

Bozarth, J. (2018). The Truth About Teaching to Learning Styles, and What to Do Instead. *The eLearning Guild. Santa Rosa, CA.* Retrieved from www.elearningguils.com/.../the-truth-about-teaching-to-learning-styles-and-what-to-do-instead

Chandler, J. (2016, October 13). *What's New in Employee Performance Evaluations?* Retrieved November 20, 2018 from https://www.councilofnonprofits.org/articles/whats-new-employee-performance-evaluations

Cheever, K. H., & Hardin, S. B. (1999). Effects of traumatic events, social support, and self-efficacy on adolescents' self-health assessments. *Western Journal of Nursing Research, 21*(5), 673–684.

Collins-Camargo, C., & Millar K. (2012). Promoting supervisory practice change in public child welfare: Lessons learned from university/agency collaborative research in four states. *Child Welfare,* 91(1): 101–124.

Cook, R. M., Welfare, L. E., & Sharma, J. (2019). Exploring supervisees' in-session experiences of utilizing intentional nondisclosure. *Clinical Supervisor,* 38(2): 202–221. https://doi.org/10.1080/07325223.2019.1608344

Dickson, G. (2018, November 12). *Research-Backed Reasons to Rethink Your Annual Employee Evaluation.* Retrieved November 12, 2018 from https://blog.bonus.ly/6-research-backed-reasons-rethink-annual-employee-evaluation

Dublino, J. (2025, December 17). *How to Implement Continuous Performance Management.* Retrieved December 29, 2025 from https://www.business.com/articles/continuous-performance-management/

Easton, V. C. (2025, January 17). *Effective Open-Ended Questions: Enhancing Client Engagement & Therapeutic Outcome.* Retrieved February, 24, 2025 from https://www.blueprint.ai/blog/effective-open-ended-questions-enhancing-client-engagement-and-therapeutic-outcomes

Eisenberger, R., Stinglhamber, F., Vandenberge, C., Sucharski, L., & Rhoades, L. (2002). Perceived supervisor support: Contributions to perceived organizational support and employee retention. *Journal of Applied Psychology,* 87(3): 565–573.

Gil, S., & Weinberg, M. (2015). Secondary trauma among social workers treating trauma clients: The role of coping strategies and internal resources. *International Social Worker,* 58(4), 551–561. https://doi.org/10.1177/0020872814564705

Hall, A. T., Goodwin, V. A., Allchurch, L., Capon, L., Farell, V., Olufunmilayo, O., & Griffin, R, (2024, November 29). Feeling valued at work: A qualitative exploration of allied health profession support workers. *BMC Health Serv Res.,* 24(1): 1511.

Hoff, N. (2025, March 14). *Why Leaders Must Make Employees Feel Valued.* Retrieved June 6, 2025 from https://www.smartbrief.com/original/why-leaders-must-make-employees-feel-valued

Kulkarni, S., Bell, H., Hartman, J. L., & Herman-Smith, R. L. (2013). Exploring individual and organizational factors contributing to compassion satisfaction, secondary traumatic stress, and burnout in domestic violence service providers. *Journal of the Society for Social Work and Research,* 4(2), 114–130.

Luest, H. (2018). *Connection—The Key to Healing and Resilience.* Retrieved December 9, 2018 from https://www.socialworker.com/feature-articles/practice/connection-key-to-healing-resilience/

Olafson, E., & Kenniston, J. (2008). Obtaining information from children in the justice system. *Juvenile and Family Court Journal,* 59(4), 71–89.

Mikkelson, A., Tiesort, C., Hinnenman, C. (2024, April 12). Employee perception of supervisor credibility: predictive effects for employee well-being outcomes. *Business and Professional Communication Quarterly,* 89(2). https://doi.org/10.1177/23294906241241668

Paru, A. E. (2022, January 13). *Supervision Matters.* Retrieved May 22, 2025 from https://www.wexnerfoundation.org/supervision-matters/

Segal, E. (2025, May 3). *How Perceptions Can Differ About the Job Experiences of Employees.* Retrieved May 13, 2025 from https://www.forbes.com/sites/edwardsegal/2025/05/23/how-perceptions-can-differ-about-the-job-experiences-of-employees/

Schwartz, E., & Shirra, A. (2018). Social connectedness moderates the relationship between warfare exposure, PTSD symptoms, and health among older adults. *Psychiatry,* 82(2): 158–172. https://doi.org/10.1080/00332747.2018.1534521

Sewell, K. M., Janse van Rensberg, M., Alschech, J., & Asakura, K. (2024). Supervision and wellness: A survey of human service practitioners. *Human*

Service organizations: Management, Leadership & Governance, 49(2), 190–207. https://doi.org/10.1080/23303131.2024.2434527

Weiss-Dagan, S., Ben-Porat, A., & Itzhaky, H. (2016). Child protection workers dealing with child abuse: The contribution of personal, social and organizational resources to secondary traumatization. *Child Abuse and Neglect*, 51, 203–211. https://doi.org/10.1016/j.chiabu.2015.10.008

STAGE THREE

Compassion and Empathy

When One Is Not Helping, Neither Is the Other

CHAPTER 7

Satisfying, Fatiguing or Distressing?

Theme

How is self-compassion related to compassion fatigue? How is compassion fatigue related to empathy distress? How is compassion fatigue actually measured? What are a few indicators that signal the onset of empathy distress? These and other questions are answered in this chapter, along with the opportunity to evaluate how well you may be doing in each of these areas.

Compassion

Put simply, the more compassionately satisfied we are, the less fatigue and distress we experience, the more effective we remain, the happier we remain. Compassion satisfaction is feeling happy being helpful, being happy about the way we are helping and providing that help in an environment that allows us to flourish. When "happy" is missing in any of these areas, satisfaction and effectiveness declines and distress increases. More specifically, compassion is fatigued by burnout conditions, toxic practices, practices that conflict with our values, low levels of engagement, absence of support for our well-being, prolonged over exposure to those in distress and/or trauma, and the absence of secondary trauma organizational practices and supervision competency.

DOI: 10.4324/9781003673699-10

In essence, everything we've discussed up to this point can either support and enrich compassion satisfaction or fatigue it.

Evaluating Fatigue

As strange as it may seem, fatigue is actually measured by our level of compassion satisfaction in addition to the presence/absence of burnout and its physical, emotional, mental and behavioral reactions and by the presence/absence of secondary trauma. Since burnout and secondary trauma have been thoroughly evaluated, we're going to have you evaluate your compassion satisfaction in detail.

Rescue Dogs

While I was preparing to write about compassion fatigue a thirty-year old memory came alive. I had been meeting with survivors of the 1995 bombing of the Federal Building in Oklahoma. I'm not sure how our conversation changed to the rescue dogs but what happened to them pretty much explains compassion fatigue. These dogs were trained to discover survivors buried under the rubble. At one point they just quit. Their nervous system just stopped working because they were unable to find any living survivors. They were unable to do what they were trained to do. When their handlers realized what was happening, they concealed workers in the rubble so the dogs could find them. This revitalized the dogs because, once they were able to successfully do what they were trained to do, they were able to continue their rescue efforts. When conditions exist, that make it difficult to do what we have been trained to do and do it well, our nervous system and our compassion also becomes fatigued. Once this physiological response is triggered our thought processes begin changing as well. The desire to help weakens as does our compassion. Our focus on our struggles continues to increase while the focus on others becomes more limited and negative. Our fatigue is experienced physically, emotionally and mentally. Compassion satisfaction becomes compassion fatigue. This is why I think it's important to identify the thoughts and feelings associated with compassion satisfaction.

Activity One: Compassion Satisfaction Survey

If I asked you to Google several sites to review their list of compassion fatigue reactions, you're likely to experience some confusion because many reactions can be attributed to other forms of stress like burnout, secondary trauma or vicarious trauma, or even medical conditions. So, let's backtrack briefly. We've isolated the reactions of burnout, secondary trauma and post-traumatic stress, so let's isolate the reactions that specifically address changes in compassion efficacy and satisfaction in order to allow you to determine the degree of satisfaction you are currently experiencing. The following statements are adapted from a variety of different sources about fatigue, burnout, secondary trauma and empathy cited throughout this work. Circle the appropriate response for the following questions using "Y" for yes, "S" for somewhat and "N" for no.

Over the last six months are you,

1. Y S N less happy about helping?
2. Y S N experiencing less satisfaction as a helper?
3. Y S N feeling less able to or unsure if you are making a difference?
4. Y S N feeling less fulfilled?
5. Y S N finding it more difficult to focus and concentrate while helping?
6. Y S N less happy about your workplace?
7. Y S N wondering how much longer you can be effective?
8. Y S N feeling more detached or disconnected from others?
9. Y S N having negative thoughts or criticism about those you are helping?
10. Y S N reacting more intensely to minor stressors?
11. Y S N feeling more tired, less energetic more often?
12. Y S N finding it more difficult to remain resilient?
13. Y S N feeling more hypersensitive?
14. Y S N thinking more about how you feel than how those you are helping feel?
15. Y S N worried more about controlling your reactions to those being helped?

    Total number of Yes___, Somewhat___, No___

Record your outcomes on the Stage Three Outcome Worksheet in Appendix B-3b.

Scoring: This is not a formal assessment tool. However, each item marked yes indicates a possible change in your level of compassion satisfaction. Five or more yes responses are definitely concerning. Even one yes should concern you. For example, if you are feeling less motivated and energetic, it could be a sign of over exposure to the distress of those you are helping. On the other hand, it could signal a reaction to burnout conditions at your workplace or an absence of daily self-care. Whatever the cause, it's a sign that it's time to do something different. You want more no responses than yes or somewhat responses combined.

If the total *yes* and *somewhat* responses outnumber *no* responses, I would also have major concerns about fatigue. If *somewhat* responses outnumber either *yes* or *no* responses, I would have the same concerns, especially if you identified any burnout and/or secondary trauma reactions earlier. In this case, fatigue would also be likely as burnout and secondary trauma is often associated with compassion fatigue. When reviewing all previous outcomes, the compassion satisfaction outcome will better help you determine the self-care that may be needed or continued. If your satisfaction outcomes are low and your overall burnout score is 700 or less, fatigue would also be likely.

Mindset: *When satisfaction begins to diminish so too does efficacy and resilience; thereafter fatigue begins to take hold.*

ProQOL

The Professional Quality of Life Scale is a widely used tool for evaluating compassion fatigue. It measures burnout, secondary trauma and compassion satisfaction. Ten questions are presented for each category. Since you have already used more extensive evaluations for burnout and secondary trauma, only the ProQOL subscale for compassion satisfaction is included in this workbook. These outcomes will be compared with those of the completed, in text, Satisfaction Survey. This provides a more extensive evaluation as the Satisfaction Survey addresses areas not addressed on the compassion satisfaction subscale.

Activity Two: ProQOL

Go to Appendix A-9 ProQOL Compassion Satisfaction Scale. Score and enter your outcome on Appendix B-3b Stage Three Outcome Worksheet and then return to the chapter for additional information.

My experience has been that the majority of people score in the average range for satisfaction. This can be misleading if other factors like burnout and secondary trauma are not considered. For now, I would suggest that if you are not in the high average range or above there is a need to examine other factors indicative of compassion fatigue. This will be discussed in *Chapter Eight*. One of these factors is our level of self-compassion.

Self-Compassion

Self-compassion is also highly correlated with compassion satisfaction. When self-compassion is low, compassion fatigue and empathy distress are more likely. Evaluating your level of self-compassion can better help you determine whether it is a possible source of fatigue or a source of compassionate strength and satisfaction. Self-compassion is also a critical practice of effective self-care and well-being, making it important to determine your level of self-compassion and the possible areas needing your attention. In fact, mindful self-compassion training is recommended to alleviate or help prevent compassion fatigue and empathy distress (Scarlett, 2024).

Activity Three: Self-Compassion Scale

Go to Appendix A-10 Self-Compassion Survey. When finished, follow the scoring instructions. Record your outcomes on the Stage Three Outcome Worksheet in Appendix B-3b and then return here for further discussion.

If presenting, and before participants take this survey, indicate that their honest responses to these questions will yield what will be the most helpful information when thinking about self-care practices. Reiterate that they will not be asked about their scores only about their reactions to the process. After completion, when talking about outcomes, suggest that if one of the self-compassion response categories is low, to go back and identify each statement associated with that category to determine what they need to change to improve that self-compassion characteristic. For example, question #7 reflects a common humanity response to being down and out as *reminding yourself that others are feeling like you.* If this is not your mindset when feeling down, it needs to be, in order to strengthen your compassion. From this perspective, this tool is an excellent resource for determining what to change to improve self-compassion.

My experience, when I've asked for a show of hands as to how many participants have previously taken a self-compassion assessment, very few hands go up; unfortunately, this seems to be the norm. When asked what surprised them the most about this assessment, the most common response is that they really haven't thought about self-compassion in the ways presented by this tool. This becomes an excellent resource for determining the different ways to respond to stressful times in order to help increase self-compassion as needed. Self-compassion is simply essential for improving or sustaining compassion satisfaction and reducing the risk for compassion fatigue and empathy distress.

Thoughts Are Revealing

Another way to approach the existence of fatigue is to examine the thoughts we are having about those we are helping. I like this next tool because, from my experience, it points to the possible existence of fatigue, secondary trauma, faulty assumptions about client's distress or limited education about the distress being presented. For example, trauma distress is an entirely different experience than the stress of grief, although trauma can include grief reactions (Steele & Malchiodi, 2012). Limited education about the different forms of distress can certainly lead to faulty thinking and be detrimental to those being helped. Fortunately, this is easily corrected if recognized. Recognizing fatigue thinking is the first step toward not only improving satisfaction but also becoming more effective in the help provided to those in distress.

Activity Four: Silencing Response Scale

Go to Appendix A-11 and complete the Silencing Response Scale. Record your outcomes on the Stage Three Outcome Worksheet in Appendix B-3b and return here when finished for additional comments.

Keep in mind, the more honest you are with your responses the easier it becomes to determine what self-care planning may be most helpful.

If presenting, ask participants how many would have thought to relate these reactions to compassion fatigue, needed education or secondary trauma. You may find very few hands go up. I would suggest that scores 0–20 might reflect little risk yet, any reaction rated 4–10 is problematic and a potential signal that compassion is likely to become fatigued if not attended to with self-care.

My experience has been that rather than processing participants' responses to this scale, it is more helpful to emphasize the normalcy of these reactions, while also indicating they signal potential problems if not addressed. This is especially the case if helpers

- ❑ are new to helping,
- ❑ have limited training related to situations or conditions they are presented with,
- ❑ are making faulty assumptions about those being helped,
- ❑ have become over exposed by the non-stop requests for help from those in distress, and
- ❑ if the distress they are being exposed to is triggering memories and emotions from some past experience(s) that have not been resolved, which is not at all uncommon.

The above responses are best discussed in supervision to determine the source of these responses, as they are detrimental to those being helped and indicators that compassion needs some help. I would mention that, if their burnout scores were even moderate, it can be difficult to stay focused and avoid becoming frustrated with some of those being helped. Dealing with personal stress outside the workplace, can also make it difficult to be at one's best when helping. If new to helping, education can significantly improve reactions. It is also possible that faulty assumptions are being made about those in distress that are triggering these responses; this is also an educational issue. If reactions are due to old memories being triggered, outside assistance may be helpful. If responses are due to over exposure and/or burnout, supervision to problem solve these may be helpful; seeing those who are less distressed and increased self-care could also be beneficial. Essentially, these silent responses do dictate the need to improve one's compassionate response.

Empathy Distress Decreases Satisfaction

The one additional factor that interferes with compassion satisfaction as well as helper effectiveness and well-being is empathy distress. Let's explore this. Empathy Distress is a self-oriented response to suffering, where one is *more upset by another's suffering than concerned for that person. This response drives one to withdraw from active listening or avoiding those individuals or situations altogether.* Too much empathy (empathy strain) leaves us drained, overwhelmed and unable to help. Compassion or "feeling for" helps to drive helping behaviors whereas too much empathy or more concern for ourselves, versus the people we are helping, drives avoidant and withdrawal behaviors. Israelashvili et al. (2020, p. 1113) stated, "There is a clear distinction between feelings of concern for others (empathic concern), versus feelings of personal concern for one's self" (personal distress). This latter component of (too much) empathy can result in an aversive, self-focused reaction, which has also been referred to as personal distress (Batson, 1991).

A simple approach to evaluating yourself for empathy distress is to ask, "Have you experienced more concern for your reactions than the reactions of those you are helping more than once?" If the answer is *yes*, there is likely a need for supervision or some compassion/empathy training. If you also find yourself engaging in avoidance behavior with persons triggering your unwanted reactions, not listening or being present when helping, further help and evaluation is needed to determine the source of this avoidance.

Others Suggest

One model of compassion fatigue challenges the idea that it is empathy that makes us vulnerable to compassion fatigue (Coetzee & Laschinger, 2017). They suggest a lack of resources, the person's response to the distress (cognitive and emotional), and inadequate positive feedback make us susceptible to compassion fatigue. Ultimately, this model suggests that positive feedback, balanced resources, and reducing self-focused personal distress when working with those we help, can mitigate compassion fatigue. Another study (Yaden et al., 2024) found that "high empathy (too much) without compassion is related to negative health outcomes, while high compassion without (too much) empathy is related to positive health outcomes and positive lifestyle choices (. . .) Such findings favor an approach to helping that is grounded in compassion rather than empathy" (p. 106). Singer & Klimecki (2014) also found that when mindfulness and meditation were used to strengthen compassion (feelings of generosity and kindness), empathy distress was significantly reduced. We also know that inadequate training in empathy leads to empathy distress and compassion fatigue (Bhagat et al., 2024).

Note: *Google "The Hidden Price of Empathy YouTube" for a very good eight-minute video about too much empathy. This will also take you to a number of additional videos regarding empathy that may interest you.*

So, what we've seen is that compassion strength (satisfaction) decreases vulnerability to empathy distress. Also, when empathy distress lingers vulnerability to secondary trauma and compassion fatigue increases. Huang et al. (2025) reported that too much empathy led to overwhelming emotional states (dysregulated emotions), increasing vulnerability to psychological distress or empathy distress, inclusive of internalizing disorders such as secondary trauma or vicarious trauma. Depending on the intensity of the exposure and the emotional status of the helper at the time of exposure (feeling terrified, helpless, powerless), post-traumatic stress can also develop.

The reality is that most helpers, at some point, will experience the need for cognitive and/or emotional regulation to maintain the balance between empathy and compassion. Remember, stress is not always a choice; things happen—like a global pandemic. COVID strained empathy, compassion, compassion satisfaction, and it led to secondary trauma and burnout for many. As helpers, your exposure to those in distress is increasing not decreasing; exposure alone is more than enough to meet the need for regulation. By regulation practices I mean self-care strategies that will be covered in the final Stage of this work.

Approach Points Aligned with Those of Self-Care (Self-care approaches are in parentheses)

- ❑ Compassion satisfaction is feeling happy being helpful, being happy about the way we are helping and providing that help in an environment that allows us to flourish (It's a way of approaching life to maintain our well-being).
- ❑ Compassion without (too much) empathy is related to positive health outcomes and positive lifestyle choices (It's a way of approaching life to maintain our well-being).
- ❑ Self-compassion is highly correlated with compassion satisfaction. Engaging in self-compassion is a critical practice of effective self-care (It's saying *yes* to what matters most-our well-being; it's about self-preservation).
- ❑ Recognizing fatigue thinking is the first step toward improving satisfaction and becoming more effective in the help provided to those in distress. (It's about applying effective effort-assessing, reflecting, doing differently).

My Final Questions

Go to Appendix B-1, My Final Questions. Record your answers for the following two questions.

1. Of all that you read or experienced in this chapter what one thought stands out the most for you?
2. Of the mindsets established in this chapter which one stands out the most for you?

If presenting, definitely spend some time on mindsets, as they reveal a good deal as to participants' thoughts and behaviors related to self-compassion, and empathy.

My experience has been that the majority of participants do not practice healthy self-compassion. This makes sense because it is a self-care practice and, as reported earlier, helpers struggle with giving themselves as much care as they give others. A number will report that although they have thought about dissatisfaction with their work experience, the satisfaction questionnaire helped them focus more specifically on the degree of their dissatisfaction. In a sense, it made their dissatisfaction more visual, motivating them to think differently about their self-care efforts.

Summary

You have now collected a comprehensive identification of those reactions that are either supporting your wellness, well-being, self-fulfillment and compassion satisfaction or causing burnout, compassion fatigue, secondary trauma, post-traumatic stress, or empathy distress. In either case, they will provide the information you need to assure that the self-care you are practicing is appropriate for what you are experiencing. In the next stage, you will be reviewing your assessment outcomes and then you will be provided with interpretations of the possible combined outcomes you have recorded. Once this is established, you'll be ready to personalize your self-care strategies using those presented in Stage Five.

References

Batson, C. D., & Oleson, K. C. (1991). Current Status of the Empathy-Altruism Hypothesis. In M. S. Clark (Ed.), *Prosocial Behavior: Review of Personality and Social Psychology* (pp. 62–85). Thousand Oaks, CA, Sage Publications.

Bhagat, P. R., Kinjal, Y. T., & Vijay, R. (2024). The empathy quandary in post-graduate medical training. *Int J Appl Basic Med Res*, 14(4): 233–238. https://doi.org/10.4103/ijabmr.ijabmr_288_24

Coetzee, S. K., & Laschinger, H. K. S. (2017). Toward a comprehensive, theoretical model of compassion fatigue: An integrative literature review. *Nursing & Health Sciences*, 20(1), 4–15. https://doi.org/10.1111/nhs.12387

Huang, C., Wu, Z., Sha, S., Liu, C., Yang, L., Jiang, P., Zhang, H., & Yang, C. (2025). The dark side of empathy: The role of excessive affective empathy in mental health. *Biological Psychiatry*, 98(5): 404–415. https://doi.org/10.1016/*j.biopsych.2024.12.020*

Israelashvili, J., Sauter, D., & Fisher, A. (2020). Two facets of affective empathy: Concern & distress have opposite relationships to emotion recognition. *Cognition and Emotion*, 34(6): 1112–1122. https://doi.org/10.1080/02699931.1724893

Scarlett, E. (2024, April 11). *How to Combat Empathetic Distress, the Shadow Side of Empathy*. Retrieved August 5, 2025 from https://www.simplepractice.com/blog/recognizing-empathetic-distress/

Singer, T., & Klimecki, O. M. (2014). Empathy and Compassion. *Current Biology*, 24(18): R875–R878. https://doi.org/10.1016/j.cub.2014.06.054

Steele, W., & Malchiodi, C. (2012). *Trauma Informed Practices with Children and Adolescents*. New York, Routledge

Yaden, D. B., Giorgi, S., Jordan, M., Buffone, A., Eichstaedt, J. C., Schwartz, H. A., Ungar, L., & Bloom, P. (2024). Characterizing empathy and compassion using computational linguistic analysis. *Emotion*, 24(1), 106–115. https://doi.org/10.1037/emo0001205

STAGE FOUR

Outcomes

Patterns and Possibilities

CHAPTER 8

Interpretations

Selecting Your Care Focus

Theme

It's time to pull everything together to see what you have discovered about yourself and about your workplace in order to determine what you believe demands your self-care the most. This chapter walks you through this process and then provides interpretations about possible outcomes.

Recording Outcomes

Activity One: Recording Outcomes

Before providing possible interpretations of your assessment outcomes, you need to record those outcomes, if you did not do so previously. To accomplish this, *Go to Appendix B-3a and B-3b, the Stage Two and Three Assessment Outcome Pages, and complete the recording of all assessment scores. When finished, return here for possible outcome interpretation.*

Note: The *Spiritual Intelligence Assessment (A-12)* is to be completed at the beginning of the next chapter on self-care as the behaviors and practices that make up the areas of spiritual intelligence are essentially preventative self-care practices associated with low stress and higher well-being.

DOI: 10.4324/9781003673699-12

About Interpretations

The interpretations that follow present a number of possible meanings based on the strength and weakness of the various categories in combination with one another. This is important because the outcome of one category can be influenced by another, either negatively or positively.

Mindset: *It is important to keep in mind that any one statement, practice, behavior or condition could be more important to you than a total score for a category because that specific factor is causing you the most stress.*

In essence, you are the one to best determine what all these outcomes mean to you personally. Some outcome interpretations may support what you already know, others may surprise you and others may meet with your disagreement. My response to any disagreement with my interpretations is that what you perceive as the correct meaning is the correct meaning for you, until you happen to find otherwise. In addition, high and low scores are pretty predictive of what is being experienced. When scores are in the *average, mid, somewhat* or *concerning* range, it will be helpful to review the outcomes from tools identifying related issues. This is when some interpretation of outcomes is most needed.

Activity Two: If possible, scan/copy your Stage Two and Stage Three Scoring Outcome Worksheets (Appendix B-3a and B-3b) and send them to your email to download and print out, so you can have outcomes visible at a glance when reading through these possible interpretations.

Possible Stage Two Outcome Interpretations

Self-Engagement

We begin with engagement because its level is associated with toxic or flourishing workplace cultures. When engagement levels are high, burnout is low and when burnout levels are high, engagement is generally low. The ideal is when both self-engagement and leader driven engagement are both high as this reflects a flourishing environment that is supportive of your wellness, well-being, professional growth and self-fulfillment. It's an environment where stress is minimal and what stress does exist is more often *eustress* or good stress.

Frequently, one level will be higher than another. For example, your self-engagement may be *high* but leader engagement only *somewhat*. This could reflect that you work in a department or program where you and your colleagues are engaged, yet the organization's support for your wellness and well-being is only *somewhat* available. This situation may sustain you for some time, especially if what you are doing is fulfilling a purpose. However, with only *somewhat* leader engagement, there may be limited support and opportunities for professional growth and well-being. If these are not currently stressful factors for you, they may become ones in the future.

Now, if leader engagement is *somewhat* and the outcome of your *Toxic Workplace Survey (A-1)* is *concerning*, I would say that you need be sure your daily self-care strategies include nervous system regulation, that you're not taking work home with you, that your purpose is being fulfilled and the outcomes of your personal well-being burnout scores are in the upper range. As the stress of that workplace environment and your personal well-being will leave you more vulnerable to compassion fatigue. If leader engagement outcomes are *somewhat* and you have high ratings for a flourishing culture, it may reflect that the environment is fulfilling your purpose and providing you with the support you consider essential. However, if, under leadership engagement, the total for *little* and *somewhat* is higher than the total for *very* engaged, vulnerability to burnout and compassion fatigue is high.

Also consider looking at compassion satisfaction. If either *self* or *leadership* engagement levels are low, compassion satisfaction may be less than satisfying. It's difficult to remain fully compassionate when engagement levels are low. Another concern would be your well-being outcomes. If outcomes of personal well-being on the *BO Scale (A-4)* are low, even though engagement is high, you may be experiencing burnout, especially if the overall BO total is 700 or less.

Burnout

Your overall *workplace* burnout score (6 categories in *Appendix A-4*) may reflect that you are doing well although one of those workplace categories is rated 70 or under. That one category, and the practices and conditions associated with it, could be causing you unnecessary stress that you are simply not willing to tolerate, especially if you have little control over changing those conditions or responding differently. I would suggest that any workplace burnout category that is rated 70, or below, be of concern as it will eventually lead to greater stress, if it hasn't already. It would be especially concerning if you also have a similar low rating for the 5 personal well-being categories total. If the relational well-being score is under 70, do be concerned as it suggests that the needed personal connections necessary to help offset a toxic environment and the vulnerability to compassion fatigue will lead to burnout. This would also be the case for those red flag statements that were scored 7 or lower. Any one of them could be a strong influencer of your satisfaction level. For example, if you are being asked to do things that go against your values, or are witnessing practices that conflict with your values, you may consider this workplace a bad fit. It certainly will be stressful and eventually reduce your level of engagement and effectiveness. This *value conflict* can cause significant stress and attack your *inner self* if endured too long. You'll want to check the outcome you recorded related to moral distress. Also, the additional red flag scores in any of the workplace categories would suggest the need for self-care attention, even if your overall burnout score is in the ideal range. Please keep in mind the following mindset.

Mindset: *Burnout is not due to resilience deficiency but to toxic workplace practices, which is a system issue (West et al., 2020) and our reaction to that system.*

If you have little influence in changing toxic practices, there are only two solutions. The first is to find a way to change how you are responding to these practices. It may be that you need to focus more on increasing experiences of joy in your personal life, that you keep your personal life free of anything associated with work, such as not responding to emails after hours, or perhaps you make sure you are taking a few minutes at work every hour to regulate your emotions. There are many possibilities. If these are not helpful, your second choice is to explore looking for a different work environment as continuing to work in a toxic environment is, well, toxic.

Although I've mentioned this several times, it needs repeating, the "S" Factor is your ultimate tool and guide to help you decide what actions you may need to take to continue to improve your situation, your condition and effectiveness.

Personal Burnout Influence

Even if you are working in a fairly flourishing environment yet are experiencing *concerning* personal stress, your effectiveness will diminish. For example, you may find it more difficult to stay in the present with those you are helping, you may find yourself being more irritable with the responses of some of those you are helping or it could be more difficult to engage with colleagues. These responses would be reflected on the Silencing Response Scale (*A-11*) so it needs your review. Whatever the case, *concerning* conditions under those personal burnout categories need your attention. Obviously, the better your personal stress scores are, the easier it will be to focus and attend to the workplace stressors. If self-compassion outcomes need attention, it's also likely that one or two areas of personal well-being also need your attention. It could require more separation from work when leaving at the end of the day, such as turning off cell notifications or needing more time away from the computer screen. Perhaps you need to do a bit more in the way of regulating your nervous system, or enhancing your social well-being or engaging in those practices associated with spiritual intelligence. Your outcomes on the Spiritual Intelligence scale will indicate the area most needing some help from you.

Review

Given these possibilities, take a few minutes to review and reflect on your Stage Two Outcomes (*B-3a*) again, as you may see something you did not catch earlier or was not addressed by these interpretations. The thought I leave you with is that what may be stressful for me may not be stressful for you. So, even if the outcomes tell you to be concerned, but they do not concern you, focus on what does and make a note about that to include it in your self-care efforts.

Possible Stage Three Outcome Interpretations

At this point, take a minute to reflect on the combined outcomes on the *Stage Three Outcomes Worksheet (B-3b)*. Our central focus in this stage is compassion satisfaction. In the text it was indicated that the strength of our compassion is associated with the strength of our self-compassion, so let's begin there.

Self-Compassion

In the text we indicated that, ideally, the compassionate responses on the *Self-Compassion Survey (A-10)* will have a higher rating than the uncompassionate responses. It was also indicated that if both corresponding responses have the same rating, self-compassion is considered low. For example, if self-kindness and self-judgement both have a score of 3, self-kindness needs your attention. The three compassion responses evaluated tell us what we may need to do more of in order to strengthen our compassion. If any one of the self-compassion responses is weaker than its corresponding uncompassionate response, it suggests that compassion satisfaction may not be at its best, which would also be reflected on the *Compassion Satisfaction Survey (A-9)* outcomes. This should also trigger consideration of your personal well-being burnout scores, as limited self-compassion can lead to increased stress in one's personal life. Low self-compassion may be reflected on the *Burnout Scale (A-4)* as taking less time to be with friends or less time to take for yourself, to pamper yourself. Do take a look at your personal well-being burnout scores and, if needed include those problem areas in your self-care efforts to support self-compassion. Limited self-compassion is also associated with lower compassion satisfaction, so let's look at that.

Compassion Satisfaction

Five or more *yes* responses on the compassion satisfaction survey are definitely concerning. Even one *yes* should concern you. For example, if you are feeling less motivated and energetic, it could be a sign of over exposure to the distress of those you are helping. On the other hand, it could signal a reaction to burnout conditions at your workplace or an absence of daily self-care. Less energy/motivation could also reflect issues with self-compassion, or absent/limited self-care efforts directed at managing your energy and/or issues under personal well-being on the Burnout Scale.

Whatever the cause, it's a sign to do something different. On the compassion satisfaction survey, you want more *no* responses than *yes* or *somewhat* responses combined. If total *yes* and *somewhat* responses outnumber *no* responses, I would also have major concerns about fatigue. If *somewhat* responses outnumber either *yes* or *no* responses, I would have the same concerns, especially if you identified any secondary trauma or post-traumatic stress reactions earlier. In this case, fatigue would also be likely as secondary trauma is often associated with compassion fatigue. When reviewing all outcomes, the compassion satisfaction outcome will better help you determine the self-care that may be needed or continued if satisfaction is not an issue. If your satisfaction outcomes are low and your overall burnout score is 700 or less, fatigue would also be likely.

ProQOL

Scoring *average* can be misleading. If your ProQOL outcome is in the mid to low range of average and burnout out levels are less than satisfactory, or secondary trauma reactions exist or the, in text, Satisfaction Survey indicates possible fatigue, I would suggest that compassion fatigue is an issue that needs your attention. This would also be the case if working in a toxic environment, if there are a number of silencing response factors rated 4 or above or if self-compassion outcomes indicate low self-compassion. Conversely, upper average to high compassion satisfaction outcomes should align with higher satisfaction on the Satisfaction Survey, areas like engagement, working in a flourishing environment, infrequent secondary trauma reactions, few silencing responses, etc. However, keep in mind that we can be compassionately satisfied yet be dealing with burnout or secondary trauma, as each can stand alone. Obviously if these are not cared for, satisfaction will be challenged.

Moral Distress

If you checked either question 27 or 37 on the *Toxic Workplace Survey (A-1)* you are experiencing some level of moral distress discussed in *Chapter Five.* Any level of moral distress is going to lower compassion satisfaction, and eat away at your well-being and sense of self-worth. It is indicative of a toxic environment, especially when that behavior goes unchallenged by leadership.

Empathy Distress, Silencing Response

When compassion satisfaction weakens, vulnerability to empathy distress increases. If your satisfaction outcomes are low—and there has been more than one incidence when you have become more concerned about your feelings versus the person you are helping—empathetic distress should concern you. Your greater concern for your reactions, versus those you are helping, would also likely be reflected in multiple responses checked on the Silencing Response Scale (*A-11*). From my experience, statements rated 4–10 on this scale may point to the possible existence of compassion fatigue, secondary trauma, or possibly faulty assumptions about client's distress, resulting from limited education about the distress being presented. If secondary trauma is a possibility, it would be reflected on the *Secondary Trauma Assessment Outcomes (A-7).* If secondary trauma is not an issue and compassion satisfaction is high, then issues with silencing responses could indicate insufficient training/education regarding those being helped. If secondary trauma is not an issue but compassion satisfaction is low, then the presence of statements rated 4–10 on the *Silencing Response Scale (A-11)* could reflect issues with empathy distress. That said, if you are in your first couple years of helping, statements rated 4–10 are more likely to be an issue with education, training and supervision related to those you are helping. However, that still leaves you vulnerable to empathy distress, secondary trauma or compassion fatigue.

Trauma Reactions

Keep in mind that secondary trauma is not a pathological response, but a not-at-all uncommon response to being directly or indirectly exposed to the distress/trauma of others. Secondary trauma is indicated when one or more reactions have been checked on the *Secondary Trauma Survey (A-7)* you completed in *Chapter Six.* Remember, there is not a certain number of reactions required to experience secondary trauma. If indicated, it's important to attend to it immediately. It's also important that the supervisor you are assigned, or have selected, is well versed in the *Secondary Trauma Supervisor Core Competencies (A-6).* That supervisor should be able to assist you with defusing those reactions and/or refer you to a trauma specialist if needed. If this is not the case, seek outside help. If experiencing post-traumatic stress, outside help is definitely recommended as a variety of interventions may be necessary.

Anyone of you working in an environment that primarily serves trauma victims, or those experiencing trauma, ought to be in an environment that is also trauma-informed. If this is not the case and supervisors are not secondary trauma competent, you need to think about being in an environment that is informed. If this is not possible or realistic for you, it would be to your benefit to join a peer support group and seek out a trauma specialist for help before secondary trauma becomes post-traumatic stress. If your environment is also more toxic than flourishing, it is vital to your well-being that stress in your personal life is minimal. If this is not the case, definitely seek help, as trying to go it alone is not an answer nor a solution.

What Demands My Self-Care

Now that you have had time to review all your outcomes and possible interpretations, record those that stand out the most in each category on the *What Demands My Self-Care worksheet in Appendix B-4.*

Up to this point you have already put a great deal of effective effort into determining your self-care needs. Your *effective effort* has involved learning, completing assessments and reflecting on the outcomes. You now have what you need to select those areas that you determine to be personal priorities in need of your self-care.

Approach Points Aligned with Those of Self-Care (Self-care approaches are in parentheses)

- ❏ Burnout is not due to resilience deficiency but to toxic workplace practices, which is a system issue and our reaction to that system (It's about sustainability; about advocating for our well-being because we are worthy of it).
- ❏ It is important to keep in mind that any one statement, practice, behavior or condition could be more important to you than a total score for

a category because that specific factor is causing you the most stress (It's personal).

- ❏ Whatever the source(s) of your stress, it's a sign that it's time to do something different (It's not an indulgence; it's a necessity, an act of self-preservation).

My Final Questions

Go to Appendix B-1 & B-1.2, My Final Questions. Answer the two questions below and record these on the worksheet.

1. Of all that you read or experienced in this chapter what one thought stands out the most for you?
2. Of the mindsets established in this chapter which one stands out the most for you?

Summary

You've accomplished a great deal. Just becoming aware of the specific thoughts, behaviors, reactions and conditions that are fueling your unwanted reactions and responses is going to make it so much easier to respond differently, and do differently, in ways that support your well-being professionally and personally. Once you prioritize what most needs your attention, in the next chapter, you'll be ready to identify, from the self-care strategies presented in that chapter, those that are most appropriate for your well-being.

References

West, C. P., Dyrbye, L. N., & Sinsky, C. (2020). Resilience and burnout among physicians and the general working population. *JAMA Network Open,* 3(7): e209385. https://doi.org/10.1001/jamanetworkopen.2020.9385

STAGE FIVE

Determining Your Personal Self-Care Strategy

CHAPTER 9

Consider These Self-Care Strategies

Making Personal Selections

Theme

You are now ready to identify your care strategies. The multiple strategies available are detailed in this chapter making it easier to align your approaches with what you have determined needs your care.

A Planned Approach to Life is Self-Caring

In *Chapter One* we detailed the importance of self-care, not as an indulgence but as a well-being necessity. We now return to self-care in order for you to select the various care practices that can be used to help you find relief from those helper stress reactions that you have determined need your attention the most. Before presenting these specific practices, it's important to appreciate that our approach to navigating our way through life also has tremendous influence on the impact stress has on our lives, our effectiveness, well-being and sustainability as helpers. For this reason, you are being asked to complete the *Spiritual Intelligence Self-Report Inventory* briefly mentioned when talking about the Spiritual Intelligence (SI) category under the Personal Well-Being category of the Burnout Scale you completed. It was indicated that "SI is not about faith or religion. SI is about how we view and respond to life and how

DOI: 10.4324/9781003673699-14

we go about achieving one that is purposeful and meaningful. It's about our approach to life in ways that embrace our *mind* and *spirit*, to avoid or effectively recover from the potentially negative impact of life's challenges, including burnout, empathetic distress, compassion fatigue or secondary trauma." The importance of how we live our lives is supported in the following mindset.

Mindset: *The practices associated with SI are associated with less stress, anxiety and depression (Pinto et al., 2023).*

Prevention

SI practices are preventative in nature. They encourage self-awareness, being honest with ourselves, living in the present, having established beliefs and values that drive our behavior, doing what deeply motivates us, pursuing our purpose, being self-compassionate and compassionate towards others, deriving satisfaction from something greater or larger than ourselves. It's about happiness and satisfaction in our personal and professional lives, self-efficacy (taking responsibility for our choices), reflection, reframing our negative thoughts, emotions, and behaviors and practicing cognitive and emotional regulation. When these essential self-care approaches are a part of how we interact with life, our reactions to stress are more positive and self-care strategies more effective.

SISR-I Evaluation

Activity One: Spiritual Self-Report Inventory

Step One: Go to Appendix A-12 and complete the Spiritual Intelligence Inventory. Follow the instructions on the inventory for scoring. Be sure to reverse score #6 as indicated in the instructions.

If presenting, review with participants the SI practices that follow. This will help clarify their understanding of the practices associated with each category measured on the SI inventory.

My experience has been that reviewing the practices below answers many of the questions participants have about SI practices. Furthermore, these practices support several of the primary care strategies we'll be recommending, such as mindfulness, reflection and reframing. It also supports that self-care is not an indulgence but an absolute necessity for overall well-being and sustainability in all areas of our lives. *Readers just continue to the next step.*

Step Two: The behaviors associated with each SI category follow. *If your score for a category is below mid-range use Worksheet B-4, What Demands*

My Self-Care, and record the behaviors associated with that category that you believe could help you improve that particular area of your approach to life. Note: Ideally you want your total score to be at least mid-range to high. The closer to the high range the better. This is also the case with the individual categories.

Critical Existential Thinking: Reflecting on our thoughts, feelings, actions, choices as to whether they align with our values and beliefs. Practicing self-compassion, taking responsibility for our choices and actions, practicing mindfulness, exploring all possibilities for what is happening before making a judgement, and seeking meaningful relationships.

Transcendental Awareness: Finding meaning and value in our actions rather than their rewards. Using meditation, mindfulness and spending time in nature to nurture the concept that we are only a small part of something larger. Being open to new challenges and viewpoints to foster a broader perspective of self and life and engaging in pro-social behaviors.

Personal Meaning Production: Defining the meaning and purpose of what we are doing, finding meaning (a teachable moment) in difficult situations, pursuing what we are passionate about, reflecting on our experiences and what they are teaching us in order to promote greater self-awareness and integration with our values and beliefs.

Conscious State Expansion: Being present, focusing on others rather than self, using mindfulness and meditation to enhance present moment awareness and clarifying thoughts and emotions in that moment in order to lead us to self-discovery and growth.

Any one or several of these SI practices may be beneficial self-care priorities for you personally. Pursuit of, and engaging in, SI practices promotes adapting to life challenges in ways that help sustain us despite those challenges life has a way of throwing at us more than once. Let's then look at those additional care strategies that are specific to minimizing and/or recovering from burnout, compassion fatigue, secondary trauma, post-traumatic stress and empathy distress. We begin with self-compassion.

Care Strategies Specific to Helper Stress

Self-Compassion

Mindset: *Limited self-compassion lowers resilience while increasing stress, anxiety, depression, avoidance behaviors, difficulty with emotional regulation and finding empathy for others (Benner, 2022).*

Stronger self-compassion is associated with improved well-being and lower stress (lower cortisol levels) (Cowand et al., 2024). Given that many helpers have difficulty with consistent self-care, being as compassionate with themselves as they are with those they are helping, it is not surprising to see higher rates of compassion fatigue among helpers. Practicing self-compassion is an essential approach to effective self-care (Conversano, 2020). Self-compassion was covered extensively in *Chapter Seven*. There are a number of excellent mindful self-compassion programs available on the internet. Self-compassion pioneer, Dr. Neff, whose work in the field of self-compassion is prolific, has a web site called *self-compassion.org.* This site is rich with educational resources, online courses, seminars, blog posts and *TED Talks*. If your self-compassion scores were indicative of needing some work, I would definitely send you to Dr. Neff. Barbara Rubel's Fabulous Transformation program (griefworkcenter.com) is also an excellent resource.

Regulation

The three areas of regulation that need our attention include our nervous system, emotions and cognition. In *Stage One: Chapter Three* we had a detailed discussion about the physiology of stress, and how our nervous system's response is not always a choice and how important it is to be able to calm and regulate our nervous systems response to stress via sensory activities, not initially with cognitive processes. The Waco children used play and comforting adults as calming techniques. Dr. Porgess pulled out from the MRI machine after reasoning didn't help with his stress response. Peter Levine responded to touch and a calm voice. And people in New York used comfort food, exercise, and other non-talking ways to regulate their nervous systems. In the face of daily distress, daily regulation of our nervous system is simply critical to sustaining what we do, and how well we do it. There are a number of basic practices regarding daily nervous system regulation. Each of the following are equally important for minimizing the negative impact of burnout, secondary trauma, compassion fatigue and empathy distress.

Daily Routine

Mindset: *Maintaining a daily routine for regulating our nervous system is essential self-care and begins with identifying what it is that helps you detach for a minute or two from stressful responses or conditions, in order to replenish your energy, lower blood pressure or re-establish productive cognitive functions, rather than being stressed by negative ones.*

This does not mean ignoring those reactions but putting them aside until you have time to reflect on what, or who, precipitated those unwanted reactions and ways you can respond differently in the future.

Reflection

Allow me to digress a minute to say a bit more about reflection and then return to daily nervous system regulation. Reflection, a self-care process, is best done before you leave work whenever possible. It's a good way to close out the work day, to leave work at work. If that is not doable then it is important to do so as part of your *End of Day Reflection* practice located in *Appendix C-1*. Reflection is a recommended approach to help reframe ways you might prepare yourself to respond differently to similar situations or experiences. For example, if you're not excited about going into work, your nervous system is already going into an alert stage. An *End of Day Reflection* is a way of preparing you for how you are going to approach the next day in order to regulate and minimize the negative or cumulative building up of stress. Okay, back to nervous sysytem regulation.

Five Minutes to Regulate

Mindset: *It only takes a minute to reduce cortisol, the stress hormone, and improve focus, concentration and energy (Hill & Bowman, 2025).*

As a helper, knowing what basic regulators work best for you is critical for maitaining your energy, concentration, attention, mental calm and clarity (Amen Clinics, 2024; Technology Networks, 2023; Weir, 2019). This effort minimizes fatigue when practiced multiple times daily. Nervous system regulation strategies can utilize numerous non-verbal approaches, or what I refer to as sensory interventions, involving breathing, movement, sounds, smells, sight and touch. In an earlier activity you took different poses and noted how each pose made you think and feel about a specific stressful situation. Those poses either calmed your reaction, or intensified it. One was more helpful than another and one may have allowed you to feel or think differently about that situation. The same holds true for the simplest of movements. Even the slightest of movements can alter what we think and feel. Let me demonstrate.

Activity Two: Regulation By Movement

You can do this as a reader by recording the instructions, pausing briefly to allow time to trace between questions. Provide 30–45 seconds of tracing while participants' process the questions for each activity.

- ❑ You need a couple plain sheets of paper and a pencil. I want you to focus on some recent stressful situation, or on a person you encountered that triggered unwanted stressful thoughts or emotions. Take a minute to focus on that situation and your reactions. Now while continuing to think about that experience, I simply want you to draw a circle on one of your papers and continue to trace that circle while thinking about your experience. Do that now. (Pause for 30–40 seconds before presenting questions.) Now as you are tracing your circle what one thought about your situation jumps out at you? (Pause between questions.) As you trace what one emotion stands out? While tracing, is it calming that reaction or intensifying it?
- ❑ Okay, staying with the same situation take another sheet of paper and draw a square or rectangle. Now continue tracing that figure and thinking about your situation. (Pause for 30–40 seconds.) Now as you think about that situation what one thought stands out? Is this different from your original thought or the same? As you continue tracing, pay attention to the reaction/feeling about that experience. Is tracing making it more intense or less intense? Are the thoughts or reactions initially associated with your situation the same or a bit different? Does tracing make them clearer or more intense?
- ❑ Now just flip your paper over for one more activity. This time while focusing on your situation and your rection I want you to just go back and forth from left to right with your pencil and keep tracing the initial line back and forth. (Pause for a moment.) Now as you think about your reaction, is this back and forth tracing making it more intense or less intense? Are any of your previous emotions or thoughts a bit different with this tracing?

If presenting, when finished simply ask for a show of hands as to how many experienced a small shift in thoughts, feelings or sensations such as body calm or tightness with various movements.

My experience, is that generally about two thirds of the participants will raise their hands indicating a change was experienced. The response will be somewhat similar when you ask how many felt it changed the way they thought about what happened.

Remember, no one intervention works for every one. It sometimes takes trying a few different approaches. Those folks who didn't experience a change may have responded differently to different sensory stimuli such as music. The point being made is that tracing was a sensory-based activity where you saw what you were doing, regulated what you were doing, touched what you were doing (pencil to paper), while thinking about what happened and your associated reactions. These brief sensory movements triggered a shift in feeling and/or thoughts about what was stressful.

Multiple Ways

There are many basic ways to regulate at a sensory level. Strategies include,

- ❑ listening to music, the sounds of nature, rubbing a "dodad" on your key chain for sensory comfort,
- ❑ getting to your favorite chair and doing a body scan of the physical sensations you're experiencing, such as shallow breathing, tight neck or shoulders, heaviness, fatigue,
- ❑ deep breathing or progressive muscle relaxation to easily and quickly release some of that tension,
- ❑ training your body to begin relaxing when you put your thumb and forefinger together, and gently squeezing out the stress, could also be beneficial,
- ❑ taking out a favorite photo and focusing on it while remembering the feeling at that time the photo was taken,
- ❑ focusing on a mindset you have written down, keep with you or someplace at work,
- ❑ taking a gratitude pause to release oxytocin the happy hormone, or
- ❑ looking at a video clip you keep on your phone that changes your mood. I love the pet and baby videos that make me laugh.

Any mini sensory process that is associated with calming the nervous system is just a part, or should be a part, of a helper's everyday self-care strategy. It takes no more than five minutes and is recommended once every hour when possible. Now sometimes our system needs activating to renew our energy. Following are some basic strategies,

- ❑ splashing cold water on your face triggers a positive polyvagal response,
- ❑ standing up and doing toe push ups will stimulate circulation and improve energy,
- ❑ Doing wall push ups and other brisk movements do the same, and
- ❑ keeping a few of your favorite quotes around or on your phone to read when you need a lift.

I'm sure you can think of many more *micro moments* that work to calm or activate your nervous system.

On the Way Out

I've suggested to many that when leaving the work environment and grabbing the doorknob on the way out, they hold onto that doorknob until they are breathing slower and feeling their body letting go of the stress of the day, and being replaced with the thought *the working day is over, now it's time for the rest of my life.* This is the use of a sensory process (grabbing the doorknob) to trigger an intentional mindset. When you get home it's then time to reset your brain using the same process. For example, as you hit whatever device you use to open the garage door, or pull into your parking spot, use those visuals or sounds to reset your focus to *being present* in your personal life.

Science confirms (Kirk et al., 2025) that these brief breaks or *micro minutes* can increase energy, cognitive clarity, focus, attention and calm, leading to lower stress and wellness. The key is doing this regularly everyday; using *effective effort* till you find what works best for you and making it a regular daily practice.

Emotional Regulation

Emotional regulation is taking any action that alters the intensity of an emotional experience. It doesn't mean suppressing or avoiding emotions. With emotional regulation skills, you can influence which emotions you have as well as how you express them. (Klynn, 2024). Essentially, emotional regulation helps to manage our energy, maintain balance, ensuring that emotions do not overwhelm or disrupt our day-to-day functioning (McRae & Gross, 2020). Thompson et al. (2022) reported studies showing that emotional dysregulation was associated with empathy distress, while emotional regulation was associated with greater cognitive empathy—staying in the present with the person in distress, rather than becoming more concerned of the feelings being triggered by that person's distress. Veerakone (2024) reported on a study from MIT that found that focusing on *social good* when experiencing negative emotions also helped to regulate those emotions. It's about

- ❑ accepting the emotions we are experiencing, not fighting them.
- ❑ disengaging or grounding ourselves for a moment as a way to calm our reactions enough to then reframe our thoughts, and
- ❑ re-engaging with the person or situation that initially triggered the dysregulation (McGarvie, 2025).

Emotional regulation is a necessity as a helper, especially in the midst of exposure to distressing or traumatic details being revealed by those you are helping. Let's look at grounding as a way to quickly regulate an unwanted reaction and regain focus on how you are attempting to help others.

Grounding

There are a number of grounding techniques that can be used to regulate our emotions until we are in a place and have the time to reflect on and process those reactions by ourselves or with the help of others such as a supervisor. For example, if a client triggers an unwanted reaction simply change your visual focus by looking at the objects on the wall or desk if in an office. Even curling your toes or pushing the soles of your feet into the floor could be the sensory trigger *that reminds you that you can deal with your rection later while continuing to focus on who you are helping.*

- ❑ a small shift in posture, tapping your foot on the floor,
- ❑ counting from 100 backward,
- ❑ deep breathing,
- ❑ picking up a pen, any object, and paying attention to its weight, feel and color may be helpful, and
- ❑ listening more intently to the sounds surrounding you can shift your focus enough to regulate your emotions and help you refocus on who you are helping.

Healthy Detachment

Healthy detachment is another way to regulate emotions, to remain empathetic without "getting emotionally entangled" (Levine, 2025, para. 9). It involves

- ❑ remaining mindful within ourselves-staying in the present,
- ❑ letting go of the need for outcomes,
- ❑ focusing on what we can control, and
- ❑ working on our old wounds.

It's not about avoidance; it's about maintaining compassion. Remember when compassion weakens, empathy distress increases.

When It's Not Helping

There are so many brief ways to regulate emotions that it just takes some exploring to find what works best for you—a visual, a sound, a smell, a touch, a posture shift and so on. However, when emotions continue to dysregulate, a combination of approaches might be recommended, while keeping in mind that what works for one does not necessarily work for others. Following are several options.

- ❑ *Meditation* is used to help calm and stablize the nervous system and to strengthen mindfulness. However, *meditation is not necessary for mindfulness to be effective. Mindfulness* is about being present in the moment with what is being experienced. Many of the following strategies use forms of meditation and/or mindfulness. I personally found reflection and mindfulness more helpful than meditation. I remember, when going through a clinical internship in social work, being required to complete a process recording after each session with a client.This was a wrtten recording of observations and responses from clients, and my thoughts and reactions about both their verbal and non-verbal responses. It was a wonderful way to help me stay present/mindful, and then be able to reflect afterwards on my immediate reactions and thoughts to that client interaction and have those evaluated by my supervisor. It was by far one of the best learning and growth experiences I had. Mindfulness practices can be very effective. For example, mindful self-compassion training is essential for minimizing and/or preventing empathetic distress, if struggling with too much empathy.
- ❑ *Cognitive Behavioral Therapy* (CBT) uses a process of reappraisal and reframing to change negative thoughts and beliefs in order to change behaviors and reactions to stressful situations. It is a very structured process.
- ❑ *Trauma Focused Cognitive Behavioral Therapy* (TF-CBT) uses the same CBT process but adds gradual exposure to, and trauma narrative processing of, trauma memories.
- ❑ *Dialectical Behavioral Training* (DBT) incorporates cognitive reappraisal/reframing techniques but also includes mindfulness practices to help regulate emotions and improve distress tolerance.
- ❑ *Experiental Emotion Focused* strategies emphasize experiencing and processing those distressful emotions and lower brain sensations and discovering how they can be regulated as needed. For example, using the body as a resource to build what Dr. van der Kolk calls islands of safety (Forte, 2020). By the way, anyone helping those with trauma, or who is themselves traumatized, must read his book *The Body Keeps the Score* (van der Kolk, 2014). It will be immensely helpful and enlightening.
- ❑ *Polyvagal Therapy* is an evidenced-based, body-based approach that helps to connect our brain with our body in order to regulate our body's stress response. Mindfulness, deep breathing, movement, visualization, imagery and co-regulation are the practices involved.

- ❑ *Mindful Awareness in Body Oriented Therapy* (MABT) teaches how to access and process sensory information from the body in order to facilitate self-awareness and emotion regulation.
- ❑ *Acceptance and Commitment Therapy* (ACT) is an approach that uses mindfulness and reframing skills to support psychological flexibility and values-based actions.
- ❑ *Eye Movement Desensitization Reprocessing* (EMDR) has also been very beneficial for those experiencing STS/PTSD and anxiety and, for many, provides faster recovery than CBT interventions. It involves bilateral stimulation allowing the brain to process negative memories and then reprocess them in healthier ways.
- ❑ *Somatic Experiencing Therapy* is another mind-body oriented approach for healing trauma and chronic stress by helping to release those physical and emotional effects stored in the nervous sytem. Somatic therapy combined with CBT can be especially beneficial.
- ❑ *Expressive Therapies* can include movement, sound, music, imagination, creativity, storytelling, guided imagery, writing, drawing, photography and other creative arts. These modalities help us safely externalize the physiological and psychological impact of our stress, fears and anxiety and by doing so makes them more manageable.

A Bit More

Allow me to say a bit more about expressive therapies because they are often discounted yet have a rich history of helping when other modalities do not. Remember, talking doesn't always work.

Mindset: *The expressive therapies help to lower stress, regulate our emotions and unwanted sensations, improve concentration and the expression of thoughts and feelings, especially when it is difficult to find the words that best describe our stress, anxiety or traumatic distress (King, 2024; Lukenda et al., 2024; de Witte et al., 2019; Murray, 2022; Nash, 2022; Emmons, 2013).*

They foster self-awareness, emotional growth, a sense of safety and empowerment and more effective mind-body integration. I can tell you personally that many would still be suffering today had it not been for the drawing activities I used to help others put their trauma experience outside themselves, in a concrete form, so they could more easily manage that experience.

One Letter

When I was going through grade school, my father and I were not close. He was a quiet man of few words. He worked two full-time jobs for a number of years so we had little contact. I really did not know much about him personally. My freshman year in high school was spent out of state. After the first couple of weeks, I received a letter from my dad. To tell you the truth I didn't even know he could write. This was a five-page letter on 8 x 11 plain paper. He wrote about everything. I was blown away. It felt like he said more in that one letter than he had said to me all the time I was at home. Those letters kept coming over the four years I was away. The point is he became real by expressing himself through writing. It was a life changing experience for both of us. We both related to one another much differently after that. Let me add a formal study about the value of writing as an expressive intervention.

Write It—Change It

Journaling has always been a non-talk healing process. We now have research to show that writing about stressful challenges is as effective and, for many, more effective than traditional talk therapy or Cognitive Processing Therapy (CPT). Sloan et al. (2018) report that research demonstrates that Written Exposure Therapy (WET) was just as effective as CPT, took half the time, and far fewer dropped out of this five-session treatment than those in the CPT group. One hundred and twenty-six male and female military and non-military victims of trauma participated. Journaling can be quite effective.

Ask veterans with PTSD what has helped them the most and you will hear about their trauma trained dog, writing, creative art, guided imagery and other expressive modalities. All can effectively help to regulate emotions and reframe thoughts to lower stress while improving well-being. If you are interested in the use of expressive therapies, I highly recommend reading *Transform Stress, Crisis & Trauma Through Creativity* by Rankin & Fibich (2024).

More detailed information for all these approaches are easily internet accessible. Many YouTube segments present the founders of these strategies and their discussions as to how they help. The effectiveness of each are well researched. Because CBT is often recommended, I do want to use it an example to address criteria that is needed to make it effective and, for some, why it is not helpful.

Cognitive Reappraisal/Reframing

The fact is, the stronger our cognitive functioning the more effective our efforts will be in mitigating ongoing stress (Crum et al., 2017). Cognitive reappraisal/reframing is a strategy where you actively identify negative thoughts and behaviors and then reframe them to shift (regulate) the emotional impact of those negative thoughts. For example, viewing a failure as a learning experience rather than a shameful experience (Buhle et al., 2014). A common stressor is feeling incompetent when things go wrong. A reframing of feeling incompetent might be "It's not that you're not competent, you just didn't know what to do in that situation." That's an easy fix, if it helps. Fear is another common stressor. One way of reframing fear is the statement, "Fear is what you are feeling, courage is what you are doing right now."

Simple, However

This seems simple enough and sometimes simple works. For example, early in my career of working with trauma victims and survivors there were times when I couldn't listen to any more of what happened to them. It was definitely a stressful reaction. At that point I had to learn how to refocus my thoughts. I found that when I said to myself, "This is not about me. I can take care of me later" it allowed me to slow down the emotional response, return to being curious about what their experience was like for them and refocus my concern on them, not myself. That worked for me because of other factors I was embracing at the time. *I was motivated to learn* all I could, which helped me *respond to that stress as an opportunity to learn* and become a more effective helper. Knowing that *I had help available*—that *I was not alone* and that this was *an opportunity to learn*—made it much easier to access that cognitive process in order to slow down my reactions. Had I not been comfortable with stress being a signal to learn, not had the motivation to learn, and if having available help was missing, I'm certain my emotional dysregulation would have continued and become problematic for myself and those I was attempting to help. Cognitive reframing is not always simple. What is essential to the effectiveness of this process is stated in the following mindset.

Mindset: *To be sustainable, reframing has to be meaningful to that person and specifically address the realities they are experiencing in their lives.*

If someone is trying to help you, but has limited experience with your realities, their efforts at helping you reframe what is happening to you may not be at all useful or sustainable. Sam's story demonstrates the need for reframing that addresses an individual's realities. It's also a good example of how this may not be possible simply because the therapist does not have the information to form reframing statements that fit within the context or reality the client is living.

Sam's Story

I've told this story many times because of the lesson it teaches about reframing being done in a way that is personally meaningful and motivating. Sam had been a high school football player and a good student. He was in great shape, strong and smart. After a few months in college, he decided he wanted to join the police force. Once he made that decision he worked out and studied what was needed to try out for acceptance into the police academy. He was accepted but it would be a few months before starting. One day he was working at the local movie theater. When the movie ended, he took his position in the hall as people exited from the screen. Almost immediately he was confronted with trouble. Before he knew what was happening, he was on the ground taking a pretty severe beating. A few weeks later I received a call from a friend close to Sam and familiar with the trauma work I was doing. He asked if I would see Sam who had isolated himself and made references to not going to the academy. There was concern about depression and suicide, since he was talking about giving up his future in law enforcement and also isolating himself. I agreed, only if Sam's friend was there with me as a way to establish some sense of safety for Sam who didn't know me.

The first thing I did was to let Sam know he could say "no" to anything I might ask him to answer or talk about in order to empower him and let him feel a bit safer. I then normalized his responses to what would be traumatic for anyone in that situation. For example, I said I wouldn't be surprised if he felt ashamed about his beating because he was big and strong but not as tough as he might have viewed himself. And of course, there is always someone who says something to further wound trauma victims. In Sam's case, someone asked, "How did you let this happen to you?"

What concerned me the most was his giving up on his future. What I will never forget is how he described what the worst part of being beaten was like for him. Again, we might assume the worst part was the pain he experienced or perhaps the fear of dying. His response was, "They're kicking and stomping on me and I can see between their legs. And when I look between their legs, there are all these people standing around and no one is helping me." He felt abandoned and utterly powerless to do anything about what was happening to him: two core feeling states of a traumatic experience. This only reinforced my concerns for his well-being. It also demonstrated that our role as helpers is being curious, not making assumptions about what anyone in distress may be experiencing or thinking. When I did bring up what he had said about not going to the academy and told him I was curious as to what was making him think this way, his response was, "If I can't take care of myself how can I take care of anyone else."

The challenge was to reframe his experience in a way to get him back to following his desire to be in law enforcement. Whatever reframing effort was made, it would have to be integrated into how his experience would make him a good cop. Had it not been for the experiences I had with police, because my son was in law enforcement, I can honestly say I don't know that I would have been able to reframe his experience in a meaningful way to motivate him to reconnect to his future dream.

My reframing began with a protocol question. “Sam, I know you’ve been on patrol rides to get a feel for what goes on, and obviously you know enough about protocols to be accepted into the academy. So, I wonder if you can tell me why standard protocol is to call for backup if you’re entering into a dangerous situation?” His response was, “I guess anyone can be taken out.” I experienced some relief when he said that because I knew how I was then going to reframe his thinking. My response was, “Sam, we don’t always have a choice as to what happens to us. We do have a choice as to what we do afterwards. And, you are absolutely right about anyone being taken out. It doesn’t matter how smart you are, how tough you might be, the one painful yet wonderful lesson you have learned is that there is safety in numbers. And the one thing I do know, without a doubt, is that given your experience, you are going to make one really good partner and one heck of a cop because you understand this.” From that point on he was on his way.

This language, the thoughts of this reframing would have never been accessible to me had it not been for my experiences with my son. It was useful, addressed his competence, his need to be reconnected to his dream, and belief in his ability and autonomy. The research of Ford & Troy (2019) indicate that reframing must be functional to be useful and sustainable. Brockman et al. (2023) also indicate that successful reframing/reappraisal depends on whether that process meets the basic needs of connection, competence and autonomy. This is so important I’ve added a shorter version of the previous mindset.

Mindset: *If a reframing is going to be sustainable it must be integrated into the context in which that individual is experiencing themselves and their environment.*

When Words Matter Most

Mindset: *Words matter most when they are personally meaningful to us and the subjective world in which we live.*

If I were spending time with a helper to help reframe their thought processes, I would be very curious about their subjective experience to better determine what specifically needs reframing. For example, it is not unusual for those who have difficulty regulating to also have little self-compassion for themselves. This absence of self-compassion leads to thoughts that attack one’s value such as,

- ❏ second-guessing competency—*If only . . . I’m not smart enough to be . . . .*
- ❏ feeling somehow responsible—*I should have known . . .*

- ❑ increased anxiety wondering what staff may be thinking about them, that . . . *I must have ignored information . . . I misread the signs . . . I didn't listen . . . No one is talking to me about it. They must think I'm incompetent.*
- ❑ distrusting view of self—*I ignored what they said. I'm so stupid. I'm a professional. I shouldn't be having all these reactions. If only . . .*
- ❑ attacking one's own psyche . . . *Had I not been so scared, maybe I could've helped the others. I'm such a coward. What's wrong with me? I should be able to control my fears. They tell me I'll be better if I talk about what happened, but I don't want to. It's too hard.*

Once one's negative and self-defeating thoughts can be identified, the reframing of those thoughts can begin.

Not for Everyone

Mindset: *Although cognitive reframing can be helpful, no one intervention works for everyone.*

Wang & Yang (2023) agree with this, as their research found limitations with cognitive reframing approaches simply because no two situations are exactly alike. What might work for one, may not work for another because of different internal and external conditions.

For example, if one is emotionally dysregulated and primarily in the lower survival brain, logic is distorted and processing thoughts can be difficult. This was extensively addressed in *Chapter Three*. Think back to the examples from Doctors Porges, Levine and Perry. Not until physiology and associated emotions are calmed, does one then have more access to cognitive processing needed for reframing. In essence, there are many variables that can determine the success of one intervention. This is why, when we talk about self-care, we approach it remembering that when one strategy is not helping, we just need to try another till we discover what is working for us.

STS/PTSD

The above practices are also beneficial for those experiencing secondary trauma when using trauma-informed techniques by trained trauma specialists. Trauma specialists will generally be certified in several trauma-based approaches. The experience of trauma is different than the experience of compassion fatigue, and therefore is best managed within a trauma-informed framework. Some do well with trauma-focused CBT, while others do better with expressive strategies and still others manage best with the development of emotional regulation skills. PTSD is more complex and may involve the need for medication along with trauma therapy. EMDR, or Experiential Emotion Focused or Exposure Therapy, has also benefited many. Exposure therapy is a process of revisiting the memories of trauma in order to learn how to regulate the emotions, sensations and thoughts of that memory. The memories do not necessarily go away but, with gradual exposure, the intensity associated with them diminishes (McDonough, 2025). Often a combination of approaches involving cognitive and emotional regulation skills, expressive therapy, body-oriented therapies and other modalities are beneficial.

Just keep in mind that, just as no one intervention is best for everyone, no one trauma specialist will be best for everyone. Before I began my own therapy, I visited three different therapists and then went with the fourth one who I felt would be most helpful. Think back about our conversation about supervisors. You need to feel safe and trust that the person you select can be helpful.

Behavioral Issues

When individual stress reactions are related to behavioral issues, such as poor time management, stress related interventions will be of limited help; learning to prioritize your time will. If you are having difficulty engaging with others, you may benefit from getting help with relationship building. If there is one specific behavior needing your attention, you may find it beneficial to search the internet for recommendations. Many of the issues specific to workplace burnout are due to toxic practices. As stated earlier, resilience alone will not prevent burnout while toxic practices go unchecked. In such a situation, I would recommend focusing your energy on your personal life. However, if individual reactions needing attention are specific to compassion, empathy, secondary trauma, the recommendations in this text that have addressed these areas will be helpful.

Self-Care—A Daily Effort

I strongly recommend a daily routine that includes the practices described below, inclusive of the *End of Day Reflection in Appendix C-1.* Stress will never go away. However, we can definitely minimize its downside with a daily routine. Having an established base line for the effectiveness of our daily care efforts, will then also help make it easier to evaluate the effectiveness of any additional self-care strategies needed. In addition, such a routine will help avoid bringing workplace stress into your personal life.

The routine below incorporates mindfulness and other SI practices, cognitive processing, reframing and nervous system regulation. Keep in mind that self-care is not so much about managing your time but harnessing your energy while staying focused on fulfilling your purpose, taking responsibility for your choices and utilizing those approaches shown to be effective in minimizing the negative effects of stress. Practice the routine below for 30 days and experience the change.

Starting the Workday

The start of the workday actually begins at the end of the previous workday. Whenever possible, before leaving work, make a *to do* list for the next day. If that is not possible, the *to-do* list can be part of the *End of Day Reflection in Appendix C-1.* Science tells us that making a *to-do* list for the next day "decreases cognitive arousal, rumination and worry" (Zucker, 2024, para. 3). You get a good night's sleep and wake up the next day with a plan; a kind of stress shield.

Reflect

Before going to bed take ten minutes to reflect on what stood out for the day. Fifteen questions in the *End of Day Reflection in Appendix C-1* will help you focus on what mattered most for the day, what did or did not happen, what got in the way, what it taught you and what you might want to pursue the next day. Reflection is the practice of looking inward to tap into and develop our strengths, our values and well-being. It's about keeping control of our life rather than allowing conditions or others to control it.

Mindset: *Reflection improves critical thinking, decision making, enriches emotional intelligence and strenthens empathy (Gupta, 2025; Morin, 2011; Avolio & Gardner, 2005).*

Reflection is also one of the SI practices. Because stress is simply a part of our professional and personal lives, I also recommend you routinely reflect on how well you are engaging in those practices associated with SI. Not only is this essential to well-being but also sustained resilience and fulfillment of purpose and meaning, which research shows leads to a longer, healthier, more satisfying life (Greenberg, 2025; Bishop, 2023; Sellig, 2021). Margaret J. Wheatley, an American writer and distinguished organizational consultant, has been honored with numerous global awards for her work in organizational leadership and change. She is quoted as saying, "Without reflection, we go blindly on our way, creating more unintended consequences, and failing to achieve anything useful" (Margaret J. Wheatly Quotes, 2018).

Micro Moments

Take micro moments at least twice in your morning work hours and twice in the afternoon. Five minutes every hour will provide the maximum benefits—cognitive clarity, focus, concentration and nervous system regulation. Experiment with movement, music, minfulness, meditation and other suggestions that were provided, to see what works best for you. Usually there will be a few that work best.

Before Leaving

Utilize a daily sensory trigger that lets the nervous system know you are ending the work day (doorknob example presented earlier). Follow that with a cognitive staement that reinforces that work is over and you are now going to live the rest of your life. Do the same when arriving home to help you be present in your personal life. This simple process is another way to regulate the nervous systen as well supporting a mindful way of life.

Gratitude

Practice gratitude daily. Practicing gratitude releases the happy hormone, improves our ability to cope better with stress, supports a stronger immune system and lower lifetime risks (Portocarrero et al., 2020; Emmons, 2013). This could be one of those micro moments where you sit quietly and reflect on what makes you grateful, a part of your End of Day Reflection or your morning coffee which helps jump start the day. It's also one of the SI practices. There was an interesting study reported by Harvard Medical School (Miller, 2012). One group was asked to write about what they were grateful for each week over a period of ten weeks. Another group was asked to do the same but write about what upset them. What they discovered was that "those who wrote about what they were grateful for, were more optimistic and felt better about their lives" (compared to the other group).

Avoid It

Try to go at least 30 minutes before going to bed avoiding all blue light sources, such as the television, iPhone, computer, video games. This is a great time to meditate or reflect on the day. Blue light stimulates the brain, making it more difficult to fall into a restorative sleep. The research is quite strong as to the negative impact of blue light on sleep patterns. This 30 minutes without blue light stimulation, will also help slow down the nervous system, help remove tension and ready your body and brain for deep restorative sleep. You will be surprised by how much easier you fall asleep and enjoy a more restful and restorative sleep. This is an important factor in fighting stress. Results from the world's largest sleep study (Wild et al., 2018) have shown that people who sleep on average between 7 to 8 hours per night performed better cognitively than those who slept less, or more, than this amount. The stronger our cognitive functioning, the more effective our efforts to mitigate the cognitive deficiencies resulting from ongoing stress (Crum et al., 2017).

Approach Points Aligned with Those of Self-Care (Self-care approaches are in parentheses)

- ❑ The practices associated with SI are associated with less stress, anxiety and depression. SI practices are preventative in nature (It's a way of approaching life to maintain our well-being).
- ❑ As a helper, knowing and using what basic regulators work best for you is essential self-care (It's about sustainability; it's an act of self-preservation).
- ❑ Science confirms that brief breaks or *micro minutes* can increase energy, cognitive clarity, focus, attention and calm, leading to lower stress and wellness.The key is doing it regularly everyday (It's about effective effort, managing our energy).
- ❑ Essentially, emotional regulation helps to maintain balance, ensuring that emotions do not overwhelm or disrupt our day-to-day functioning (It's about managing our energy, our well-being, staying within our window of tolerance).
- ❑ Reframing, to be successful, has to be meaningful to us and specifically address the realities we are experiencing in our lives (It's personal).

At the conclusion of every chapter, you were asked to record your responses to two final questions. A lot was presented in this chapter, so you are being asked to do the same in order to complete what matters most to your self-care efforts.

My Final Questions

Answer the two questions below and record these on the *My Final Questions worksheet in Appendix B-1 & B-1.2.* This worksheet will be used in the next activity.

1. Of all that you read or experienced in this chapter what one thought stands out the most for you?
2. Of the mindsets established in this chapter which one stands out the most for you?

Return here for one additional activity.

Activity Three: My Thoughts, My Mindsets

As you reflect on the thoughts you recorded for each chapter in *Appendix B-1,* including this last chapter, ask yourself, "What do these thoughts suggest I need to do differently (think, respond, etc.)?" Record your response on the *What Demands My Self-Care worksheet Appendix B-4.*

Activity Four

Review Chapter Nine Mindsets listed on *My Final Questions worksheet in Appendix B-1.* From all mindsets listed, select the three that are now the most meaningful for you. Record these on the *End of Day Reflection worksheet in Appendix C-1.*

Ready to Prioritize and Select Self-Care Strategies

Why Prioritize?

Some of your self-care efforts will need to be integrated with those other priorities in your life, such as driving the kids to baseball or gymnastics practice, changing the oil in the car, paying bills, returning phone calls, getting to that doctor's appointment on time, grocery shopping, meeting with friends and so on. Life is busy. If we do not keep our self-care priorities in our sights, it's very easy to be pulled in other directions. Workplaces today demand multitasking and responding to unrelenting demands, day-to-day crises. Under these stressful conditions it is very easy to lose sight of what is important, to get sucked into what others want, even when it is not pertinent to our work or our responsibilities; that makes for lost time, energy and performance inefficiency. Keeping our self-care priorities in view helps to counter these demands and the stress they induce. Focusing on our priorities also helps avoid physical and emotional fatigue, especially in organizations engaged in practices associated with burnout.

Ultimately, prioritizing gives us more time to harness our energy for those things in life that matter the most to us personally. However, for this to happen we need to daily remind ourselves of those priorities. Establishing and reviewing these priorities on a regular basis, reinforces our efforts and commitment to be at our best, our most effective and our healthiest, physically, psychologically, emotionally, socially, in our relationships and in the work we do.

Prioritizing Self-Care Needs

Step One: Review *What Demands My Self-Care worksheet (B-4)* and numerically prioritize, as best you can, which of the helper stressors listed are presenting the greatest amount of stress for you. These can cut across the categories listed. For example, both burnout and compassion fatigue can stand alone but may also co-exist. Compassion may be problematic yet issues with a supervisor are causing the greatest stress. What our initial thoughts tell us we need to do is sometimes our best advice. Give these "to do's" the appropriate rating.

Use the following rating scale for all outcomes listed on the *What Demands My Self-Care worksheet.*

1 = Those needing my most immediate attention because they are interfering with my happiness, my energy levels, my wellness, my desire to help . . .

2 = Those interfering with parts of my life but not with the same intensity as those rated #1

3 = Those associated with a specific situation or person that is not constant or cannot be changed yet need my attention because my emotional, cognitive response is upsetting for me.

Assigning Self-Care Strategies

I suggest starting with those issues rated #1. Some may argue and suggest beginning with the issues that may be the easiest to resolve. The choice is purely subjective. Do what you believe is best for you at the time.

Whatever you decide, I do hope your very first care strategy begins with initiating a daily self-care routine. If you do currently practice one, I again recommend that it contains the practices included in the previous example under *Starting the Workday* inclusive of *The End of Day Reflection.* This daily routine may, in fact, have a very positive effect on any one of your stressors, regardless of the rating you assigned to it.

What I can tell you is that selecting care strategies for helper stress, other than burnout, is fairly straightforward. For example, compassion fatigue can benefit from enhanced self-compassion, mindful self-compassion and/or mindful compassion training in addition to your daily care routine. If these are not helpful then you may need to utilize one of the more formal strategies like DBT. It may take time to find what works best. Burnout is a bit more complex because it is the result of toxic workplace practices such as issues you have little control over, performance behaviors and/or relational issues especially around engagement. Engaging in the practicing of a daily self-care routine will help to buffer some of downsides of this stress, in addition to specific practices resolving these issues. Searching the internet for how others have responded to issues like staff conflict, fairness, workload, supervision, may also prove somewhat helpful. However, if toxic practices and low engagement continues, stress relief will be limited. This is another reason for having a SI, mind-body-spirit self-care approach to living life that defuses the downsides of stress no matter the source.

From This Point Forward

You have abundant information as to what needs your care and those strategies that have proven to be beneficial for many experiencing the stress of helping others. Priorities do change over time, and sometimes suddenly, due to unexpected conditions or situations. That's understandable. What is most important is enhancing and sustaining your self-care, wherever your efforts take you or whatever conditions challenge you. For this reason, it can be helpful to periodically review your self-care efforts. *There is a Self-Care Efforts Checklist in Appendix C-2* that you may find useful and a way to stay focused.

Hopefully, if nothing else, you walk away from this work realizing you do have the resources and the ability to determine what stress can do for you—improve well-being, effectiveness sustainability and self-fulfillment when used as a signal for positive change and growth professionally and personally. From this point on it's all about *effective effort.* Begin by selecting what you believe will be helpful, giving it a try and maybe even *tinkering* with it until the results tell you whether it's helpful or not. If it's not helpful, you take what you learned, *furrow your brow* and start over again until you find what works.

It's all about giving yourself what you deserve—the same compassion, support and attention you work so hard to give others.

References

Amen Clinics. (2024, August 27). *Cognitive Rest: 4 Reasons Why Your Brain Needs a Break.* Retrieved August 18, 2025 from https://www.amenclinics.com/blog/cognitive-rest-4-reasons-why-your-brain-needs-a-break/

Avolio, B. J., & Gardner, W. L. (2005). Authentic leadership development: Getting to the root of positive forms of leadership. *The Leadership Quarterly,* 16(3), 315–338.

Benner, C. (2022, October 26). *Why Is Self-Compassion So Hard for Some People?* Retrieved August 10, 2025 from https://greatergood.berkeley.edu/article/item/why_is_self_compassion _so_hard_for_some_people

Bishop, R. (2023, March 15). *Does Purpose Play a Positive Role in Mental Health?* Retrieved August 25, 2025 from https://www.mayoclinichealthsystem.org/hometown-health/speaking-of-health/purpose-and-mental-health

Brockman, R., Ciarrochi, J., Parker, P., & Kashdan, T. (2023, February). Behaving versus thinking positively: When the benefits of cognitive reappraisal are contingent on satisfying basic psychological needs. *Journal of Behavioral Contextual Science,* 27(11): 120–125. https://doi.org/10.1016/j.jcbs.2023.01.005

Buhle, J., Silvers, J., Wagner, T., Lopez, R., Onyemekwu, C., Kober, H., Weber, J., & Ochsner, K. (2014). Cognitive reappraisal of emotion: A meta-analysis of human neuroimaging studies. *Cerebral Cortex,* 24(11): 2981–2990. https://doi.org/10.1093/cercor/bht154

Conversano, V. (2020, July 30). Mindfulness, compassion and self-compassion among health care professionals: What's new? *Sec. Psychology,* 11(2020): 1683. https://doi.org/10.3389/fpysd.2020.01683

Cowand, A., Amarsaikhan, U., Ricks, R. F., Cash, E. D., & Sephton, S. E. (2024). Self-compassion is associated with improved well-being and healthier cortisol profiles in undergraduate students. *Mindfulness,* 15(7): 1831–1845. https://doi.org/10.1007/s12671-024-02383-w

Crum, A., Akinila, M., Martin, A., & Faith, S. (2017). The role of stress mindset in shaping cognitive, emotional and physiological responses to challenging and threatening stress. *Anxiety, Stress, Coping,* 30(4), 379–395. http//dx.doi.org/10.1080/10615806.2016.2755585

de Witte, M., Spruit, A., van Hooren, S., Moonen, X., & Stams, G-J. (2019). Effects of music intervention on stress related outcomes: a systematic review and two meta-analyses. *Health Psychology Review, 14(*2): 294–324. https://doi.org/10.1080/17437199.2019.1627897

Emmons, R. (2013). Gratitude as a psychotherapeutic intervention. *Journal of Clinical Psychology,* 69(80): 856–855.

Ford, BQ., & Troy, AS. (2019). Reappraisal reconsidered: A close look at the costs of an acclaimed emotional-regulation strategy. *Current Directions in Psychological Science, 28*(2): 195–203.

Forte, T. (2020, October 22). *The Body Keeps Score: Brain, Mind and Body in the Treatment of Trauma (Book Summary).* Retrieved August 14, 2025 from https://fortelabs.com/blog/the-body-keeps-the-score-summary/

Greenberg, S. (2025). *The Importance of Living a Purpose-Driven Life.* Retrieved August 25, 2025 from https://www.viacharacter.org/topics/articles/the-importance-of-living-a-purpose-driven-life

Gupta, S. (2025, July 3). *How Self-reflection Benefits Your Mental Health.* Retrieved August 25, 2025 from https://www.verywellmind.com/self-reflection-importance-benefits-and-strategies-7500858

Hill, D., & Bowman, K. (2025, April 13). *Here's how to train your brain to crave movement more than screen time.* Retrieved August 20, 2025 from https://www.npr.org/2025/04/13/g-s1-59848/sitting-scrolling-screens-brain-exercise-habit

King, J. (2024, Sept 26). *Arts for Well-Being: A Self-Directed Stress Relief Exercise for Local Officials.* Retrieved August 10, 2025 from https://www.nlc.org/article/2024/09/26/arts-for-well-being-a-self-directed-stress-relief-exercise-for-local-officials/

Kirk, B. J., Mavropalias, G., J Blazevich, A. J., Cochrane-Wilke, J. L., Molan, A., & Nosake, K. (2025, March 25). Effects of home based 5-minute eccentric exercise program on physical fitness, body composition, and health in sedentary individuals. *Eur J Appl Physiol,* 125(8): 2241–2255. https://doi.org/10.1007/s00421-025-05757-7

Klynn, B. (2024, November 28). *Emotional Regulation: Skills, Exercises and Strategies.* Retrieved May 5, 2025 from https://www.betterup.com/en-gb/blog/emotional-regulation-skills

Levine, A. (2025, May 12). *Healthy Detachment Without Losing Yourself.: How Therapists Stay Present, Empathetic and Grounded Even in the Toughest Sessions.* Retrieved September 5, 2025 from https://www.psychologytoday.com/gb/blog/things-to-consider/202505/healthy-detachment-caring-without-losing-yourself

Lukenda, K., Sulzenbruck, S., & Sutter, C. (2024). Expressive writing as a practice against work stress: A literature review. *Journal of Workplace Behavioral Health,* 39(2024): 106–137

McDonough, V. T., (2025). *Secondary PTSD or Secondary Traumatic Stress Should Not Be Underestimated.* Retrieved August 25, 2025 from https://www.brainline.org/article/secondary-ptsd-or-secondary-traumatic-stress-should-not-be-underestimated

McGarvie, S. (2025 January 9). *Emotional Regulation: 5 Evidenced Based Emotional Regulation Techniques.* Retrieved August 25, 2025 from https://positivepsychology.com/emotion-regulation/

McRae, K., & Gross, J. (2020). Emotion regulation. *Emotion,* 20(1): 1–9. https//doi.org/10.1037/emo0000703

Margaret J. Wheatly Quotes. (2018). Retrieved November 10, 2018 from https://www.brainyquote.com/authors/margaret_j_wheatley

Miller, M. C. (2012, November 21). *In Praise of Gratitude.* Retrieved September 1, 2025 from https://www.health.harvard.edu/blog/in-praise-of-gratitude-201211215561

Morin, A. (2011). Self-awareness part 1: Definition, measures, effects, functions, and antecedents. *Social and Personality Psychology Compass,* 5(10), 807–823.

Murray, B. (2022, June 27). *Writing to Heal.* Retrieved August 10 from https://www.apa.org/monitor/jun02/writing

Nash, J. (2022, Oct. 16). *Expressive Art Therapy: 15 Creative Activities Techniques.* Retrieved August 10, 2025 from https://positivepsychology.com/expressive-arts-therapy

Pinto, C. T., Velga, F., Guedes, L., Pinto, S., & Nunes, R. (2023, November). Models of spiritual intelligence interventions: A scoping review. *Nurse Education in Practice,* 73(Nov.): 103829. https://doi.org/10.1016/j.nepr.2023.103829

Portocarrero, F. F., Ginzalez, K., & Ekema-Agbaw, M. (2020). A meta-analytic review of the relationship between dispositional gratitude and well-being. *Personality and Individual Differences,* 164(Oct.): 110101. https://doi.org/10.1016/j.paid.2020.110101

Rankin, A., & Fibich, M. (2024). *Transform Stress Crisis & Trauma Through Creativity: An Art Therapy and Writing Workbook to Activate Wellbeing Strategies.* Baltimore, Maryland, Sidran Press.

Sellig, M. (2021, August 23). *10 Powerful Benefits of living With Purpose: Wealth, Health, Longevity and More.* Retrieved August 25, 2025 from https://www.psychologytoday.com/gb/blog/changepower/202108/10-powerful-benefits-of-living-with-purpose

Sloan, D., Marx, B., Lee, D., & Resick, P. (2018, January 17). A brief exposure-based treatment vs cognitive processing therapy for posttraumatic stress disorder: A randomized noninferiority clinical trial. *JAMA Psychiatry,* 75(3): 233–239. https://doi.org/10.1001/jamapsychiatry.2017.4249

Technology Networks. (2023, July 5). *A 5 Minute Unstructured Break Can Help Restore Attention.* Retrieved August 18, 2025 from https://www.technologynetworks.com/neuroscience/news/a-five-minute-unstructured-break-can-help-restore-attention-375755

Thompson, N. M., van Reekum, C. M., & Chakrabarti, B. (2022). Cognitive and affective empathy relate differentially to emotion regulation. *Affective Science,* 3(Nov.), 118–134. https://doi.org/10.1007/s42761-021-00062-w

van der Kolk, B. (2014). *The Body Keeps the Score: Brain, Mind, and Body in the Healing of Trauma.* New York, Penguin Books.

Veerakone, R. (2024 July 8). *A New Strategy to Cope with Emotional Stress.* Retrieved August 25, 2025 from https://news.mit.edu/2024/new-strategy-cope-emotional-stress-0708

Wang, Y. X., & Yang, B. (2023, April 17). A new understanding of the cognitive reappraisal technique: an extension based on the schema theory. *Front Behav Neurosci,.* 17(April): 1174585. https://doi.org/10.3389/fnbeh.2023.1174585

Weir, K. (2019, January 1). *Give Me a Break.* Retrieved August 18, 2025 from https://www.apa.org/monitor/2019/01/break

Wild, C. J, Nichols, E. S., Battista, M. E., Stojanoski, B., & Owen, A. M. (2018). Dissociable effects of self-reported daily sleep duration on high-level cognitive abilities. *Sleep,* 41(12): zsy182. https://doi.org/10.1093/sleep/zsy182

Zucker, R. (2024, December 26). *How to Stop Thinking About Work at 3 A.M.* Retrieved August 10, 2025 from https://hbr.org/2019/12/how-to-stop-thinking-about-work-at-3am

CHAPTER 10

Accessing Additional Sources for Additional Solutions

Theme

Had we had a chance to sit down together and talk about the issues you might be dealing with, I would have certainly provided a number of recommendations. One of those recommendations would be that it is really up to you to determine what may be best for you and then to begin the process of effective effort. Because self-care is a personal issue, you are the best one to determine what resources or approaches to self-care may work best for you. If the recommendations that were made throughout the text are limited or simply do not seem to apply to your situation, I can suggest how you might use the internet to search for additional possibilities and provide a few additional resources you may find helpful

What I Suggest

What I suggest is searching for *free websites that help with (insert topic—compassion fatigue, self-compassion, burnout, toxic workplaces, secondary trauma, etc.).* I would then also search for *free websites that help (insert your profession—first responders, law enforcement, healthcare, etc.) with (topic—secondary trauma, burnout, fatigue, etc.).* One example might be: *free websites that help social workers with compassion fatigue.*

DOI: 10.4324/9781003673699-15

For first responders be specific, for example, *free websites that help . . . (firefighters, police, emergency room nurses, cardiologists, etc.).* These two combined searches will yield some similar sources as well as different ones, so it's to your benefit to conduct two searches. You'll find that many of the sites provide free toolkits, online courses, webinars, YouTube segments, blogs and numerous articles.

Training

You can also search for free websites that provide *free training for compassion, self-compassion, mindful compassion, compassion fatigue, burnout, etc.* The number of excellent resources is amazing.

Specific Behaviors

You may be struggling with a specific issue in any of the areas that were presented. For example, one of the red flags that showed up on the Burnout Scale may have been dealing with staff conflict. Simply search *How to deal with staff conflicts* and you will be presented with a multitude of strategies. You could do the same for self-engagement issues, problems with a supervisor or practices related to fairness. Use the same process for any of the helper stress categories. For example, maybe you're experiencing intrusive thoughts/memories of what you were exposed to while helping someone in distress. Simply search for *help with intrusive thoughts* and again you'll be presented with multiple solutions.

YouTube

And then there's YouTube where you can watch and listen to experts directly for brief periods at a time. It can also be used to access brief segments of meditation or mindfulness, music to calm or to energize your nervous system. *TED Talks* are also a wonderful way to hear from experts in greater depth.

Books

Simply search for *the 10 best books about*. . . Search for them on Amazon, which will usually allow you to read a sufficient enough selection from a book to decide if that's the one for you. Of course, asking colleagues for their recommendation can also be helpful. Several books have also been mentioned in the text because they are rich with help, suggestions and information that matters. I learned a good deal from books over the years. Sometimes it would take several chapters before one statement jumped out, as if it were written for me personally, and proved quite helpful. My favorites in the area of stress are *The Body Keeps the Score* by Bessel van der Kolk, *A Boy Raised as a Dog* by Bruce Perry, *Magical Moments of Change* by Lenore Terr, *Man's Search for Meaning* by Viktor Frankl, *In an Unspoken Voice* by Peter Levine, T*he Upside of Stress* by Kelly McGonigal, *Trauma and Expressive Arts Therapy* by Cathy Malchiodi, *Radical Self-Care for Helpers, Healers and Changemakers* by Nicole Steward, *Transform Stress, Crisis & Trauma Through Creativity* by Rankin & Fibich, and Anna Baranowsky & Eric Gentry's (2026 pending publication) *Cognitive Behavioral Somatic Therapy Skills Workbook for PTSD.* All are inspirational in the hope they provide and practical with the techniques they present. Of course, there are many others that are equally helpful. Search until you find what fits you best.

Apps

I am not an app person. Relying on some device to tell me it's time to breathe or stretch means I'm not getting good at listening to the wisdom of my body. However, something is better than nothing, if that something helps you to relax, refocus, etc. I would just recommend it as a way to start a habit until you become your own app. The only three I would recommend, because the reports by reputable folks are very good, are Virgin Pulse, Calm and Happify.

Getting Help

If what you are learning or trying is not helping, or even making it worse, do please seek help from credentialed and certified professionals by searching *professional helpers for (compassion fatigue, etc.) near me.* Share what's happening with colleagues; you'll find you are not alone. The support of others is always beneficial.

Additional Resources I Found Useful

To save time searching various titles, Google the titles below to access numerous self-care practices in many of the areas evaluated in the assessments you completed.

17 ways to take care of yourself
Changing Our Perceptions
Finding Inner Calm jackkornfield.com
Finding Purpose Strategies
How To Overcome Empathy Overwhelm
Overcoming Burnout in the Workplace
The Mindful Self-Compassion Program
Websites: Using the websites listed below simply type in a topic as needed. For example, *BetterUp Compassion Fatigue or Polyvagal Institute Exercises.* Each site will generate a number of resources.

A Caregiver's Toolbox, Carol Bradley Bursack	American Institute of Stress
American Psychological Association (APA)	BetterUp
Brain First Institute	CoffeePals
Engagement Multiplier	Forbes Leadership
Gallup Press	Griefworkcenter.com
Harvard Health, Harvard Education	Mental Health Today
Traumatology Institute	Mindful Compassion Focused Therapy
National Center for PTSD	Polyvagal Institute
Very Well Mind	Psychology Today
SAMHSA	The Stress and Resilience Institute
Mindful Awareness in Body-Oriented Therapy (MBAT)	Positive Psychology-Stress and Burnout Prevention

A final word of encouragement: May your self-care journey bring you the best of what you deserve in your personal and professional lives.

References

Baranowsky, A. B., & Gentry, E. J. (2026). *Cognitive Behavioral Somatic Therapy Skills Workbook for PTSD.* Oakland, CA, New Harbinger Publications.
Frankl, V. E. (2006). *Man's Search for Meaning.* Boston, MA, Beacon Press.
Levine, P. A. (2010). *In an Unspoken Voice: How the Body Releases Trauma and Restores Goodness.* Berkeley, CA, North Atlantic Books.
Malchiodi, C. A. (2020). *Trauma and Expressive Arts Therapy: Brain, Body, and Imagination in the Healing Process.* NY, Guilford Press.

McGonigal, K. (2015). *The Upside of Stress: Why Stress is Good for You, and How to Get Good At It.* NY, Avery.

Perry, B. D., & Szalavitz, M. (2006). *The Boy Who Was Raised as a Dog: And Other Stories from a Child Psychiatrist's Notebook.* NY, Basic Books.

Rankin, L., & Fibich, T. (2023). *Transform Stress, Crisis & Trauma Through Creativity: Creative Interventions for Mental Health Professionals.* NY, Routledge.

Steward, N. (2021). *Radical Self-Care for Helpers, Healers, and Changemakers.* San Jose, CA, Nicole Steward Consulting.

Terr, L. C. (1990). *Magical Moments of Change: How Psychotherapy Turns Kids Around.* NY, W. W. Norton.

van der Kolk, B. A. (2014). The Body Keeps the Score: Brain, Mind, and Body in the Healing of Trauma. NY, Viking.

Appendix A-1

Chapter 4: Activity 2—Toxic Workplace Stress Survey

(The following toxic workplace conditions that trigger stress are adapted from the following sources: Gallup, 2016; Stone, 2024; Heinz, 2024; DSG Global 2025.)

Simply check or circle the number that applies to your workplace. If your immediate response to a question is *somewhat* consider it a *yes* response as multiple *somewhat* responses equals toxicity. (The term "client" refers to anyone you are helping or responding to.)

1. My workload is constantly heavy.
2. Most days I feel time pressures for all I have to do.
3. I have little say as to how I do my job.
4. I go hours with little social contact from other employees.
5. The majority of clients I see or conditions I respond to are stressful.
6. I respond to the same client issues every day; there's little variety.
7. I often work through lunch.
8. I am expected to respond to work-related texts/emails outside work hours.
9. Managers/supervisors are difficult to access. They seem too busy to take time for me.
10. Supervision is inadequate.
11. My voice doesn't matter much.

12. I am not reimbursed for outside training pertinent to what I do.
13. I am not provided time for regular skill building training.
14. There's very little flexibility in my workplace.
15. Once assigned a supervisor, I cannot change to another if issues arise.
16. I have little control over my work and or those I am asked to help.
17. There is little recognition for what I do.
18. My boss sees my results and gives me more work, not new opportunities.
19. There's a lot of gossiping and complaining in my workplace.
20. Manager/supervisor shows favoritism with some employees
21. Expectations of me are erratic.
22. I'm not sure what values my workplace supports.
23. There is little employee social interaction during or after work hours.
24. Performance evaluations are not based on preset agreed upon, measurable objectives.
25. There is a lot of negativity.
26. Performance evaluation criteria are unclear.
27. I observe others doing what I consider inappropriate as a helper.
28. Educational resources pertinent to my work are lacking.
29. There is very little participation in decision-making.
30. There are fellow employees not being held to the same standards expected of me.
31. We are sometimes criticized publicly for what we did or didn't do.
32. Other employees work late or on weekends.
33. There's little promotion from within.
34. Less experienced employees are promoted over more experienced ones.
35. We are all off doing our own thing, not as a team supporting one another.
36. Limited benefits place additional stress on me financially.
37. Some of what I am expected to do with or about clients goes against my values.
38. There always seems to be changes being made in policies, practices, reporting, etc.
39. Rarely do leaders engage with us, ask for our opinions, problem solve together.
40. I am micromanaged, given little room to try different ways to help others.

Scoring

This is not a diagnostic tool but a way to help reflect on your environment's source of stress.

Simply add the total number of items checked/circled and record that number below.

Minimal 1–10 ______, Concerning 11–19 ______, Toxic 20+ ______

***If you circled either #27 or #37 please record your response on the Stage Three Worksheet in Appendix B-3b*

Interpretation

A score of 1–10 reflects some toxicity. Your satisfaction associated with accomplishing your purpose in that environment may allow you to tolerate and manage without experiencing burnout. However, stay alert to new stress reactions and or changes in workplace practices especially related to burnout.

A score of 11–20 reflects concern over toxicity and its impact on your stress levels that needs additional evaluation for other contributing factors presented in this work to determine added stressors that can intensify the impact of these toxic stress sources. This will be done in Chapter Eight.

A score of 20 or above reflects workplace toxicity as a major contributor to dissatisfaction, higher stress and greater vulnerability to compassion fatigue and the downsides of stress inclusive of performance. It also should raise the question, "Should I find a different workplace environment?" especially if you cannot say you are satisfied despite these factors. *It's also important to reflect on each item checked as any one item could be causing you enough stress to be thinking about finding a new workplace or even interfering with home-life balance.

References

DSG Global. (2025). Four Questions to Ask Before the Great Resignation. Retrieved April 14, 2025 from www.dsgco.com>focus-questions-to-ask-before-

Gallup (2016). Why is Employee Engagement So Important? Retrieved July 11, 2025 from https://www.engagementmultiplier.com/blog/why-is-employee-engagement-so-important/

Heinz, K. (2024). Toxic Work Environment: 18 Examples and How to Improve It. Retrieved May 20, 2025 from https://builtin.com>bad-company-culture

Stone, K. (2024). Transforming a Toxic Workplace Culture. Retrieved May 26, 2025 from https://diversio.com>toxic-workplace-culture

Appendix A-2

Chapter 5: Activity 1—Self-Engagement Survey

Self-Engagement Survey
© 2025 Steele

The items in this scale reflect the items most frequently cited in sources identifying characteristics of engagement (Quantum Workplace, 2025; Harvard Business Review, 2021; Gallup, 2016; Engagement Multiplier, 2014). It is not a diagnostic tool but an indicator of the level of engagement, which is associated with wellness, well-being, sustained effectiveness, self-fulfillment, retention and support of the organization.

1. Am I aware of the expectations of my job? Yes___ Somewhat ___ Rarely ___
2. Am I supported by leadership/manager/supervisor to help meet these expectations? Yes___ Somewhat ___ Rarely___
3. Is my progress, my efforts, the work I do discussed/reviewed at least every two weeks? Yes___ Somewhat___ Rarely___
4. Am I given opportunities to enhance/develop my skills? Yes___ Somewhat ___ Rarely___
5. Are my peers supportive in helpful ways to me? Yes___ Somewhat___ Rarely___
6. Do I feel my "voice", my comments and opinions are taken seriously? Yes___ Somewhat___ Rarely___

7. My supervisor/manager connects/checks with me via email, text, phone, a brief note or brief visit regularly without micromanaging? Yes__ Somewhat___ Rarely___
8. Leadership demonstrates its concern for my well-being? Yes___ Somewhat___ Rarely___
9. I feel appreciated/recognized for the work I am doing? Yes___ Somewhat___ Rarely___
10. I enjoy working in this organization? Yes___ Somewhat___ Rarely___
11. I think about getting another job weekly___, monthly ___, every few months ___, rarely ___?

Scoring

A. Add the number of "Yes" responses to the first 10 statements.
Total = ___ (Very engaged)
B. Add the number of "Somewhat" responses to the first 10 statements.
Total = ___ (Only somewhat engaged)
C. Add the number of "Rarely" responses to the first 10 statements.
Total = ___ (Rarely engaged)

#11. If you are thinking about looking for another job weekly add "4" to category "C" total; if monthly add "3" to total. If thinking about looking for another job every few months add "2" to category "B" total. If rarely thinking about another job add "2" to category "A"

The highest total represents the level of engagement. *Yes* responses for #s 1–10 are favorable responses.

My level of engagement ____________________________________

Positive engagement generally supports retention, higher levels of performance and engaging in activities that support the organization with minimal stress. *Somewhat* engagement will be reflected in more sporadic performance and attendance, less involvement in support of the organization, more frequent thoughts/searches for another job and a higher stress level. *Rarely* is not beneficial to your well-being.

References

Engagement Multiplier. (2014). *Employee Engagement vs. Employee Well-being.* Accessed Dec. 16, 2025. https://www.engagementmultiplier.com/blog/employee-engagement-vs-employee-well/

Gallup (2016). *Why is Employee Engagement So Important?* Retrieved July 11, 2017 from https://www.engagementmultiplier.com/.../why-is-employee-engagement-so-important.

Harvard Business Review. 2021 How Companies Can Improve Employee Engagement. Retrieved April 12, 2025 from https://hbr.org>2021/10>how>companies-can-improv...

Quantum Workplace: What Is Employee Engagement? Retrieved January 15, 2025. https://www.quantumworkplace.com>future-of-work

Appendix A-3

Chapter 5: Activity 2—Employees Will Engage When

Simply circle the corresponding number to those statements that reflect your culture.

Employees will engage when leaders

1. encourage collaboration, working together as a team,
2. are respectful and considerate of each other,
3. give and seek useful feedback from one another as needed,
4. stress the importance of quality service and provide ongoing resources that support service quality,
5. demonstrate their passion for quality at all levels,
6. keep employees informed about what is occurring in the organization and consistently report on its strengths, what is being accomplished with clients and in the community (To be engaged employees need to feel proud of their organization and that they are part of something larger than themselves.),
7. have the tough conversations about employees taking responsibility for resolving conflict among themselves rather than shifting blame or complaining to others,

8. encourage staff, when mistakes are made, to immediately bring them to the attention of their supervisor/manager so they can be corrected quickly and become teachable moments for all to learn from,
9. encourage employees to share their ideas, seek new experiences within the organization and take the initiative to improve skills,
10. develop a culture where employees feel safe (physically, emotionally, mentally) and connected to the mission, values and beliefs of the organization.

Employees Will Engage When Their Supervisor/Manager

11. identifies problem areas and possible ways to correct those problems, for example time management techniques, completing written records (It's amazing how many employees can verbalize client interactions but find it difficult to translate those interactions into writing. It takes practice and support for some to become comfortable and confident with preparing written documents.),
12. establishes monthly progress goals,
13. provides information and resources related to the work they do but also to help enhance their professional growth,
14. assists them with their self-care/well-being needs and strategies.
15. addresses their strengths,
16. helps them find ways to improve on those strengths,
17. helps them find ways to utilize those strengths in the workplace (Opportunities might include mentoring newer employees, writing and presenting reports about new trends, what other similar organizations have found helpful, preparing YouTube segments, conducting trainings, completing certification training; the opportunities are endless. Employees will have suggestions of their own that, when allowed to pursue, will further enhance their level of engagement.),
18. hears weekly from their supervisors/managers via face-to-face, email or text or through the organization's social network.

We all have four universal brain-based needs (Brendtro & Mitchell, 2015; van Bockern & McDonald, 2015). These needs are belonging, mastery, independence and generosity. When these are acknowledged, we connect with and feel cared for (engaged) by those who take the time to meet our needs. These needs can be easily addressed on a regular basis. Examples are listed below. Check those needs your culture fulfills.

Employees Will Engage When Their Universal Needs Are Being Met

19. Mary: It is always good to see you (Belonging),
20. Lorenzo: I didn't realize how much you know about . . . (Mastery),
21. Juanita: I really appreciated the way you took the initiative to . . . (Independence),
22. Chris: That was really nice, the way you helped out Susan (Generosity).

Scoring

Count the number of practices circled and then place that total in the appropriate category.

Little Engagement 1–8 _____, Somewhat Engaged 9–13_____, Very Engaged 14–22 _____

*This is not a formal tool. It is meant as guide. However, it does reflect the level of engagement you may be experiencing. You want to be at least *somewhat* engaged; *Somewhat* engaged may be workable if burnout factors are minimal, and you are experiencing a sense of fulfillment and support in areas important to you. However, this level of engagement suggests there are problems with toxicity or the lack of support for your wellness and well-being. If the total for *Little* and *Somewhat* is higher than the total for *Very* engaged, vulnerability to burnout and compassion fatigue is high.

References

Brendtro, L., Mitchell, M. (2015). Deep Brain Learning: Evidence-Based Essentials in Education, Treatment, and Youth Development. Albion, MI: Starr Commonwealth.

van Bockern, S., and McDonald, T. (2015). Creating circle of courage schools. Reclaiming Children and Youth, 20(4), 13–17.

Appendix A-4

Chapter 5: Activity 3—Burnout Assessment

The Burnout Assessment is based on research findings across the globe. The Burnout Assessment is comprised of two parts.

1. The Professional Profile looks at six work categories that can contribute to burnout. The following categories are based on the research of Christina Maslach and Michael P. Leiter. All questions are original content.
   a) Workload refers to the amount of work one is responsible for managing.
   b) Control refers to the level of autonomy one experiences at work.
   c) Reward refers to the intrinsic and extrinsic edification of one's work.
   d) Community refers to the quality of the relationship between one's manager, co-workers and employer.

   e) Fairness refers to equity across economic, gender and ethnic lines and the opportunity for upward mobility.
   f) Values refers to one's personal values in relation to the organization's values.
2. The Personal Profile looks at five categories of well-being that can be affected by your work.
   a) Physical well-being.
   b) Mental well-being.
   c) Emotional well-being.
   d) Spiritual well-being.
   e) Relational well-being.

Each category consists of ten questions, for a total of 110 questions. Read each statement carefully and answer on a scale of 1–10.

1 = Disagree & 10 = Agree. The scale is on a continuum, with 5 being neutral or unable to decide. Please avoid using N/A (not applicable) as much as possible for greater accuracy.

Example 1

I spend time with close friends regularly.

Disagree Neutral Agree
1 2 3 4 5 6 7 8 9 10 N/A

Example 2

I do not think about unfinished work after leaving for the day.

Disagree Neutral Agree
1 2 3 4 5 6 7 8 9 10 N/A

At the end of each category, calculate your score by adding the number you have chosen in each line. Here is an example:

I do not think about unfinished work after leaving for the day.
1 2 **3** 4 5 6 7 8 9 10 N/A

My workplace invests in my professional growth.
1 2 3 4 5 6 7 **8** 9 10 N/A

I enjoy working with my manager & co-workers.
1 2 3 4 5 **6** 7 8 9 10 N/A

Add up your score. Total: **17** / 30

How to Use the Assessment at Work

The Burnout Assessment provides an effective tool for evaluating employee burnout risk, thereby providing a wealth of information to help prevent burnout on your team. Burnout is more than just a work-life balance issue. It reflects company culture priorities around workload, autonomy, reward, connection, equity and values. Employee wellness incorporates both healthy workplace culture and personal self-care. The first step is opening the conversation with employees about burnout. This assessment provides you with essential questions that uncover relevant information for understanding the strains and stress within your organization. Learn what causes your employees the most significant stress so you can implement effective measures. This can positively impact employee well-being and increase productivity. Further, you can prevent costly leaves of absence and termination by stopping burnout before it happens. Happy, healthy employees create healthy organizations that thrive. If you have any questions, please reach out to us at https://www.break-through.ca/contact.

Disclaimer

The Burnout Assessment does not provide a diagnosis. The scores do not reflect any particular diagnosis or course of treatment. The Burnout Assessment is a tool to help assess burnout potential using a series of questions. If you have concerns about your health, well-being, mental health, or if you think you may be experiencing burnout, please contact your medical doctor.

The information contained herein is not offered as a substitute for professional mental health or medical care and is not intended to diagnose, treat or cure any mental health or medical conditions. Please consult with your physician or mental health care provider before making changes to your lifestyle.

Burnout Assessment

Professional Section—WORKLOAD Disagree Agree

1. I have the capacity to keep up with my work & do so with excellence.
   1 2 3 4 5 6 7 8 9 10 N/A
2. I have the training necessary to excel at my job.
   1 2 3 4 5 6 7 8 9 10 N/A

3. I do not feel burned out from my work.
   1 2 3 4 5 6 7 8 9 10 N/A
4. I am able to finish my responsibilities without working overtime.
   1 2 3 4 5 6 7 8 9 10 N/A
5. I have time to plan and prioritize my work.
   1 2 3 4 5 6 7 8 9 10 N/A
6. I have time to work on my most important responsibilities.
   1 2 3 4 5 6 7 8 9 10 N/A
7. I do not take work home to complete on evenings, weekends, or vacations.
   1 2 3 4 5 6 7 8 9 10 N/A
8. I do not think about unfinished work after leaving for the day.
   1 2 3 4 5 6 7 8 9 10 N/A
9. I have the support & resources needed to perform my job with excellence.
   1 2 3 4 5 6 7 8 9 10 N/A
10. My work does not take precedence over my personal interests.
   1 2 3 4 5 6 7 8 9 10 N/A

Total Score ______/100

CONTROL Disagree Agree

1. I can handle the pace & my amount of work long term.
   1 2 3 4 5 6 7 8 9 10 N/A
2. My work environment & tasks feel predictable.
   1 2 3 4 5 6 7 8 9 10 N/A
3. I am equipped to meet the challenges of my work.
   1 2 3 4 5 6 7 8 9 10 N/A
4. I have clarity regarding expectations & priorities.
   1 2 3 4 5 6 7 8 9 10 N/A
5. Communication in my organization is effective, authentic, clear & adequate.
   1 2 3 4 5 6 7 8 9 10 N/A
6. I feel positive about my job.
   1 2 3 4 5 6 7 8 9 10 N/A
7. I have influence with my team.
   1 2 3 4 5 6 7 8 9 10 N/A
8. I have control over where, when & how I do my work.
   1 2 3 4 5 6 7 8 9 10 N/A
9. I have a proper work setup to perform my responsibilities.
   1 2 3 4 5 6 7 8 9 10 N/A

10. I have adequate decision-making influence over my work.
    1 2 3 4 5 6 7 8 9 10 N/A

Total Score ______/100

REWARD Disagree Agree

1. I feel inspired and take pride in my work.
   1 2 3 4 5 6 7 8 9 10 N/A
2. I make a significant contribution at work.
   1 2 3 4 5 6 7 8 9 10 N/A
3. I feel my effort is noticed & rewarded.
   1 2 3 4 5 6 7 8 9 10 N/A
4. My manager or team encourages & appreciates my efforts.
   1 2 3 4 5 6 7 8 9 10 N/A
5. I feel fairly compensated monetarily for my work.
   1 2 3 4 5 6 7 8 9 10 N/A
6. I receive adequate health benefits to support myself & family.
   1 2 3 4 5 6 7 8 9 10 N/A
7. I can save for the future rather than living from paycheck to paycheck.
   1 2 3 4 5 6 7 8 9 10 N/A
8. My workplace invests in my professional growth.
   1 2 3 4 5 6 7 8 9 10 N/A
9. I feel appreciated for my contribution to my team or organization.
   1 2 3 4 5 6 7 8 9 10 N/A
10. I have sufficient time away from work & feel in control of my time off.
    1 2 3 4 5 6 7 8 9 10 N/A

Total Score ______/100

COMMUNITY Disagree Agree

1. I enjoy working with my manager/supervisor & co-workers.
   1 2 3 4 5 6 7 8 9 10 N/A
2. The culture of my organization is positive.
   1 2 3 4 5 6 7 8 9 10 N/A
3. I do not get irritated easily by my work or co-workers.
   1 2 3 4 5 6 7 8 9 10 N/A
4. I treat people at work with care & respect.
   1 2 3 4 5 6 7 8 9 10 N/A
5. I feel comfortable sharing my concerns with my manager.
   1 2 3 4 5 6 7 8 9 10 N/A
6. I feel heard & that my voice counts with my manager & team.
   1 2 3 4 5 6 7 8 9 10 N/A

7. I feel psychologically safe at work.
   1 2 3 4 5 6 7 8 9 10 N/A
8. I trust my co-workers.
   1 2 3 4 5 6 7 8 9 10 N/A
9. My co-workers do not adversely affect my work.
   1 2 3 4 5 6 7 8 9 10 N/A
10. My team is free from conflict.
   1 2 3 4 5 6 7 8 9 10 N/A

Total Score ______/100

FAIRNESS Disagree Agree

1. I feel compensated relative to others in my organization & field.
   1 2 3 4 5 6 7 8 9 10 N/A
2. I have adequate opportunities to move upward in my organization.
   1 2 3 4 5 6 7 8 9 10 N/A
3. I feel respected regardless of my gender or sexual orientation.
   1 2 3 4 5 6 7 8 9 10 NA
4. I have the same opportunities as people of other genders or orientations.
   1 2 3 4 5 6 7 8 9 10 NA
5. I feel respected regardless of my spiritual orientation.
   1 2 3 4 5 6 78 9 10 N/A
6. I have the same opportunities as people of other spiritual orientations.
   1 2 3 4 5 6 7 8 9 10 N/A
7. I feel respected regardless of my ethnic identity.
   1 2 3 4 5 6 78 9 10 N/A
8. I have the same opportunities as people of other ethnicities.
   1 2 3 4 5 6 7 8 9 10 N/A
9. My organization wholeheartedly embraces diversity, equity & inclusion.
   1 2 3 4 5 6 7 8 9 10 N/A
10. I can climb the ladder at work while keeping my integrity.
   1 2 3 4 5 6 7 8 9 10 N/A

Total Score ______/100

VALUES Disagree Agree

1. My personal values align with the values of my organization.
   1 2 3 4 5 6 7 8 9 10 N/A
2. My organization's mission, vision, & values are authentically lived out.
   1 2 3 4 5 6 7 8 9 10 N/A
3. My responsibilities align with my organization's values.
   1 2 3 4 5 6 7 8 9 10 N/A

4. I am treated with respect at work.
   1 2 3 4 5 6 7 8 9 10 N/A
5. Team successes are acknowledged & shared by the entire team.
   1 2 3 4 5 6 7 8 9 10 N/A
6. I make a positive contribution to my organization.
   1 2 3 4 5 6 7 8 9 10 N/A
7. I make a positive contribution to society through my work.
   1 2 3 4 5 6 7 8 9 10 N/A
8. I feel engaged in my role at work.
   1 2 3 4 5 6 7 8 9 10 N/A
9. My organization's goals fit well with my career ambitions.
   1 2 3 4 5 6 7 8 9 10 N/A
10. I am growing personally & professionally within my organization.
    1 2 3 4 5 6 7 8 9 10 N/A

Total ______/100

Personal Section - PHYSICAL WELL-BEING Disagree Agree

1. I sleep well & feel rested upon waking.
   1 2 3 4 5 6 7 8 9 10 N/A
2. I do not experience stress-related dreams or nightmares.
   1 2 3 4 5 6 7 8 9 10 N/A
3. I exercise at least three times per week.
   1 2 3 4 5 6 7 8 9 10 N/A
4. I generally feel healthy & well.
   1 2 3 4 5 6 7 8 9 10 N/A
5. I am satisfied with my level of health.
   1 2 3 4 5 6 7 8 9 10 N/A
6. I do not get sick more often than I used to.
   1 2 3 4 5 6 7 8 9 10 N/A
7. I rarely take sick days due to work-related stress.
   1 2 3 4 5 6 7 8 9 10 N/A
8. I do not feel physically run down or drained.
   1 2 3 4 5 6 7 8 9 10 N/A
9. I feel good about my current energy levels.
   1 2 3 4 5 6 7 8 9 10 N/A
10. I have the energy required to work at peak performance & feel good outside of work.
    1 2 3 4 5 6 7 8 9 10 N/A

Total Score ______/100

MENTAL WELL-BEING Disagree Agree

1. The stress I experience feels manageable long-term.
   1 2 3 4 5 6 78 9 10 N/A
2. I do not feel mentally run down or drained.
   1 2 3 4 5 6 7 8 9 10 N/A
3. My mind is calm & at rest most of the time.
   1 2 3 4 5 6 7 8 9 10 N/A
4. I feel hopeful & optimistic about the future.
   1 2 3 4 5 6 7 8 9 10 N/A
5. I do not think about my work during my time off.
   1 2 3 4 5 6 78 9 10 N/A
6. I have good boundaries between work & the rest of my life.
   1 2 3 4 5 6 7 8 9 10 N/A
7. I turn off my cell notifications at night.
   1 2 3 4 5 6 7 8 9 10 N/A
8. My thoughts toward both my job & my life are positive.
   1 2 3 4 5 6 7 8 9 10 N/A
9. I know & utilize effective stress management techniques.
   1 2 3 4 5 6 7 8 9 10 N/A
10. I do not feel anxious or depressed due to work-related stress.
    1 2 3 4 5 6 7 8 9 10 N/A

Total Score ______/100

EMOTIONAL WELL-BEING Disagree Agree

1. I do not feel emotionally run down or drained.
   1 2 3 4 5 6 7 8 9 10 N/A
2. I have fun & engage in restorative activities daily.
   1 2 3 4 5 6 7 8 9 10 N/A
3. I feel peaceful & calm most of the time.
   1 2 3 4 5 6 7 8 9 10 N/A
4. I feel positive about my work-life balance.
   1 2 3 4 5 6 7 8 9 10 N/A
5. I have designated screen-free time every day.
   1 2 3 4 5 6 7 8 9 10 N/A
6. I enjoy my job & do not feel like quitting.
   1 2 3 4 5 6 7 8 9 10 N/A
7. I have enough emotional reserve for family & friends.
   1 2 3 4 5 6 7 8 9 10 N/A

8. When I wake up in the morning, I feel excited about work.
   1 2 3 4 5 6 7 8 9 10 N/A
9. I engage in a creative outlet weekly.
   1 2 3 4 5 6 7 8 9 10 N/A
10. I have strong self-confidence.
    1 2 3 4 5 6 7 8 9 10 N/A

Total ______/100

SPIRITUAL WELL-BEING Disagree Agree

1. I volunteer at something that feels fulfilling.
   1 2 3 4 5 6 7 8 9 10 N A
2. I invest in personal growth weekly.
   1 2 3 4 5 6 7 8 9 10 N/A
3. I actively engage in spiritual practice.
   1 2 3 4 5 6 7 8 9 10 N/A
4. I regularly enjoy inspiring texts, podcasts or music.
   1 2 3 4 5 6 7 8 9 10 N/A
5. I feel connected to a faith community.
   1 2 3 4 5 6 7 8 9 10 N/A
6. I know I have intrinsic worth outside of what I accomplish.
   1 2 3 4 5 6 7 8 9 10 N/A
7. I do not feel shame or guilt related to my work.
   1 2 3 4 5 6 7 8 9 10 N/A
8. I have time & energy to passionately engage in a cause outside of work.
   1 2 3 4 5 6 7 8 9 10 N/A
9. I find meaning in something greater than myself.
   1 2 3 4 5 6 7 8 9 10 N/A
10. I spend time in nature every week.
    1 2 3 4 5 6 7 8 9 10 N/A

Total ______/100

RELATIONAL WELL-BEING Disagree Agree

1. I spend time with close friends regularly.
   1 2 3 4 5 6 7 8 9 10 N/A
2. I spend time with close family or people whom I identify as family.
   1 2 3 4 5 6 7 8 9 10 N/A
3. I have a rich & rewarding social life.
   1 2 3 4 5 6 7 8 9 10 N/A

4. My work hours make it easy to connect with loved ones on weekends and holidays.
   1 2 3 4 5 6 7 8 9 10 N/A
5. I make a positive contribution to another person's life.
   1 2 3 4 5 6 7 8 9 10 N/A
6. I feel loved & appreciated.
   1 2 3 4 5 6 7 8 9 10 N/A
7. I feel physically & psychologically safe in my relationships outside work.
   1 2 3 4 5 6 7 8 9 10 N/A
8. I rarely feel alone or isolated.
   1 2 3 4 5 6 7 8 9 10 N/A
9. I have enough time for my family & friends.
   1 2 3 4 5 6 7 8 9 10 N/A
10. I have enough energy for my family & friends.
   1 2 3 4 5 6 7 8 9 10 N/A

Total ______/100

NOTES

SCORING & INTERPRETATION

Scoring serves as a guide rather than a definitive measure. The numbers provide objective data to encourage investigation into the reasons behind the score. Generally, a higher score indicates greater health in that area. For mid to low scores, it's important to ask insightful questions to uncover the reasons for lower overall, category and red-flag scores. Lastly, the measure provides trajectory data when repeated over time, such as quarterly, or on a biannual, or annual basis.

YOUR OVERALL SCORE

Add the category totals together. This total provides overall score out of a possible 1100 (11 categories x 10 questions for a possible 10 points per question).

900–1100 out of 1100 is ideal. You are doing well overall in terms of burnout risk.

601–899 out of 1100 means you have areas of concern that could potentially lead to burnout if not addressed. Now is the time to implement prevention measures.

1–600 out of 1100 means your burnout risk is moderate to high. Your challenges may indicate you are experiencing burnout or could potentially lead to it. Now is the time to implement measures to prevent and overcome burnout.

YOUR OVERALL SCORE___________/1100

CATEGORY SCORE

Beyond your overall score, it is important to note any category with a total under **70 out of 100.**

Your score may be 80 out of 100 in one category but only 30 in another. You can begin to implement measures to prevent burnout for the low category.

CATEGORIES UNDER 70/100

RED FLAGS

Finally, note any individual question you scored at a 7 or under. This indicates a warning sign to take seriously and start implementing measures to improve this score. Red flags indicate a larger issue that, if neglected, can grow over time.

RED FLAGS UNDER 7

This author's suggestion: Given that the accumulation of scores across categories could also reflect burnout risks, I suggest using the following overall category scores as well.

Workplace Score	Possible Total—600 for all 6 categories
(Six Categories)	____ 500–600 Ideal
	____ 400–499 Concerning
	____ 1–399 At risk

PERSONAL STRESS CATEGORY BO SCORES—FIVE CATEGORIES

Total possible score 500
Your total score _____400–500 Ideal
_____200–400 Concerning
_____200 and below At Risk

Categories 70 or under-name & score

____________________, ____________________

____________________, ____________________

Personal BO Red Fag 7 or under statements

____________________, ____________________

____________________, ____________________

Record all scores on the Stage Two Scoring Outcome Worksheet in Appendix B-3a and then return to the chapter for further comments.

Reference

Bonita, E. (2022, January). Burnout Assessment. Retrieved May 5, 2025, from https://www.break-through.ca/burnout-assessment.

Appendix A-5

Chapter 6: Activity 1—STS Reactions

Prepared 2025 by Dr. William Steele

The criteria for Secondary Traumatic Stress (STS) consist of symptoms of intrusion, avoidance, arousal and alteration in cognition and mood. Unlike PTSD there is no specific number of symptoms required to meet STS diagnosis. *STS is the result of indirect exposure experienced via a client's story, or what you witnessed when responding to a situation that was traumatic and/or hearing about the trauma of a close family member or friend.* In other words, you were not directly victimized.

STS can have a sudden onset, for example listening to one client's experience, or develop over multiple indirect exposures. This is not a diagnostic tool. The items have been adapted from Bride's STS scale (Bride et al., 2004) and the most current DSM-5-TR (American Psychiatric Association, 2013) criteria for PTSD which added criteria "D", alterations in cognitions and mood.

Directions: Simply check those reactions under each category that you are experiencing and then review scoring instructions for results.

Intrusion

___ I have unexpected upsetting thoughts/memories/images of what happened with/to clients.

___ At times it feels like I am experiencing what my client experienced.

___ I think about what happened to some clients even when I do not want to.
___ I sometimes have disturbing dreams related to client situations/materials.
___ I have unwanted, strong physical reactions (heart pounding, sweating, etc.) when something or someone reminds of that traumatic situation.
___ Things that remind me of that situation causes me unwanted distress.

Avoidance

___ I am avoiding people, places, situations, reading of material that reminds me of traumatic client situations.
___ I avoid certain clients/client conditions that remind me of that trauma situation.
___ I find I am not socializing as much as I used to.
___ I find I'm not as active as I have been in the past.
___ There are times when I try to move clients away from talking about what happened because I do not want to hear it.
___ I'm drinking more and or using other substances to get me through.

Arousal

___ I'm jumpy, easily startled.
___ I'm irritated more often.
___ I'm having trouble sleeping.
___ It feels like I'm constantly ready or waiting for something bad to happen.
___ It's harder to concentrate, to focus.

Cognitive or Mood Changes

___ I find that at times I'm numb, detached.
___ I have more negative thoughts about myself, others or life since this happened.
___ It's harder to be positive about people, places, things.
___ I'm not doing the things I once enjoyed doing.
___ There are things I can't remember as to what happened with clients.
___ I'm blaming myself or others for what happened.

Scoring:

Record number of items checked under each category.

Intrusion ____, Avoidance ____, Arousal ____, Cognitive/Mood alterations ____

If you are experiencing at least one reaction in intrusion and avoidance, two or more under arousal and alterations in cognitions and mood, further screening is recommended to determine if you may be also experiencing PTSD. Keep in mind that there remains a great deal of discussion as to what constitutes STS and the gap between STS and PTSD. **What matters** is that you take whatever reactions you checked seriously and discuss them with your supervisor or an outside trauma specialist if you do not feel comfortable bringing them to your supervisor. In most cases brief intervention can help resolve STS reactions if present, additional efforts may be needed to treat PTSD.

All professionals experience the reactions listed above at some point. If you are having a stressful time in your personal life, it certainly will be harder to deal with client traumas or situations. There will be some clients who call that cause you, on a stressful day, to say "not today". However, when experiencing STS you will have multiple reactions across the above categories. Your reactions may follow interaction with one client or they be as a result of assisting and or responding to multiple clients/situations over time.

References

American Psychiatric Association. (2013). Diagnostic and Statistical Manual of Mental Disorders (5th ed.). Washington, DC, American Psychiatric Publishing.

Bride, B.E., Robinson, M.R., Yegidis, B., & Figley, C.R. (2004). Development and validation of the Secondary Traumatic Stress Scale. Research on Social Work Practice, 14, 27–35.

Appendix A-6

Chapter 6: Activity 2—NCTSN Core Competencies of Trauma-Informed Supervisors

Reprinted with permission from NCTSN Core Competencies for Secondary Trauma-Informed Supervision
https://www.nctsn.org/resources/using-secondary-traumatic-stress-core-competencies-trauma-informed-supervision

Adapted as a Checklist Form retaining all original content. *If leadership is seeking supervisors who are trauma-informed, this is an excellent tool for evaluating candidate competency. Trauma-informed supervisors need to be competent in all nine areas. Supervisees should expect their supervisor to engage these practices and/or provide the information as described below.

Directions: As a supervisor, simply check those practices you are competent in providing. Those practices not checked become areas for competency training. **If you are helpers providing direct care/responses and experiencing any STS reactions check those areas your supervisor has discussed with you or helped you with.**

1. **Knowledge of the signs, symptoms, and risk factors of STS and its impact on employees; Knowledge of agency support options, referral process for employee assistance, or external support resources for supervisees who are experiencing symptoms of STS.**

The Supervisor is able to do the following:

___ Recognize the signs of STS in their supervisees.
___ Address observed STS with symptomatic employees in a supportive manner that normalizes their responses, promotes resiliency, and is supportive of the supervisee and does not pathologize, demean, or threaten the supervisee.
___ Delineate what the STS-informed services and support options are available from the organization.
___ Facilitate the referral process for accessing available, quality services for symptomatic employees.
___ Identify other resources that provide STS prevention or intervention services and is able to assist the employee into accessing those resources.
___ Encourage the consistent use of organizational supports for the mitigation/prevention of STS symptoms as a normalized part of doing this work.
___ Act as an advocate within the organization for STS support, training, or other needed adjustments needed by supervisees indicated by supervisory monitoring of STS symptoms in supervisees.
___ Differentiate STS, PTSD, and burnout symptoms, and describe the differential varying responses to each condition.
___ Identify how race, historical trauma, implicit bias, and/or culture impacts the way STS manifests at the individual and organizational levels.

2. **Knowledge and capacity to self-assess, reflective capacity to monitor, and address the supervisor's own personal STS.**

The Supervisor is able to do the following:

___ Recognize the effect of race, historical trauma, implicit bias, culture and/or other trauma exposure upon themselves him/herself and describe how it may manifest in the supervisory process.
___ Self-assess for signs and symptoms of secondary traumatic stress that is affecting their, his/her own functioning on a regular basis.
___ Define a plan for regular reflection to identify and self-assess secondary traumatic stress.
___ Address secondary traumatic stress signs and symptoms of STS when they arise in their own lives.
___ Willingly seek support from peers or own supervisor.

3. **Knowledge of how to encourage employees in sharing the emotional experience of doing trauma work in a safe and supportive manner.**

The Supervisor is able to do the following:

___ Employ skills to enhance the psychological safety of supervisees during supervision.
___ Describe common emotional responses to trauma work.
___ Skillfully employ reflective listening as part of supervisory practice.
___ Identify and utilize supervisees' strengths in order to use data to increase supervisee self-awareness, competence, and resilience.
___ Describe common emotional responses to trauma work and integrate these into discussions with supervisees.
___ Normalize common emotional responses to trauma work during supervision.
___ Provide emotional support to supervisees, and determine what method may be most helpful to supervisees.

4. **Knowledge of skills to assist the employee in emotional re-regulation after difficult encounters; capacity to assess the effectiveness of intervention, monitor progress and make appropriate referrals, if necessary**

The Supervisor is able to do the following:

Educate supervisees

___ Define self-regulation;
___ Teach self-regulation skills;
___ Normalize emotional responses to difficult situations.

Assess supervisees

___ Evaluate the immediate current well-being of the supervisee;
___ Identify negative self-appraisals, cognitive distortions and ineffective coping behaviors that the supervisee may be demonstrating;
___ Observe continuously and over time the emotional response of the supervisee over time to assess recovery and the potential need for added supports or referrals.

Coach and support supervisees

___ Assist with self-regulation, including cognitive skills (e.g., thinking about a situation differently), and behavioral recovery (e.g., distraction, self-soothing, and physical relaxation and redirection of energy).
___ Communicate concern and support.
___ Support the supervisee toward the development of skills for managing intense affect, and to prompt supervisees to utilize these strategies when needed.
___ Provide concrete suggestions regarding emotional regulation strategies, and emphasize their importance by allowing supervisees the time needed to implement their chosen strategies.

5. **Knowledge of basic Psychological First Aid (PFA) or other supportive approaches to assist staff after an emergency or crisis event.**

The Supervisor is able to do the following:

___ Assure the psychological, physical, and emotional safety of staff following an emergency or crisis event incident, including a discussion of physical and psychological and emotional safety.
___ Know the eight Core Actions of PFA approach.
___ Recognize the different ways staff may respond to an emergency or crisis event.
___ Invite questions from staff in a manner that supports individuals' need for emotional safety and by respecting individuals' choice to share or not share as they see fit.
___ Provide accurate information regarding secondary traumatic stress, signs to self-monitor the signs and symptoms, and strategies to enhance coping.
___ Inquire about the immediate needs of staff following an event.
___ Assist supervisees in the development of an action plan to address identified needs.
___ Facilitate access to up-to-date information on resources available to staff who have experienced direct/indirect trauma exposure, including EAP information, insurance empaneled providers, and specific recommendations related to referral sources familiar with secondary traumatic stress.

6. **Ability to both model and coach supervisees in using a trauma lens to guide case conceptualization and service delivery.**

The Supervisor is able to do the following:

___ Educate supervisees regarding how trauma may alter functioning of a trauma-exposed client.

___ Assure that the supervisee has formulated the role of trauma in the clinical presentation.

___ Redirect the supervisee from focusing on what is wrong with a trauma-exposed client (i.e., diagnosis and symptoms) to what happened in the client's life (i.e., consideration of how behaviors/symptoms may make sense when the client's trauma exposure is assessed.)

___ Guide supervisees to a recognition of a client's trauma history and symptoms in a way that explains what the client may be experiencing and serves to guide service delivery.

___ Redirect supervisees when they drift into attitudes/beliefs about clients that are inconsistent with the trauma-focused "lens".

___ Educate supervisees about key trauma concepts, support them in incorporating these concepts into a trauma-informed case formulation, and in guiding the supervisee when they drift into an approach inconsistent with the trauma lens.

___ Promote fidelity to trauma-responsive, and evidence-supported/based models in daily practice.

___ Encourage supervisee to bring forth multiple perspectives of the presenting problem(s), priorities, focus, and goals of treatment by encouraging supervisee's active engagement of the client, the client's significant others/family, and extended supports in the assessment, intervention planning, and ongoing service delivery process.

7. **Knowledge of resiliency factors and ability to structure resilience-building into individual and group supervisory activities.**

The Supervisor is able to do the following:

___ Facilitate the supervisee's experience of a developing sense of mastery of the management of trauma-related issues with clients.

___ Identify and develop the supervisee's strengths and help supervisee him or her to apply those strengths to job-related activities.

___ Connect the individual to his or her team to guard against isolation and to develop a sense of shared ownership of difficult circumstances.

___ Support the development of compassion satisfaction in the supervisee via the following:

___ Assisting with the analysis of supervisee perceptions regarding complex case situations, and supporting acceptance of situations that cannot be changed.

___ Assisting the supervisee to reframe situations to allow for the recognition of partial successes.
___ Assisting the supervisee to adopt a positive view of him or herself and their skill level.
___ Encouraging the supervisee to notice, acknowledge, and savor positive moments with clients.
___ Reinforcing the benefits of engaging in pleasurable activities at work and off hours.

8. Ability to distinguish between expected changes in supervisee perspectives and cognitive distortions related to indirect trauma exposure.

The Supervisor is able to do the following:

___ Recognize when changes in a supervisee's perspectives occur.
___ Successfully engage a supervisee in the discussion of observed changes and obtain his or her perspectives/thoughts regarding these changed views.
___ Normalize the changes in worldview (e.g., bad things do happen to innocent children) that will naturally occur during trauma work.
___ Assist the supervisee by challenging unhelpful cognitive distortions about self, work, or the world (e.g., thinking "This is useless", "The world is unsafe", "I'm the only one", or displaying hypervigilance).
___ Provide support towards replacing cognitive distortions with more accurate assessments.

9. Ability to use appropriate self-disclosure in supervisory sessions to enhance the supervisee's ability to recognize, acknowledge, and respond to the impact of indirect trauma.

The Supervisor is able to do the following:

___ Normalize STS responses through timely use of self-disclosure related to their, his or her own experiences dealing with trauma work.
___ Employ self-disclosure as a tool to help supervisees recognize, acknowledge, and respond to the impact of indirect trauma.
___ Willingly disclose when asked directly by a supervisee, thereby avoiding a posture of withholding, and facilitating emotional relatedness and equality in the relationship.
___ Monitor their, his or her own motivation and intentions as a critical factor in weighing the ethical force of self-disclosure, particularly whether the goal of such disclosure is primarily for the supervisee's benefit.

Scoring: There is no scoring for this tool. It is used to identify STS areas of supervisor competency. However, supervisors should be expected to be competent in the majority of the above areas. **For Our Purpose: Supervisors** who are trauma-informed and competent in STS interventions will engage the majority of the above practices. There are 64 total items. Add the number of items checked and divide that number by 64 to arrive at a %. For example, 39 checked items divided by 64 = 60% competency. You can do better. You need to do better. Seek out training and literature related to areas that need developing.

My Competency % = _____

Helpers use the same scoring method above. If you are helping traumatized individuals and or responding to trauma-inducing situations, the higher the percentage of the STS factors checked, the more effective the support you are receiving from supervision.

My Support Level % = _____

If you are providing help to traumatized individuals, your well-being deserves at least a support level of 50% or higher (my opinion). This is not only critical to your well-being, it is critical to your efficacy in helping trauma victims.

The NCTSN is funded by the Center for Mental Health Services (CMHS), Substance Abuse and Mental Health Services Administration (SAMHSA), US Department of Health and Human Services and jointly coordinated by UCLA and Duke University. The views, policies, and opinions expressed are those of the authors and do not necessarily reflect those of SAMHSA or HHS.

Appendix A-7

Chapter 6: Activity 5—Secondary Traumatic Stress-Informed Organizational Assessment (STSI)

Reprinted and adapted by permission from Dr. Ginny Sprang, Center on Trauma and Children, University of Kentucky.

This tool identifies six specific areas of strength and opportunities to implement STS-informed policies and practices. It is an assessment tool that can be used by organizational representatives at any level to evaluate the degree to which their organization is STS-informed and able to respond to the impact of secondary traumatic stress in the workplace. It can be downloaded at no cost by visiting www.uky.edu/CTAC/STSI-OA

Sprang, G., Ross, L., Blackshear, K., Miller, B., Vrabel, C., Ham, J., Henry, J., & Caringi, J. (2014). The Secondary Traumatic Stress-Informed Organization Assessment (STSI-OA) Tool. Lexington, Kentucky: University Center on Trauma and Children, #14-STSOO1.Retrieved May 5, 2025 from www.uky.edu/CTAC/STSI-OA

Directions: Simply check those items that you are currently aware are in place at your organization. If you do not know or are unsure use "u" to indicate further investigation is needed.

The organization promotes resilience-building activities that enhance the following:

___ Basic knowledge about STS
___ Monitoring the impact of STS on professional well-being

___ Maintaining a positive focus on the core mission for which the organization exists
___ A sense of hope: e.g., a belief in a client's potential for trauma recovery, healing and personal growth
___ Specific skills that enhance a worker's sense of professional competency
___ Strong peer support among staff, supervisors and staff and/or outside consultants
___ Healthy coping strategies to deal with the psychological demands of the job

To what degree does the organization promote a sense of safety?

___ The organization protects the physical safety of staff using strategies or techniques to reduce risk (e.g., panic buttons, security alarms, multiple staff, etc.)
___ Staff in the organization are encouraged to not share graphic details of trauma stories unnecessarily with co-workers
___ Periodically, the organization conducts a safety survey or forum that assesses worker perceptions of psychological safety
___ Organizational leaders manage risk appropriately and protect workers as much as possible from dangerous clients and/or situations
___ The organization provides training on how to manage potentially dangerous situations (e.g., angry clients)
___ The organization has a defined protocol for how to respond to staff when critical incidents occur

How STS-informed are organizational policies?

___ The organization has defined practices addressing the psychological safety of staff
___ The organization has defined practices addressing the physical safety of staff
___ The organization has a risk-management policy in place to provide interventions to those who report high levels of STS
___ The organization has defined procedures to promote resilience building in staff (e.g., self-care workshops)
___ The organization's strategic plan addresses ways to enhance staff resiliency
___ The organization's strategic plan addresses ways to enhance staff safety

How STS-informed are the practices of leaders (executive directors, CEOs, COOs, administration, etc.)?

___ Leadership actively encourages self-care
___ Leadership models good self-care
___ Supervisors promote safety and resilience to STS by routinely attending to the risks and signs of STS
___ Supervisors promote safety and resilience to STS by offering consistent supervision that includes discussion of the effect of the work on the worker
___ Supervisors promote safety and resilience to STS by intentionally managing caseloads and case assignments with the dose of indirect trauma exposure in mind
___ Staff provide input to leaders on ways the organization can improve its policies and practices regarding STS
___ Supervisors address STS by referring those with high levels of disturbance to trained mental health professionals
___ Supervisors promote safety and resilience to STS by offering additional supervision during times of high risk for STS
___ Leadership responds to STS as an occupational hazard and not a weakness

How STS-informed are other routine organizational practices?

___ The organization provides formal trainings on ways to enhance psychological safety
___ The organization provides formal trainings on ways to enhance physical safety
___ The organization provides formal trainings on enhancing resilience to STS
___ The organization offers activities (besides trainings) that promote resilience to STS
___ The organization discusses STS during new employee orientation
___ The organization has regular opportunities to provide team and peer support to individuals with high levels of exposure
___ The organization provides release time to allow employees to attend trainings focused on resilience building or STS management

How well does the organization evaluate and monitor STS policies and practices?

___ The organization assesses the level of STS in the workplace
___ The organization routinely monitors workforce trends (e.g., attrition, absenteeism) that may signify a lack of safety or an increase in STS

___ The organization responds to what it learns through evaluation, monitoring and/or feedback in ways that promote safety and resilience

___ The organization routinely seeks feedback from the workforce regarding psychosocial trends that may signify an increase in STS (e.g. increased conflict, social isolation)

This survey has no formal scoring format but is used to identify areas needing attention. However . . .

Note (author's opinion): **For our purpose** you want a sense as to how well your organization is addressing STS, how well leadership is demonstrating concern for your well-being and their skill in helping trauma victims. In a trauma-informed organization **you should expect that at least 75% of the items are checked.** There are 40 items. Total only those that you have checked and divide by 40 for a percentage. If 30 items were checked the % would = 75%. Do not count those items you marked as "u" for uncertain.

Score ____%

Scoring: Obviously, those items not checked or scored as "u" for uncertain/ I don't know, need to be further pursued. It is not uncommon to find that some of these items may be in place yet the organization has not effectively communicated their availability. In some cases, it reflects that supervisors/managers are not reviewing this information with supervisees. In either case, a lack of awareness and/or not being informed increases staff's negative perception of STS from leadership.

Appendix A-8

Chapter 6: Activity 6—PTSD Survey

This is not meant to be a diagnostic tool but a way to check for any reactions you may be having that are associated with PTSD and the need for a more clinical evaluation. One practical reason for a clinical evaluation is that most insurances will cover treatment for a formal diagnosis of PTSD.

PTSD is the result of direct exposure to a traumatic incident happening to yourself or directly witnessing trauma happening to others. Learning of what happened to a close family member or friend also qualifies. Keep in mind that witnessing and/or hearing about another's tragedy can also trigger STS but not meet the full criteria for a PTSD diagnosis. Another PTSD criteria is being exposed multiple times to aversive incidents and/or details of traumatic incidents like abuse.

A formal diagnosis requires one or more reactions under intrusion and avoidance and two or more under arousal and negative alterations in cognition and mood. Duration of reactions must be one month or more. Delayed reactions that begin six months after exposure also meet the criteria.

Directions: simply circle those that apply.

Intrusion (one or more)

❑ Recurrent, involuntary, and intrusive distressing memories of the traumatic event

- ❏ Flashbacks
- ❏ Nightmares related to event
- ❏ Intense psychological distress when exposed to cues that resemble aspects of the traumatic event
- ❏ Physiological reactions to cues that remind one of what happened

Avoidance (one or more)

- ❏ Avoidance of distressing memories, thoughts, feelings associated with the traumatic event
- ❏ Avoidance of people, conversations, client material or places associated with traumatic event

Negative alterations in mood or cognition (two or more)

- ❏ Inability to remember important aspects of the traumatic event
- ❏ Diminished interest in activities previously enjoyed
- ❏ Feelings of detachment
- ❏ Feeling numb, hopeless, or disconnected
- ❏ Unable to experience positive emotions
- ❏ Struggling with guilt or shame
- ❏ Distorted world view, negative view of self

Arousal (two or more)

- ❏ Feeling constantly on edge
- ❏ Panic attacks
- ❏ Having trouble sleeping
- ❏ Problems concentrating
- ❏ Easily startled
- ❏ Experiencing sudden bursts of anger or irritability

Record number of reactions in each category . . . Intrusion (1 needed for full criteria) ___,

Avoidance (1 needed for full criteria) ___, Arousal (2 needed for full criteria) ___,

Alterations in Cognition/Mood (2 needed for full criteria) ___

If you do not meet full criteria for PTSD yet are experiencing reactions in any of these areas you are likely experiencing STS. If you meet the criteria for specific reactions, definitely seek help from a qualified trauma-informed clinical specialist who can also evaluate additional criteria and provide the appropriate care.

Reference

DSM-5-TR, American Psychiatric Association. (2020). *Diagnostic and Statistical Manual of Mental Disorders* (5th ed., text rev.).

Appendix A-9

Chapter 7: Activity 2—Professional Quality of Life Scale (ProQOL-5) 2009

Permission to use granted by Dr. Stamm, The Center for Victims of Torture, www.ProQOL.org. Compassion Satisfaction Subscale Only adapted from Version 5 of the ProQOL

Consider each of the following questions about you and your current work situation. Select the number that honestly reflects how frequently you experienced these things in the last 30 days.

1 = Never, 2 = Rarely, 3 = Sometimes, 4 = Often, 5 = Very Often

___ I get satisfaction from being able to [help] people.
___ I feel invigorated after working with those I [help].
___ I like my work as a [helper].
___ I am pleased with how I am able to keep up with [helping] techniques and protocols.
___ My work makes me feel satisfied.
___ I have happy thoughts and feelings about those I [help] and how I could help them.
___ I believe I can make a difference through my work.
___ I am proud of what I can do to [help].
___ I have thoughts that I am a "success" as a [helper].
___ I am happy that I chose to do this work.

To find your score for Compassion Satisfaction, total your scores.
My Sum = ___

My Outcome: Check appropriate level
22 or less = Low compassion satisfaction ___
23–41 = Average ___
42 plus = High ___

Appendix A-10

Chapter 7: Activity 3—Self-Compassion Scale © 2003 Kristin Neff

Reprinted with permission from Dr. Kristen Neff, self-compassion.org

HOW I TYPICALLY ACT TOWARDS MYSELF IN DIFFICULT TIMES

Please read each statement carefully before answering. To the left of each item, indicate how often you behave in the stated manner, using the following scale:

Almost never = 1 2 3 4 5 = Almost always

1. I'm disapproving and judgmental about my own flaws and inadequacies.
2. When I'm feeling down, I tend to obsess and fixate on everything that's wrong.
3. When things are going badly for me, I see the difficulties as part of life that everyone goes through.
4. When I think about my inadequacies, it tends to make me feel more separate and cut off from the rest of the world.
5. I try to be loving towards myself when I'm feeling emotional pain.
6. When I fail at something important to me, I become consumed by feelings of inadequacy.

7. When I'm down and out, I remind myself that there are lots of other people in the world feeling like I am.
8. When times are really difficult, I tend to be tough on myself.
9. When something upsets me, I try to keep my emotions in balance.
10. When I feel inadequate in some way, I try to remind myself that feelings of inadequacy are shared by most people.
11. I'm intolerant and impatient towards those aspects of my personality I don't like.
12. When I'm going through a very hard time, I give myself the caring and tenderness I need.
13. When I'm feeling down, I tend to feel like most other people are probably happier than I am.
14. When something painful happens, I try to take a balanced view of the situation.
15. I try to see my failings as part of the human condition.
16. When I see aspects of myself that I don't like, I get down on myself.
17. When I fail at something important to me, I try to keep things in perspective.
18. When I'm really struggling, I tend to feel like other people must be having an easier time of it.
19. I'm kind to myself when I'm experiencing suffering.
20. When something upsets me, I get carried away with my feelings.
21. I can be a bit cold-hearted towards myself when I'm experiencing suffering.
22. When I'm feeling down, I try to approach my feelings with curiosity and openness.
23. I'm tolerant of my own flaws and inadequacies.
24. When something painful happens, I tend to blow the incident out of proportion.
25. When I fail at something that's important to me, I tend to feel alone in my failure.
26. I try to be understanding and patient towards those aspects of my personality I don't like.

Scoring: **We are only scoring for the Subscales in order to determine which specific area of self-compassion needs your attention.** Subscale scores are computed by calculating the mean (average) of each subscale item responses by adding up the sum and then dividing the sum by the total number of items in that subscale. For example, if your sum total for Self-kindness is 20, divide it by the 5 items in that subscale for a mean/average of 4, meaning you are almost always kind to yourself during difficult times.

Self-Kindness Items: 5, 12, 19, 23, 26 = Sum Total ___ divide by 5 = ____ mean average

Self-Judgment Items: 1, 8, 11, 16, 21 = Sum Total ___ divide by 5 = ____ mean average

Common Humanity Items: 3, 7, 10, 15 = Sum Total ___ divide by 4 = ____ mean average

Isolation Items: 4, 13, 18, 25 = Sum Total ___ divide by 4 = ____ mean average

Mindfulness Items: 9, 14, 17, 22 = Sum Total ___ divide by 4 = ____ mean average

Over-identified Items: 2, 6, 20, 24 = Sum Total ___ divide by 4 = ____ mean average

Interpretation

This scoring method provides you with very specific detail as to your mindset during stressful times. Remember it's our mindset that drives our behavior and our nervous system responses to stress. You want the Compassionate mean scores to be high and the Uncompassionate mean scores to be low.

Compassionate Response Score Uncompassionate Response Score

Self-kindness _____ self-judgement _____
Common Humanity _____ isolation _____
Mindfulness _____ over identification _____

If mean scores are the same for a compassionate response and corresponding uncompassionate response it suggests that self-compassion is low. You want compassionate mean scores to be higher than uncompassionate scores. If one compassionate response category is low, it will be important to identify the specific statements in that category to determine the responses needed to strengthen your compassionate response.

Being self-compassionate is really about having those mindsets that direct compassionate behavior and help reduce stress and compassion fatigue during difficult times. Approaching this tool from a mindset perspective makes it quite easy to identify mindsets in each statement that either support self-compassion or are counter-productive to compassion satisfaction.

Appendix A-11

Chapter 7: Activity 4—Silencing Response Scale

Anna Baranowski (© 2011, Routledge)
Reprinted with permission from Taylor & Francis, 'The silencing response in clinical practice: On the road to dialogue', in C.R. Figley (ed.), *Treating Compassion*
Fatigue, 2002, pp. 155–170, Routledge, New York.

This author's Note: Keep in mind even seasoned professionals will occasionally experience any one of these responses. *They are opportunities for change.* Seasoned professionals understand this and engage in self-reflection as to the possible meaning/source of their response rather than ignore or minimize that response.

INSTRUCTIONS: This scale was developed to help caregivers identify specific communication struggles in their work. Choose the number that best reflects your experience. Answer all items to the best of your ability as they reflect your feelings. Use the following rating system.

0 = rarely or never___ 1___2___3___4___5___6___7___8___9___10 = very often

(1) ____ Are there times when you believe your client is repeating emotional issues you feel were already covered?
(2) ____ Do you get angry with client(s)?
(3) ____ Are there times when you react with sarcasm toward your client(s)?

(4) ____ Are there times when you fake interest?
(5) ____ Do you feel that listening to certain experiences of your client(s) will not help?
(6) ____ Do you feel that letting your client talk about their trauma will hurt them?
(7) ____ Do you feel that listening to your client's experiences will hurt you?
(8) ____ Are there times that you blame your client for the bad things that have happened to them?
(9) ____ Are there times when you are unable to believe what your client is telling you because what they are describing seems overly traumatic?
(10) ____ Are there times when you feel numb, avoidant or apathetic before meeting with certain clients?
(11) ____ Do you consistently support certain clients in avoiding important therapeutic material, despite ample time to address their concerns?
(12) ____ Are there times when sessions do not seem to be going well or the client's treatment progress appears to be blocked?
(13) ____ Do you become negatively aroused when a client is angry with you?
(14) ____ Are there times when you cannot remember what a client has just said?
(15) ____ Are there times when you cannot focus on what a client is saying?

Scoring

There is no scoring for this tool. In my opinion any item rated 4 or above could benefit from further exploration as to what may be triggering that response and needing your attention as it could signal issues leading to compassion fatigue, empathy distress or the need for training. Return to the chapter for further discussion. Also review Chapter Eight under the heading Empathetic Distress, Silencing Response for additional interpretation.

Total statements rated 4 or above _____

Specific Statements rated 4 or above ___, ___, ___, ___, ___, ___, ___, ___

Appendix A-12

Chapter 9: Activity 1—SISRI

The Spiritual Intelligence Self-Report Inventory © 2008 David King. Reprinted with permission from Dr. David B. King

Note: Why do you want to evaluate your spiritual intelligence? Those who have a higher level of spiritual intelligence **are more flexible and self-conscious, and have a holistic attitude to existence and hardships of life** (Evans, 2000). Those with higher spiritual intelligence are benefiting from several capacities, for instance, they have **the power to cope with stress, change the threats of life into opportunities, and finally they have a better mental health status** (Wigglesworth, 2006; Thakadipuram, 2023).

The following statements are designed to measure various behaviors, thought processes and mental characteristics. Read each statement carefully and choose which one of the five possible responses best reflects you by checking the corresponding number. If you are not sure, or if a statement does not seem to apply to you, choose the answer that seems the best. Please answer honestly and make responses based on how you actually are rather than how you would like to be. The five possible responses are:

0—Not at all true of me, 1—Not very true of me, 2—Somewhat true of me, 3—Very true of me, 4—Completely true of me. For each item, check the one response that most accurately describes you.

1. I have often questioned or pondered the nature of reality. ___0___1___2___3___4

2. I recognize aspects of myself that are deeper than my physical body. ___0___1___2___3___4
3. I have spent time contemplating the purpose or reason for my existence. ___0___1___2___3___4
4. I am able to enter higher states of consciousness or awareness. ___0___1 ___2___3___4
5. I am able to deeply contemplate what happens after death. ___0___1 ___2___3___4
6. It is difficult for me to sense anything other than the physical and material. ___0___1___2___3___4
7. My ability to find meaning and purpose in life helps me adapt to stressful situations. ___0___1___2___3___4
8. I can control when I enter higher states of consciousness or awareness. ___0___1___2___3___4
9. I have developed my own theories about such things as life, death, reality and existence. ___0___1___2___3___4
10. I am aware of a deeper connection between myself and other people. ___0___1___2___3___4
11. I am able to define a purpose or reason for my life. ___0___1___2___3___4
12. I am able to move freely between levels of consciousness or awareness. ___0___1___2___3___4
13. I frequently contemplate the meaning of events in my life. ___0___1 ___2___3___4
14. I define myself by my deeper, non-physical self. ___0___1___2___3___4
15. When I experience a failure, I am still able to find meaning in it. ___0___1___2___3___4
16. I often see issues and choices more clearly while in higher states of consciousness/awareness. ___0___1___2___3___4
17. I have often contemplated the relationship between human beings and the rest of the universe. ___0___1___2___3___4
18. I am highly aware of the nonmaterial aspects of life. ___0___1___2 ___3___4
19. I am able to make decisions according to my purpose in life. ___0 ___1___2___3___4
20. I recognize qualities in people, which are more meaningful than their body, personality, or emotions. ___0___1___2___3___4
21. I have deeply contemplated whether or not there is some greater power or force (e.g., god, goddess, divine being, higher energy, etc.). ___0___1___2___3___4
22. Recognizing the nonmaterial aspects of life helps me feel centered. ___0___1___2___3___4

23. I am able to find meaning and purpose in my everyday experiences. ___0___1___2___3___4
24. I have developed my own techniques for entering higher states of consciousness or awareness. ___0___1___2___3___4

Total Spiritual Intelligence Score and examples of subscale meaning

Sum all item responses or subscale scores (after accounting for *reverse-coded item/question #6 . . . a score of 0 = 4, 1 = 3, 2 = 2, 3 = 1 and 4 = 0). *Reverse this scoring before adding your total scores.*

24 items in total; Range: 0–96; mid-range = 48 . . . My overall score = ___
Four Factors/Subscales:

I. **Critical Existential Thinking** (CET): Sum items 1, 3, 5, 9, 13, 17, and 21.
Seven items in total; range: 0–28; mid-range = 14 . . . My score = ___
Reflects that: I think about the purpose of my life and the meaning of things I've experienced, the meaning of what has happened to me, and the reason(s) for living. I also think about a greater power.

II. **Personal Meaning Production** (PMP): Sum items 7, 11, 15, 19, and 23.
Five items in total; range: 0–20; mid-range = 10 . . . My score = ___
Reflects that: Even when I fail, I find meaning in the loss—I learn. I do have purpose and meaning in my life. I make my decisions based on what is meaningful for me; what supports my purpose, my values, and beliefs.

III. **Transcendental Awareness (TA):** Sum items 2, 6*, 10, 14, 18, 20, and 22.
Seven items in total; range: 0–28; mid-range = 14 . . . My score = ___
***Prior to summing scores reverse the score on #6–0 = 4, 1 = 3, 2 = 2, 3 = 1 & 4 = 0**
Reflects that: I think about things that go beyond the material or physical. I think about myself in ways that are not about how I look, my physical strengths or attributes. I recognize qualities in others that go beyond how they look, beyond their personality.

IV. **Conscious State Expansion (CSE):** Sum items 4, 8, 12, 16, and 24.
Five items in total; range: 0–20; mid-range = 10 . . . My score = ___
Reflects that: I meditate, reflect, practice mindfulness. I have an awareness beyond myself.

How I Use

The higher our score across all four subscales the greater our resilience. The categories with scores below mid-range demand attention. They suggest you may need to change your mindset, the way you think about life, yourself, your purpose. Return to the main text to now identify the behaviors associated with those categories that had mid to below range scores. These can then be recorded on **the What Demands My Self-Care the Most Worksheet in *Appendix B-4*.**

Use of the SISRI is unrestricted so long as it is for academic, educational or research purposes. Unlimited duplication of this scale is allowed with full author acknowledgement only. Alterations and/or modifications of any kind are strictly prohibited without author permission. For additional information, please visit http://www.dbking.net/spiritualintelligence/ or e-mail David King at davidking2311@gmail.com

References

Emmons, R. A. (2000). Is spirituality an intelligence? Motivation, cognition and the psychology of ultimate concern. *Int J Psychol Religion*, 2000: 3–26.

King, D. B. (2008). *Rethinking claims of spiritual intelligence: A definition, model, and measure* (M. Sc.). Trent University, Canada.

Thakadipuram, T. (2023). *Leadership Wholeness, Volume 1: A Model of Spiritual Intelligence (Palgrave Studies in Workplace Spirituality and Fulfillment)* Switzerland, Palgrave MacMillan.

Wigglesworth, C. (2006). Why spiritual intelligence is essential to mature leadership. *Integral Leadership Review*, 6(2006): 206–208

Appendix B1.1

My Final Questions: Question One

Q. Of all that you read or experienced in this chapter what one thought stands out the most? *Record your first answer for each chapter on this page.*

Chp1____
Chp2____
Chp3____
Chp4____
Chp5____
Chp6____
Chp7____
Chp8____
Chp9____

Proceed to the next page B-1.2 to write down your response to Question Two

Appendix B-1.2

My Final Questions: Question Two

Q. Of the mindsets posted for each chapter, which one mindset from each chapter stands out the most for you? Put a check by the mindset that stands out for you.

Chapter One Mindsets

___ *Different stressors will demand different solutions.*

___ *It only takes one particular stressor and/or one particular way of responding to that stressor to decrease our effectiveness, erode our sense of well-being and challenge our thoughts about self, what we do and who we help.*

___ *The fact is helper stress is unavoidable; what we do with it, or how we approach it, is what matters most. It can be an enemy or a friend.*

___ *There is no one intervention or strategy that fits every individual or every situation.*

___ *It's not the terminology that matters most to our self-care, it's what we are specifically experiencing that matters most.*

___ *Secondary trauma is not a pathologic condition but a response/reaction considered not to be at all unusual among those caring for trauma populations and/or responding to potentially trauma inducing incidents.*

___ *Despite all the possibilities of the reactions you are or may experience, these do not reflect an illness; they are opportunities to enrich your sustained effectiveness and resilience as helpers by doing what you are doing differently.*

___ *Assessments can be very helpful in identifying potential stress indicators. However, sometimes it takes asking, "What is happening when you have this reaction?" in order to get at what may be triggering your behavior, in order to determine the most appropriate self-care strategy.*

Chapter Two Mindsets

___ *Our reactions to stress at any given time are not always a choice but a bio-neurological response often impossible to control cognitively.*

___ *"A stressful situation, whether something environmental, such as a looming work deadline, or psychological, such as worry about losing a job, can trigger a cascade of stress hormones that produce well-orchestrated physiological changes" (Harvard Health Publishing, 2018).*

___ *When our stress level remains constant the release of cortisol continues and becomes the primary cause of memory and concentration problems, anxiety, depression, weight gain and numerous health issues including life-threatening ones like heart disease.*

___ *Stress alters the way we think and process information and subsequently how we behave. When that stress piles up, what we think and how we behave only gets worse. Everyone caring for others is vulnerable to several types of stress no matter their knowledge or experience.*

___ *The quality of our performance on any task, whether physical or mental, is related to our level of stress (emotional arousal). If we are feeling either very low or very high levels of emotion arousal, then our performance is likely to be impaired.*

___ *Our bodies, our physiology is the first to respond to trauma and, as such, needs to be attended to or, said differently, needs to be regulated and calmed, often daily for helpers exposed to individuals in distress and/or in response to stress inducing incidents.*

___ *It's the subjective ways you are experiencing stress that matter most in determining the self-care strategies most appropriate for you.*

Chapter Three Mindsets

___ *There is no one intervention or self-care strategy that fits every individual or every situation.*

___ *"Effective Effort is purposeful and targeted. When I am really trying effectively, I am doing a LOT! I pause and quietly think. I problem-solve. I research. I tinker. I figure out what isn't working and change my strategy. I furrow my brow, and I don't stop until I figure it out" (Diehl, 2017).*

___ *Effective effort is a wonderful example of good stress or eustress; it motivates, inspires, teaches, enhances performance, self-fulfillment and well-being.*

Chapter Four Mindsets

___ *The stress I am experiencing as a helper is not always because of me but because of the practices and policies of my workplace.*

___ *Put simply, a purpose that is fulfilled (satisfied) leads to less stress (Sutin et al., 2023).*

Chapter Five Mindsets

___ *When my workplace gives me the opportunity to grow and contribute to society and my community in a meaningful way, I experience a greater sense of fulfillment.*

___ *The more engaged I am, the more passionate I am about what I do with those I am helping and the more committed I am to my organization.*

___ *When my values align with my organization's values and practices I do well; when they do not, my well-being suffers.*

Chapter Six Mindsets

___ *If you are assisting those in trauma, responding to trauma situations and/or to those presenting emotionally challenging situations, you want to be working in an organizational culture that demonstrates it understands the stressful impact of the work you will be doing by providing you the appropriate STS support.*

___ *Secondary trauma is not a pathological condition; it is not at all an uncommon response to helping those in trauma and distress.*

Chapter Seven Mindsets

___ *Self-compassion increases resilience, compassion satisfaction and resistance to empathetic or personal distress.*

___ *When satisfaction begins to diminish so too does efficacy and resilience.*

___ *To be sustainable, reframing has to be meaningful to that person and specifically address the realities they are experiencing in their lives. If someone is trying to help you, but has limited experience with your realities, their efforts at helping you reframe what is happening to you may not be at all useful or sustainable.*

___ *The primary approach to stress needs to be grounded in the belief that stress is an opportunity to grow our effectiveness, competence and over all well-being.*

___ *If a reframing is going to be sustainable it must be integrated into the context in which that individual is experiencing themselves and their environment.*

Chapter Eight Mindsets

___ *It is important to keep in mind that any one statement, practice, behavior or condition could be more important to you than a total score for that category because that specific factor is causing you the most stress.*

___ *Burnout is not due to resilience deficiency but to toxic workplace practices, which is a system issue.*

Chapter Nine Mindsets

___ *The practices associated with SI are associated with less stress, anxiety and depression.*

___ *Limited self-compassion lowers resilience while increasing stress, anxiety, depression, avoidance behaviors, difficulty with emotional regulation and empathy for others (Benner, 2022).*

___ *Maintaining a daily routine for regulating our nervous system is essential self-care and begins with identifying what it is that helps you detach for a minute or two from stressful responses or conditions, in order to replenish your energy, avoid getting stuck in the negative, to lower blood pressure or re-establish productive cognitive functions rather than being stressed by negative ones.*

___ *It only takes a minute to reduce cortisol, the stress hormone, and improve focus, concentration and energy.*

___ *If a reframing is going to be sustainable it must be integrated into the context in which that individual is experiencing themselves and their environment.*

___ *Although cognitive reframing can be helpful, I just want to reiterate that no one intervention works for everyone. Wang et al. (2023) agree with this as their research found limitations with cognitive reframing approaches as no two situations are exactly alike. What might work for one, may not work for another because of different internal and external conditions.*

___ *The expressive therapies help to lower stress, regulate our emotions and unwanted sensations, improve concentration and explore thoughts and feelings especially when it is difficult to find the words that best describe our stress, anxiety or traumatic distress.*

___ *Reflection improves critical thinking, decision making, enriches emotional intelligence and strengthens empathy.*

Appendix B-2

Chapter 3: Activity 4—My Subjective Experience Worksheet

At this point I want you to take a few minutes to answer the following questions about your subjective experience to a stressful difficulty you are experiencing. Focus on the details of the unwanted stress response you are or may have experienced. Ask yourself who was involved and what happened that made it stressful. Then complete the questions below. Allow your responses to be as spontaneous as possible. If you do not have an immediate response to a question, move to the next question and return to that unanswered one before completing the activity. When finished return to the main text for additional information.

What's the worst part of the difficulty/stress you are experiencing?

____

What is the worst part of that worst part?

____

When do you feel it the most?

____

Where do you feel it the most in your body?

____

Who or what intensifies it?

____

Who or what helps to reduce it?

What does that stress make you feel like doing?

How does it change what you think about yourself, the work you are doing?

If that stress could talk, what would it say to you?

If it could listen, what would you say to it?

If you could name it, what name would you give it?

Does anyone else know about your stress?

When they found out, what did they say to you?

What do you wish they would have said to you?

What worries you the most about your stress?

In comparison with other worries you may have, would you put this worry in the top third of your biggest worries, the middle third or lower third?

So, being as spontaneous as possible for you, where do you need to direct your self-care effort; what would say you need to do right now to help yourself out?

Appendix B-3a

Stage Two Scoring Outcomes (207)

Burnout Scale Scores Chapter 5

Overall Score ____ 900–1100 Doing well
____ 601–899 Concerning
____ 1–600 At risk

Workplace Score (Six Categories) Possible Total 600 for all 6 categories
____ 500–600 Ideal
____ 400–499 Concerning
____ 1–399 At risk

Categories under 70
Score & Title ( ) ____________________, ( ) ____________________,
( ) ____________________

Individual Red Flag
Score of 7 or under Statement ____________________, ____________________
____________________, ____________________
____________________, ____________________

Toxic Survey Chapter 4

Total Score 40   Your score 1–10 Minimal ____; 11–19 Concerning ____; 20+ Toxic ____

Self-Engagement Chapter 5 (highest # ='s level of self-engagement)

Total Number of *Yes (I'm engaged)* ____, Total *Somewhat* ____, Total *Rare* ____

Leader Engagement Chapter 5

Total circled 1–8 Little ____; 9–13 Somewhat ____; 14+ Very ____

STS/PTSD Chapter 6

Number of STS Reactions by Category by Category

- Intrusion ____
- Avoidance ____
- Arousal ____
- Cognitive/Mood Changes ____
  (2 or more required) ____

Number of PTSD Reactions

- Intrusion (1 required) ____
- Avoidance (1 required) ____
- Arousal (2 or more required) ____
- Cognitive/Mood Changes

STS Supervisor Core Competency Chapter 6

% scored ____ 75% plus ideal

Secondary Traumatic Stress Informed Organizational Assessment Chapter 6

% scored ____ 75% plus Ideal

Appendix B-3b

Stage Three Scoring Outcomes (133)

Self-Compassion

Compassionate Response Scores		Uncompassionate	
Self-Kindness	______	Self-judgement	______
Common Humanity	______	Isolation	______
Mindfulness	______	Over-Identification	______

Silencing Response Score

Total statements rated 1–3 ______ Compassionate
Total statements rated 4–7 ______ Somewhat
Total statements rated 8–10 ______ Training Needed

Compassion Satisfaction (In Text Chapter 7)

ProQOL

Total *Yes* ______ At risk (5 or more)
Total *somewhat* ______ Moderate (7 or more)
Total *No* ______ Satisfaction (12+)

Compassion Satisfaction
Low _____(22 or less)
Average _____ (23–41)
High _____(42+)

Empathy Distress

Experienced More than once

Yes ______
No ______

Moral Distress (Chp. 5-Circled #27 or 37)

Yes _____
No _____

Personal Stress Category BO Scores—Five Categories.

Total possible score 500.
Your total score _____400–500 Ideal
_____200–400 Concerning
_____200 and below At Risk
Categories 70 or under—name & score
____________________, ____________________
____________________, ____________________

Personal BO Red Flag 7 or under statements

____________________, ____________________
____________________, ____________________
____________________, ____________________

Appendix B-4

What Demands My Self-Care the Most as Indicated from All Assessment Outcomes

Concern may be about single or multiple personal reactions, thoughts, behaviors, practices for each of the areas below.

What Matters Most About Results from Burnout Scale:

Workplace

____

____

____

____

Personal Life

____

____

____

____

From Toxic Workplace Practices

From Flourishing Environments/Engagement Practices

Regarding Trauma Serving Environments—Supervision, STS/PTSD, STS Informed Environment

About Compassion, Self-Compassion, Satisfaction, Fatigue, Empathy Distress

From Spiritual Intelligence Assessment—practices in each category I need to initiate

Critical Thinking

Transcendental Awareness____

Personal Meaning____

Conscious Expansion____

What my combined thoughts from each chapter suggest I need to do differently (there may be multiple responses)

____

Appendix C-1

Chapter 9: Brief End of Day Reflection or Difficult Week

The following questions can be used to reflect on all aspects of your day—work, personal and professional growth, family/social, health, finances and spiritual. *If interested in additional reflective questions* simply Google "end of day" or "end of week" reflective questions and you will be introduced to a number of excellent resources.

Remember: *Helper self-care is not an indulgence; it is an ethical responsibility, an act of self-preservation, sustainability and continued effectiveness as a helper. It is personal, not about managing my time but harnessing my energy for what matters most to me personally and professionally.*

- ❑ What was the best part of my day today and who or what made it the best part? What did this teach me?
- ❑ Who or what am I most grateful for today?
- ❑ What did I spend too much time doing today that was not necessary? Who or what caused this to happen and what can I do tomorrow to use my time more effectively?
- ❑ What did I not spend enough time doing? Who or what prevented me from taking the time I needed and what can I do to tomorrow to change this?

❑ Did I remain focused on what matters most to me and if not, what can I do tomorrow to reset my focus?

❑ Was there a person or situation that triggered an unwanted emotional reaction today? What did I learn from this and what do I need to do or change in order to better regulate my reaction should this happen again?

❑ How can I use today to help me tomorrow?

❑ Am I staying in line with those mindsets below that stood out the most for me, or do I need to establish newer ones that may now be more appropriate?

❑ My Three

❑ Mindsets: 1.______________________________
2.______________________________
3.______________________________

Reflection for a Difficult Week As Needed

❑ What was my worst experience(s) this week?

❑ Who or what specifically made it the worst experience?

❑ What was my physical reaction? My emotional reaction?

❑ What did I do to regulate these reactions?

❑ Did I remain focused on what matters most to me and if not, what can I do to reset my focus?

❑ Do I need to do something different?

❑ What did this teach me?

How am I reframing this into a positive learning experience? (What I need more of or need to do differently, in order to be better prepared to respond more effectively should something similar happen again—and they will)

Appendix C-2

Chapter 9: Self-Care Strategies Checklist

These strategies are listed from those you can initially do on your own, to those that will involve additional help if your individual efforts have not been helpful.

- ❑ Check your approach to self-care. Is it that self-care is not an indulgence but an ethical responsibility and an act of self-preservation, sustainability, effectiveness and well-being; a personal approach, not about managing my time but harnessing my energy for all that matters most to me? *Review Chapter One for approaches to self-care.*
- ❑ Check your approach to stress. Is it in line with the mindsets established in Chapters Two and Three—stress as a friend letting us know it's time to do different and that stress is as much a physiological as a psychological response and in need of daily regulation?
- ❑ Check your approach to living life. Do your practices reflect the body, mind, spirit practices presented in this work?
- ❑ Are you working in an environment that allows you to flourish, pursue your purpose, experience a sense of fulfillment and well-being? If not, are you at least in an environment that allows you to fulfill your current purpose *while you harness your energies to support satisfaction and joy in your personal life?* If the answer is *no*, what are you doing to pursue changing this?

- ❑ Are you utilizing subjective questioning to identify the source driving your unwanted reactions to the stress that you experience?
- ❑ Are you in a supervisory relationship you trust, one that is educating you, enhancing your skills, helping you regulate the stress of helping? If not, are you in a support group or seeing someone individually to assist you with whatever helper stress you are experiencing?
- ❑ Are you practicing a daily self-care routine similar to the practices presented in Chapter Nine under Daily Routine?
- ❑ Are you experiencing satisfaction from what you are doing, where you are doing it, who you are doing it with and how you are doing it? The *how* is usually related to education and training. If you are experiencing dissatisfaction, in any of the other three areas, are you receiving help with identifying what you can do to change this dissatisfaction before it leads to burnout or fatigue?
- ❑ If already experiencing compassion fatigue and or empathetic distress, have you explored mindful self-compassion or a mindful compassion training? If so, and these have not been helpful, have you the explored the other strategies presented in Chapter Nine—CBT, DBT, ACT, Experiential Emotion Focused, for more difficult, longer standing emotional dysregulation or Somatic Experiencing, EMDR or Expressive Therapies for trauma related stress?
- ❑ Are you committed to an *effective effort* approach for not only lowering your stress but enhancing your well-being, fulfilling your sense of purpose and experiencing joy and satisfaction in your personal life and life as a helper?

Appendix C-3

Chapter 9: Prevalence of STS and PTSD

Note: Updated data for some helpers, such as law enforcement, judges, court workers, are limited. However, at the same time, new articles and blogs have been written about the trauma these helpers are experiencing across all fields. When possible, the most recent data is provided with older data showing that prevalence has existed over the years. I believe it is safe to say that the level or severity of helper stress has increased especially since COVID-19.

Child Welfare

- ❑ Research by Rienks (2020) indicated high levels of STS in Child Welfare Workers with 29% of those presenting severe levels.
- ❑ University of California, Center for Human services studied 363 child welfare workers. One half or 50% of 363 child welfare workers had scores indicative of experiencing post-traumatic stress disorder (PTSD) due to STS (Conrad et al., 2006).
- ❑ In a previous study 34% of child welfare workers met criteria for PTSD due to STS (Salston & Figley, 2003). In addition, 75% of these workers reported having fair or poor health compared to peers not caring for trauma victims.

- ❑ Health issues, such as heart disease, diabetes, depression, do emerge as a result of prolonged stress in those who do not engage in consistent self-care (APA, 2023; Griffin, 2014) Additional studies showed similar STS and health results among child welfare supervisors (Collins, 2018).

Judges/Attorneys/Court Workers

- ❑ Judges and court workers in criminal, family and juvenile court experience similar frequency of STS (Schrever et al., 2024; Smith, 2017).
- ❑ In a study of 800 judges, 45% reported experiencing STS (Judicial Edge, 2017)
- ❑ Vrklevski & Franklin (2008) found that criminal lawyers scored significantly higher on measures of vicarious trauma and depression when compared to non-criminal lawyers.
- ❑ Symptoms of secondary traumatic stress, such as sleep disturbances and nightmares, loss of appetite, hypervigilance and feelings of depression have also been identified among judges (Jaffe et al., 2003).

Social Workers/Mental Health Workers

- ❑ 45% of workers in 2024 reported feeling emotionally drained 51% expressed feeling "used up at the end of the day" (Muldoon, 2025).
- ❑ 42% of social workers were found to be suffering from secondary traumatic stress (Ratcliff, 2024).
- ❑ One review of case managers in mental health settings found that 1 in 5 had PTSD symptoms (Meldrum et al., 2018).
- ❑ Another study found that approximately one third of individuals working in residential treatment experience symptoms of compassion fatigue (Eastwood & Ecklund, 2008).
- ❑ 72% of mental health workers who provided clinical services to Katrina victims reported experiencing anxiety (Culver et al., 2011).

Nursing/Medical/First Responders

- ❑ A recent study (Ilihan & Kupeleli, 2022) found that 71% of emergency health care workers experienced Secondary Traumatic Stress.
- ❑ Among hospice nurses Abendroth & Flannery (2006) found that 79% experienced moderate to high rates of compassion fatigue.

- ❑ Other studies indicate that 85% of emergency department nurses experience symptoms of STS (Hooper et al., 2010; Gomez & Rutledge, 2009).
- ❑ Hooper (2010) found that 85% of all nurses regardless of role, experience CF.
- ❑ In another study, more than 25% of ambulance paramedics were identified as having severe ranges of post-traumatic symptoms (Beck, 2011).
- ❑ It is estimated that 30% of first responders develop behavioral health conditions including, but not limited to, depression and posttraumatic stress disorder (SAMHSA, 2018).
- ❑ According to the Journal of Occupational Health, approximately 20% of fire fighters and paramedics experience PTSD (DeMarco, 2018).

Law Enforcement

- ❑ Police retention is in a crisis as a result of trauma-based factors (Drew et al., 2024).
- ❑ Studies of PTSD and law enforcement can show anywhere from 5–50% presence depending upon what officers are exposed to and the frequency of that exposure. Some studies show that of the 900,000 police officers in the country, 19% or 180,000 experience PTSD (Craddock & Telesco, 2021; Kirschman, 2017).
- ❑ Other studies suggest that 34% of law enforcement experience STS symptoms but do meet the criteria for PTSD (Kirschman, 2017).
- ❑ Forensic investigators, and those working on internet crimes against children, 36% experienced moderate to high levels of secondary trauma (Perez et al., 2010).
- ❑ One study of 715 police officers found that 7–19% of frontline police officers had PTSD. A 2006 study found that 20% of officers who responded to September 1, 2011 showed such severe difficulties they were referred for mental health support (Brady, 2012).
- ❑ Investigating child physical and sexual abuse cases is ranked as the third leading stressor behind being involved in a shooting and the shooting of an officer. The officers exposed to these situations experience higher levels of PTSD/STS/CF than found in other law enforcement roles, although this does not preclude experiencing moderate to severe STS/PTSD following exposure to other situations (Brady, 2012).

Educators

- ❑ 44% of K-12 teachers burned out more than any other profession, and 75% reported stress-related issues. Teachers are 40% more likely to experience anxiety than most other professions, including health care workers (Peck, 2025).

Ministers

- ❑ 63% of pastors report stress as their number one challenge (Henslee, 2022).

Veterinarians

- ❑ According to the American Veterinary Medical Association (Larkin, 2024) burnout rate among veterinarians is similar to the general population. Exhaustion is the most frequently mentioned stressor and higher than the general population and 17% of younger veterinarians (up to age 34) indicate psychological distress-trauma, compassion fatigue.

Burnout

- ❑ Of the 150,000 physicians who answered the 2024 Medscape annual physician survey, 49% reported being burned out (Medscape, 2018).
- ❑ Another study of registered nurses in 2024 (Statista Research Department, 2024) reported over two thirds of those surveyed reported having feelings of burnout. The percentage of hospital nurses, nursing home nurses, and nurses working in other settings had high degree of emotional exhaustion.
- ❑ Nationally, child welfare worker turnover is estimated between 30% and 40% with an average tenure of fewer than two years, according to a US General Accounting Office report (Kim et al., 2024).
- ❑ A 2016 study by California State University, San Bernardino, found that social workers appear to be potentially more burned out and have less feelings of personal accomplishment than other human service workers (APA, 2018).

References

Abendroth, M., & Flannery, J. (2006). Predicting the risk of compassion fatigue: A study of hospice nurses. *Journal of Hospice and Palliative Nursing,* 8(6), 346–356.

APA. (2018). *Research Roundup: Burnout in Mental Health Providers.* Retrieved August, 9, 2018 from https://www.apaservices.org/practice/update/2018/01-25/mental-health-providers

APA. (2023). *Stress in America 2023: A Nation Recovering From Collective Trauma.* Retrieved May 4, 2025 from https://www.apa.org/news/press/releases/stress/2023/collective-trauma-recovery

Beck, C. (2011). Secondary traumatic stress in nurses: A systematic review. *Archives of Psychiatric Nursing,* 25(1): 1–10.

Brady P. Q. (2012). Crimes Against Caring: Compassion Fatigue, Burnout and Self-Care Practices Among Professionals Working with Crimes Against Children. *Boise State University Scholar Works, Criminal Justice Graduate Project and Thesis.*

Collins, J. (2018). *Addressing Secondary Traumatic Stress.* Retrieved August 9, 2018 from https://www.cwla.org/addressing-secondary-traumatic-stress/

Conrad, D., & Kellar-Guenther, Y. (2006). Compassion fatigue, burnout, and compassion satisfaction among Colorado child protection workers. *Child Abuse & Neglect,* 30(10), 1071–1080.

Craddock, T. B. & Telesco, G (2021). Public stress and deleterious outcomes: Efforts towards improving police mental health. *J Police Crim Psychol,* 37(1) : 173-182.

Culver, L., McKinney, B., & Paradise, L. (2011). Mental health professionals' experiences of vicarious traumatization in post-Hurricane Katrina New Orleans, *Journal of Loss and Trauma,* 16(1), 33-42.

DeMarco, H. (2018). The Other Victims: First Responders to Violent Disasters Often Suffer Alone. Retrieved August 4, 2018 from https://www.npr.org/sections/health-shots/2018/07/04/625784687/the-other-victims-first-responders-to-violent-disasters-often-suffer-alone

Drew, J. M., Sargeant, E., & Martin, S. (2024). Why do police consider leaving the profession? The interplay between job demand stress, burnout, psychological distress, and commitment. *Policing: A Journal of Policy and Practice,* 18(March): paae036.

Eastwood, C. D., & Ecklund, K. (2008). Compassion fatigue risk and self-care practices among residential treatment center childcare workers. *Residential Treatment for Children & Youth,* 25(2), 103–122.

Gomez, D., & Rutledge, D. N. (2009). Prevalence of secondary traumatic stress among emergency nurses. *Journal of Emergency Nursing,* 35(3), 199–204.

Griffin, M.R. (2014, March 31). *10 Health Problems Related To Stress You Can Fix.* Retrieved July 29, 2018 from https://www.webmd.com/balance/stress-management/features/10-fixable-stress-related-health-problems

Henslee, M. (2022, June 8). *3 Areas of Stress for a Pastor.* Retrieved June 3, 2025 from https://research.lifeway.com/2022/06/08

Hooper CI., Craig J., Janvrin DR., Wetsel MA., Reimels E. (2010). Compassion satisfaction, burnout, and compassion fatigue among emergency nurses compared with nurses in other selected inpatient specialties. *J. Emerg Nur,* 36(5): 420-427.

Ilihan, B., Kupeleli, I. (2022, February). Secondary traumatic stress, anxiety, and depression among emergency healthcare workers in the middle of COVID-19 outbreak: A cross sectional study. *Am J Emerg Med,* 55: 99–104.

Jaffe, P. G., Crooks, C. V., Dunford-Jackson, B. L., & Town, J. M. (2003). Vicarious trauma in judges: The personal challenge of dispensing justice. *Juvenile and Family Court Journal,* 54(4): 1–9.

Judicial Edge, (2017). *Nearly Half of All Judges Have Suffered From This Condition.* Retrieved August 4, 2018 from www.judges.org/nearly-half-judges-suffered-condition/

Kim, J., Pierce, B., & Park, T.K. (2024). Secondary traumatic stress and public child welfare workers' intention to remain employed in child welfare: The interaction effect of job functions. *Human Service Organizations: Management, Leadership & Governance,* 48(2), 136–149.

Kirschman, E. (2017). Cops and PTSD: Why you should care, what you can do. Retrieved July 30, 2018 from https://www.psychologytoday.com/us/blog/cop-doc/201706/cops-and-ptsd-0

Larkin, M. (2024, January 22). *American Veterinary Profession Heading in Right Direction with Mental Health.* Retrieved August 10, 2025 from https://www.avma.org/news/veterinary-profession-heading-right-direction-mental-health

Medscape. (2018). *Medscape National Physician Burnout & Depression Report.* Retrieved August 10, 2018 from https://www.medscape.com/slideshow/2018-lifestyle-burnout-depression-6009235

Meldrum, L., King, R., & Spooner, D. (2018). Secondary traumatic stress in case managers working in community mental health services. In: Figley C. R, editor. *Treating Compassion Fatigue.* (pp. 85–106.) New York, NY, Routledge.

Muldoon, C. (2025). *Stress and Burnout in the Workplace: What Organizations Can Do to Help.* Retrieved April 5, 2025 from www.webmdhealthservices.com>blog>christin

Peck, D. (2025, January 3). *Teacher Burnout Statistics: Why Teachers Quit in 2025.* Retrieved August 25, 2025 from https://www.devlinpeck.com/content/teacher-burnout-statistics

Perez, L. M., Jones, J., Englert, D. R., & Sachau, D. (2010). Secondary traumatic stress and burnout among law enforcement investigators exposed to disturbing media images. *Journal of Police and Criminal Psychology,* 25(2), 113–124.

Ratcliff, M. (2024). Social workers, burnout, and self-care: A public health crisis. *Dela J Public Health,* 10(1): 26–29.

Rienks, S. (2020). An exploration of child welfare caseworkers' experience of secondary trauma and strategies for coping. *Child Abuse and Neglect,* 110(3): 104355.

Salston, M., & Figley, C. R. (2003). Secondary traumatic stress effects of working with survivors of criminal victimization. *Journal of Traumatic Stress,* 16, 167–174.

SAMHSA. (2018). *First Responders: Behavioral Health Concerns, Emergency Response, and Trauma.* Retrieved August 4, 2018 from https://www.samhsa.gov/.../supplementalresearchbulletin-firstresponders-may2018.pdf

Schrever, C., Hulbert, C., & Soudin, T. (2024). The privilege and pressure; judges and magistrate's reflections on the sources and impacts of stress in judicial work. *Psychiatry, Psychology and Law,* 31(3): 327–380.

Smith, W. (2017). *Secondary or Vicarious Trauma Among Judges and Court Personnel.* Retrieved August 17, 2018 from https://ncsc.contentdm.oclc.org/digital/api/collection/hr/id/171/page/0/inline/hr_171_0

Statista Research Department (2024). Nurses with Burnout or Depression. Retrieved November, 27, 2024 from https://www.statista.com/topics/11131/burnout-among-physicians-and-nurses-in-the-united-states/#topicOverview

Vrklevski, P.L., & Franklin, J. (2008). Vicarious trauma: The impact on solicitors of exposure to traumatic material. *Traumatology,* 14(1), 106–118.

Index